The World's Classics

405
ENGLISH
CRITICAL ESSAYS
TWENTIETH CENTURY

Oxford University Press, Amen House, London E.C. 4

GLASGOW NEW YORK TORONTO MELBOURNE WELLINGTON
BOMBAY CALCUTTA MADRAS KARACHI CAPE TOWN IBADAN

Geoffrey Cumberlege, Publisher to the University

ENGLISH CRITICAL ESSAYS

TWENTIETH CENTURY

SELECTED
WITH AN INTRODUCTION
BY
PHYLLIS M. JONES

Geoffrey Cumberlege
OXFORD UNIVERSITY PRESS
London   New York   Toronto

The present selection of English Critical Essays (*Twentieth Century*) *was first published in* The World's Classics *in* 1933 *and reprinted in* 1935, 1940, 1942, 1947, 1950, 1954, *and* 1956

PRINTED IN GREAT BRITAIN

Introduction

THE impulse from which criticism arises is that which prompts the much-maligned man who says 'I know what I like'. But the critic as he becomes professional, as (that is) he professes his liking more and more publicly and officially, becomes evangelistic. To his ardent spirit the next step from knowing what he likes is the conviction that others ought to be converted to that preference: that here, in fact, is the true faith in Literature, and the sooner others realize it the sooner will they be saved, not from future damnation but from present embarrassment—the possession of an undesirable taste in literature. Sometimes the undesirable is also unfashionable, and to the fear of being unfashionable the contemporary critic owes in every age his happy dictatorship. He, unlike the modest user of the cliché, doesn't say that 'he doesn't know much about Literature' or Music or whatever: on the contrary, almost his first endeavour is to convince us as subtly as possible of the catholicity of his knowledge and the justice of his principles in order to prove his right to his chair of doctrine. Criticism then, on the lowest plane, might be said to be the effort of the individual mind to persuade the mass mind that his faith is that one most worthy of all men to be received. And the reader is apt to feel at times that, like some other missionary spirits, the critic believes that the end justifies the sometimes tedious means. In so doing, the critic, if he succeeds at all, accomplishes one of three main things: (1) he instructs us in the accidents of his subject by elucidating obscure passages and references, by purifying the text, by deciding bibliographical details, and in numerous other ways bringing order out of what was textual chaos; or (2) he acts as a guide to our emotions—those emotions, that is to say, which are aroused by art—classifying them according to their causes and deciding in the light of his own experience what particular quality of each work is responsible for each particular emotion; or (3) and most important of all, he brings about some kind of unity between the experiences which we connect with Life and those we associate with Literature. It is unnecessary to add that these three accomplishments are not exclusive—a critic may do one, two, or all three of them in the space of one essay.

Of the first two it is perhaps superfluous to try to assign the more important place. A long tradition, mostly and necessarily academic, attributes to the first an honourable if cloistered name; a name which, if it never receives the highest honours, is seldom discredited. True, Bentley did alter

They hand in hand, with wandering steps and slow,
Through Eden took their solitary way

to

They, hand in hand, with social steps their way
Through Eden took, with heavenly comfort cheered;

but we owe to Theobald

for his nose was as sharp as a pen, and a' babbled of green fields.

INTRODUCTION

The first you can take or leave as you like. Bentley liked it: we do not. But the second few will want to reject. It is constructive criticism at its best, taking something which was obviously nonsense and making not so much sense as inspiration. If the modern reader is sometimes apt to underrate the value of the textual critic it is probably because he has never had anything but a good text to read. Future generations may not find so much use for that kind of criticism. Good texts of even the worst authors are stored in all but indestructible security: contemporary critics of contemporary authors will have elucidated all the obscure references long before the man is dead, let alone before time has proved him worth explaining. Elucidatory notes of this kind are like sauces; one takes them or one doesn't. If one does, they are ready to hand; if one prefers the author unexplained and unaccompanied, he is always there. But even in the latter case you can hardly fail to honour the man who gives you your plain text as perfect as he can make it.

To the second class belong the majority of present-day critics. It includes a large body of writers, from the rare best to the more frequent worst. The critic of this kind at his best is a guide to our sensitiveness. He knows that there are certain passions common to all men, and that these can be worked on by certain qualities in art; the reader is not always aware of this—he may not even recognize the quality though he is conscious of the emotion: the critic will be his guide. For example—there is, in effect, says Mr. Saintsbury, 'some quality of verse which we are agreed to call the "Grand Style": the masters of this style are A, B, C, &c.; they bring it to perfection in the following quotations. When you read these phrases or passages you are under the influence of 'the perfection of expression in every direction and kind', and when this perfection works in such a way that it transports and transmutes the subject, then the 'Grand Style' exists. It may be the metre that is affecting you, or an evoked double or single image, or superb diction—or a hundred other causes. But when it exists its effect is infallible. It is true; only, when you have said that

> She has been fairer, Madam, than she is,

is in the Grand Style, and partly produces its effect by 'the double meaning' and 'pathetic moderation and modulation of the disguised and deserted mistress', you still don't know what it is that is the essence of the effect, except that it can be labelled the 'Grand Style', and there you are back at the beginning, deeply grateful to Mr. Saintsbury for having carried you thus far, but with the unsatisfied feeling that all has not yet been explained, and that the secret lies deeper, only to be come at by prayer and fasting and long hours of watching, not with the critics, but with the poets themselves. The emotion we know: a similar acute experience (not necessarily an identical one) can be aroused by the line of the Wiltshire Downs, by a Bach aria, by a Renoir painting—each a perfection of expression. But what is there peculiar to an arrangement of words, more especially to poetry, that it can produce an emotion as deep as any that life has to offer? (It has been thought convenient here to except in all cases man's relation to God, which may or may not be so very different from his relation to Letters, more particularly to poetry, save that for Letters some native inborn desire may or may not exist, but for the former we must believe that a native inborn desire does exist.)

Criticism as a tradition in England might be thought to have begun and ended with Arnold: before him was splendid chaos, after him the overwhelming flood. Up to and including Arnold criticism in England was concerned with assessing and discovering certain values which it considered to be important, but which varied from time to time. It may have misjudged them; in some cases it certainly over-estimated them: but what they were in each century it certainly knew—even when the value sunk as low as mere conventional morality. Modern criticism has no hierarchy among the qualities it seeks—if indeed it seeks any qualities at all; it appears to know as little what it wants from Letters as the modern generation does of what it wants from Life. The finest effects of the traditional critics—say of Johnson or Lamb—were to a large extent brought about by the production in the reader of an equivalent emotion. The most popular, and one of the finest, examples is De Quincey's essay on the *Knocking at the Gate in Macbeth*. A similar effect is in Johnson's sentence on the same play: 'He that peruses Shakespeare looks round alarmed and starts to find himself alone.' This kind of writing communicates by its own style the virtues it is engaged in assessing. We think that Johnson was very often wrong about Shakespeare: we are quite certain he was wrong about *Lycidas*; and yet there is in that wrongness something which is nearer to Shakespeare and Milton than many more correct estimates of these poets will ever be. You may learn nothing from him or Arnold (though usually you may learn much), but you will get a reflection of what you felt when you read the original. You will know that reflection, and the original image will be reduplicated in your mind.

The present chaotic state of criticism has been enhanced by several accidental things. No period has ever been so free from a prejudice against any of the past as our own; we do not object to Elizabethans or Augustans, Romantics or Victorians—we enjoy them all. It is much to our good, but our catholicity has helped to abolish principles as well as prejudices. The chaos is enormously increased by the tacit assumption that reviewing is criticism. Reviewing may or may not be criticism, but when a reviewer states that 'this is the worst novel I have read for a long time' no one imagines that he has even begun to criticize—that he has done more than say 'I know what I like—and this is not it'. (That reviewing may be criticism it is hoped has been proved by the inclusion here of some essays which originally appeared in that form.) Again writing has become the favourite form of self-expression; and of all forms of writing the essay-critical, sown at school and fostered and watered

INTRODUCTION

in the Universities, is second only to the novel in commonness. To be a reviewer or a publisher's reader is the ideal and inward conceit of every young man or woman who was ever said to be good at Literature. That very few reviewers have even begun to know what they are looking for is quite obvious; but that is mostly a reflection of life. When a generation arises that knows quite surely what it is looking for in life so soon will it know what it wants in Literature; and just as soon, probably, will it get it.

The terms Life and Literature are usually used to denote separate experiences. But the significance of Literature is that it is not only a part of life, but a life itself and in some sense an equivalent of the greater one; 'the complementary life', as Alice Meynell called it. To reconcile these three facts is the final task of the critic. 'Our destiny, our being's heart and home, Is with infinitude', says Wordsworth. It is with

> Effort, and expectation and desire
> And something evermore about to be.

If the mind of man is only capable of grasping finite things, yet its destiny, according to Wordsworth, is with something which it will never entirely apprehend. It is the true business of the critic, as of the poet, to make this apprehension as complete as possible, but his boundaries are more clearly marked; he has to bring about a unity of experience between what we call Life and what we distinguish in the great traditional word Letters—*orbis litterarum humaniorum*. It is a world which, to those who choose to know it, is more real and more substantial than the world of perceptible objects in which we move. Who has not walked down a street and felt that the houses, the pavements themselves, were unreal? But who of any that have loved Milton has ever felt that

> Thus with the year
> Seasons return; but not to me returns
> Day, or the sweet approach of even or morn,
> Or sight of vernal bloom, or summer's rose,
> Or flocks, or herds, or human face divine,

was anything but reality itself? Every storm we have ever known may pass from our recollection, but we remember every incident from the appearance of the 'very remarkable sky', in the storm that destroyed Steerforth. A man may very well choose not to know, or to reject this world (just as surely as Satan chose Evil instead of Good), but that is a matter of choice and not of knowledge. If a man knows anything of Shakespeare and others he will know that they have 'Voices more than all the winds with power'. What that power is we shall almost certainly never know (unless perhaps by attending to that subject which this essay has excepted from its concern): it may be that the power itself lies in just that capacity to arouse in us a consciousness of 'something evermore about to be'; that, *exceptis excipiendis*, there is nothing in this life which more arouses in our souls a knowledge of their origin and their nature than the contemplation of poetry. We know things first of all in life and we know them again more fully and more clearly in poetry: in poetry it is possible to know even

INTRODUCTION

pain and desolation—our own pain and desolation—as fruitful rather than sterile things. At the end of the *Prelude* Wordsworth, speaking of the purpose of the poets, says:

> Prophets of Nature, we to them will speak
> A lasting inspiration, sanctified
> By reason, blest by faith: what we have loved
> Others will love, and we will teach them how;
> Instruct them how the mind of man becomes
> A thousand times more beautiful than the earth
> On which he dwells, above this frame of things
> (Which 'mid all revolution in the hopes
> And fears of men doth still remain unchanged)
> In beauty exalted, as it is itself
> Of quality and fabric more divine.

Would it be too much to say that, at its highest, this was the office of criticism?

Contents

INTRODUCTION v

ROBERT BRIDGES, 1844–1930
Poetic Diction in English . . . 1

GEORGE SAINTSBURY, 1845–1933
Shakespeare and the Grand Style . . 10

ALICE MEYNELL, 1850–1922
Dickens as a Man of Letters . . 38

A. C. BRADLEY, 1851–1934
The Reaction against Tennyson . . 59

GEORGE MOORE, 1852–1933
George Eliot 87

W. P. KER, 1855–1923
Pope 109

A. C. BENSON, 1862–1925
Theodore Watts-Dunton . . 129

Sir E. K. CHAMBERS, 1866–1954
Matthew Arnold 145

MAX BEERBOHM, 1872–1956
Ouida 174

J. A. CHAPMAN, 1875–
Wordsworth and Literary Criticism . 184

H. W. GARROD, 1878–
The Profession of Poetry . . . 213

ROBERT BRIDGES
1844–1930
Poetic Diction in English
The Forum, May 1923; *Collected Essays*, II, III, 1930

POETIC Diction is a wide subject, and this paper will deal with only one little corner of it; it will examine the dislike which poets of to-day exhibit towards the traditional forms: and since even this, to be thorough, would involve a completer description of the traditional forms than a short discourse allows of, we must be contented to outline the situation with a few typical illustrations.

The revolt against the old diction is a reaction which in its general attitude is rational: and it is in line with the reaction of 'The Lake School' of Poetry, familiar to all students in Wordsworth's statement, and Coleridge's criticism and correction of that statement in his *Biographia Literaria*. Both movements alike protest against all archaisms of vocabulary and grammar and what are called literary forms, and plead for the simple terms and direct forms of common speech.

As my method is to be by illustration, I will begin with an extreme example, Milton's *Lycidas*, a poem which, though Dr. Johnson's common sense condemned it without reserve, has in spite of the extravagance of its conventions grown in favour, and firmly holds its claim to be one of the most beautiful of the great masterpieces of English verse.

Only a few days ago I received a new German

translation of it, in the preface whereto it is stated to be 'Ein Gipfel, vielleicht der Gipfel aller schäferlichen, aller Renaissancelyrik, unerreicht die Schönheit u. s. w.'

The undisguised conventionality of *Lycidas* is sufficiently obvious in its properties. Muses, Fauns, Satyrs, and Nymphs, with Druids and River-gods associate with St. Peter and the Pope, and in their company a new River-god, Camus, invented on a bogus etymology: but the remoteness from common sense which offended Dr. Johnson can be fully exposed by quoting a single line: the poet bewailing the death of a college friend by shipwreck in the Irish Channel, concludes the section of his lament over the unburied body in these words:

And O ye dolphins, waft the hapless youth!

We have to face the fact that this strange and meaningless invocation does not sound frigid or foolish in the poem. Rather it is evident that it was the very strength of the poet's feeling that has forced the transmutation of his memories and of the practical aspects of life into a dreamy passionate flux, where all is so heightened and inspired that we do not wonder to find embedded therein the clear prophecy of a conspicuous historical event: though the whole of literature can scarcely show any comparable example.

This is poetic magic. Certainly it was not to common sense that Milton turned for consolation; and a work of sheer beauty was the only worthy offering that Poetry could make.

After reading *Lycidas* let us see how it is with

Shelley's *Adonais*. Though as a whole this poem cannot compete with Milton, yet it contains lines and passages of unsurpassable beauty, both of diction and verse, and it is worthy to be compared; and since (especially towards the end) it is in closer contact with our natural expression of feeling, it appeals more strongly to some tastes. Well, the properties are as literary as in Milton. We have the Muses and Urania: Milton's 'where were ye Nymphs when the remorseless deep?' becomes 'where wert thou mighty Mother, when he lay?' and in company with Urania we have Albion and Cain and Apollo and the Wandering Jew and living persons, all magisterially blended by Shelley's usual phantasmagoria. And in one respect he is even more conventional or pedantic than Milton, because he borrows more directly from his Greek models, and with marvellous Englishing makes Hellenic beauties his own. Moreover, he works Bion's machinery: Aphrodite bewailing Adonis becomes Urania bewailing Keats—the difference in the circumstances needing all the resources of his free symbolism to adapt it. We must not, however, be led away from the question of mere diction, and I mentioned this point merely to show that Shelley's diction is more conventional than Milton's and sometimes when it least appears to be so, because many of its beauties are more directly borrowed. He has, indeed, no one line to match Milton's call to the dolphins, but many which common sense would rate as equally extravagant.

Thirdly, let us look at Arnold's *Thyrsis*, a Victorian poem in direct line with *Lycidas* and

Adonais, consciously affiliated with them and plainly inspired by Milton. I remember many years ago how Ingram Bywater, when we were both young, contended against me that *Thyrsis* was as good a poem as *Lycidas*: I do not know how far he was in earnest.

Now in Arnold's poem he and his friend are Corydon and Thyrsis, they have their shepherd's pipes, and the Hellenic properties are practically the same as Milton's and Shelley's; but they are frankly set in a modern English landscape and introduced naturally as actual figures of the mental world wherein the two friends had lived and loved. Their mutual sympathy in this symbolism makes it possible almost to confound Enna with Cumnor, and that is skilfully accomplished, but amid the strong details of native colour and homely affections we have an Ionian folk-tale of obscure antiquity, the relevancy of which is hardly cleared up by a long note. Since there is no trace of Christian symbolism in the poem, the Properties are simpler than Milton's or Shelley's, and the Diction may be styled Wordsworthian; it would hardly have offended Dr. Johnson: it is plainly not intended to be in what Arnold has called 'the grand style', and he was never in danger of attempting Shelley's heavenward flights, which he thought ineffectual. Thus we may say that, compared with *Lycidas* and *Adonais*, Arnold's *Thyrsis* is in simplified diction.

What then is the effect of such a diction? In judging this we must remember that Arnold is not Milton, and I am probably myself too much biased in favour of the greater poet: but if a 'rational' diction is any decided poetic advantage, then that advantage should appear, whereas the impression that *Thyrsis* makes on me when I compare it with *Lycidas* is that it lacks in passion, as if it were a handling of emotions rather than the compelling utterance of them, and so far as that must have the effect of insincerity it is the last thing that we should expect from the exclusion of conventions. It does not carry the same conviction of distress that *Lycidas* does; neither the friendship nor the sorrow seems so profound, and the whole poem, though it is agreeable reading, leaves one cold at the end. This might in great part be accounted for by its fanciful argument and by the poet's mentality, nor can I pretend to decide how much is due to the diction: the example must remain a negative one; but in illustration, I will quote a passage from *Thyrsis* where Arnold follows Milton in moralizing on the 'vanity' of the sincerest human effort in the search for ideal Truth; he has

> This does not come with houses or with gold,
> With place, with honour, and a flattering crew;
> 'Tis not in the world's market bought and sold!
> But the smooth-slipping weeks
> Drop by, and leave its seeker still untired;
> Out of the heed of mortals he is gone,
> He wends unfollow'd, he must house alone;
> Yet on he fares, by his own heart inspired.

Milton has

> *Fame* is the spur that the clear spirit doth raise
> (That last infirmity of Noble mind)
> To scorn delights, and live laborious dayes;

> But the fair Guerdon when we hope to find,
> And think to burst out into sudden blaze,
> Comes the blind *Fury* with th' abhorred shears,
> And slits the thinspun life, 'But not the praise,'
> *Phoebus* repli'd, and touch'd my trembling ears. . . .

and so on, and this in spite of old *Phoebus* and the bad grammatical inversion in the first line.

It is difficult to dissociate the quality of Diction from two other matters, namely, Properties and Keeping. Properties is a term borrowed from the stage. The mixture of Greek and Christian types in *Lycidas* and *Adonais* is a good example of Properties. The term Keeping is taken from Painting and has no convenient synonym, but it may be explained as the harmonizing of the artistic medium, and since Diction is the chief means in the harmonizing of Properties, it would seem that any restriction or limitation of the Diction must tend to limit the Properties, since without artistic keeping their absurdities would be exposed.

Dr. Johnson's common sense might contend that all Properties were absurd if their absurdity were merely disguised by Keeping. But in aesthetic no Property is absurd if it is in Keeping. This does not decide what Properties should be used. Different Properties are indispensable for different imaginative effects. Good Keeping is a first essential in all good writing, and especially in poetry. Perhaps it is evident here that the poorer the Properties are, the less call will they make on diction for their keeping, although the simplest Properties are on their own plane no less exigent: and again the higher the poet's command of diction, the wider may be the field of his Properties. Also, and this is a very practical point, if a writer with no command of imaginative diction should use such Properties as are difficult of harmonization, he will discredit both the Properties and the Diction.

This is as it should be. In all fields of Art the imitators are far more numerous than the artists, and they will copy the externals, in poetry the Versification and the Diction, which in their hands become futile. Criticism does not assist art by exposing such incompetencies: nor can it be praised for philanthropic intention, because dabbling in the arts is one of the most harmless pleasures of life: there may be more to be said for it than for dabbling in criticism as I am doing here.

We may now fairly put the following question: Is this protest against poetic diction intended to confine Properties to actualities? No poet would consent to that. Is it then merely a protest against archaic and literary forms of speech? Supposing this to be intended, we may inquire how far it can, on any poetic plane, be practically enforced. We cannot hope to get very far through with this business, but we can insert the thin end of the wedge.

The adverb *hither* has gone almost entirely out of use in common speech, and except in the idiom 'hither and thither' is rarely found in modern prose. Yet though obsolescent it is without obscurity and is a pretty word. No purist in diction could object to it.

And if *hither* be admitted, what of *wherein*,

whereto, whereby, &c. To forbid them and insist on the alternatives *in which, to which, by which,* &c., would discredit any honest grammarian; his hope would be that familiarity with the better and more convenient forms in poetry might lead to their more frequent use in prose, and that they might thus, through the journals and current literature, win restoration into our common speech.

But if it should happen that such simple obsolescent forms actually became quite common again, it is certain that they would lose some of their poetic and literary value, and a writer who had maintained his elevation partly on such cheap stilts would miss them and unconsciously feel about for something to take their place. And their natural substitutes would be other words which had the same obsolescent quality as his old friends used to have before they had been too familiarized. One can imagine that this process of restoring good obsolescent forms might thus go on *ad infinitum*. On the other hand, as things are now, the self-denial of our common speech may be regarded as the generous and jealous guardian of our literary style.

Since poetic language is essentially a rarity of expression of one sort or another, it is unreasonable to forbid apt and desirable grammatical forms merely because they are not read in the newspapers or heard at the dinner-table. And if once such unusual forms are admitted they will colour the keeping of the diction and invite a kindred vocabulary. It has lately become a fashion to use dialectal words in poetry. Such words are generally free from the stain of conventionality and since they are often better English words than their familiar synonyms, the only objection against them is that they are unknown or obscure, and have the same sort of effect as some of Burns's Scottish words have to English ears—they need translation. But if, for instance, such good old English words as *inwit* and *wanhope* should be rehabilitated (and they have been pushing up their heads for thirty years), we should gain a great deal; for we should not only win back towards a closer relationship with our older literature, but these words would soon differentiate themselves from their Latin synonyms *conscience* and *despair*, just as we have differentiated *fatherly* and *paternal*; and we should thus add to that subtlety in the expression of ideas which by like means has become a peculiar excellence of our tongue.

It might be urged that with Milton and Shelley, who were educated by Hellenic models and had come by reading and meditation to have panoramic views of History and Truth, it was natural to write at that height—their poetic diction may be the spontaneous utterance of their subconscious mind—but that it is nevertheless regrettable because common folk whom they might otherwise delight and instruct cannot understand it. This is a wrong notion. It was not Dr. Johnson's ignorance or deficient education that made him dislike *Lycidas*. It was his unpoetic mind that was at fault, and his taste in Music or Painting would probably have been at the same level. Moreover, children do not resent what they cannot understand in Poetry, and they generally have a keener sense for beauty than Dr. Johnson had—indeed, if he would have become again as a little child, he might have liked *Lycidas* very well. Anatole France has put this matter so admirably that I will end my paper by transcribing the words in which he tells his own experience:

'Il y avait dans ce récit un grand nombre de termes que j'entendais pour la première fois et dont je ne savais pas la signification; mais l'ensemble m'en sembla si triste et si beau que je ressentis, à l'entendre, un frisson inconnu; le charme de la mélancolie m'était révélé par une trentaine de vers dont j'aurais été incapable d'expliquer le sens littéral. C'est que, à moins d'être vieux, on n'a pas besoin de beaucoup comprendre pour beaucoup sentir. Des choses obscures peuvent être des choses touchantes, et il est bien vrai que le vague plaît aux jeunes âmes.'

GEORGE SAINTSBURY
1845–1933

Shakespeare and the Grand Style[1]

Essays and Studies, vol. i, 1910

THE adventure of this paper may appear extravagant, but it has seemed to me perhaps not unfitting, if not for myself, yet for the person whom the English Association has thought fit to choose for its president in the third centenary year of the publication of the *Sonnets*. Nor is the adventurer, however moderate his prowess, quite

[1] Presidential address to the English Association, January 1910.

untried in the kind, at any rate, of the quest. Some years ago, at the request of the Dante Society, I wrote and read a paper, as yet unpublished, on the relation of that great poet to the mysterious entity called the Grand Style; and last year I ventured to deal with Milton in the same way, before the Royal Society of Literature. The opportunity of completing the trio was tempting, and I can only hope that I have not been tempted to too great a failure.

It is always in such a case as a ceremony desirable, though except as a ceremony it can hardly be necessary, to disclaim any intention of direct controversy. Such controversy would be, in this case, with the founder or re-founder of all recent discussion on the present subject, Mr. Matthew Arnold.[1] I do not share his views: but controversy in detail would be quite out of place in such a paper as this, and, in reference to a dead antagonist, it would lack even the piquancy which, when carried on between the living, it seems to possess for many, I cannot say I think to the best, tastes. It is sufficient to remind you that Mr. Arnold could only accord to Shakespeare what I have elsewhere called a sort of 'uncovenanted' Grand Style—an occasional magnificence, chequered if not checkmated by styles the reverse of grand. It appears to me on the contrary that Shakespeare held the Grand Style in the hollow of his hand, letting it loose or withholding it as good seemed to him: and further, that the seeming almost always *was* good.

It has been often said in various forms, but

[1] See the lectures *On Translating Homer.*

hardly ever without truth, that all dispute turns upon difference of definition—and that, if people were only clear-witted enough and even-tempered enough, the arrival at definition would be the conclusion of the whole matter. For their differences of opinion would either disappear in the process, or they would be seen to be irreconcilable, and to possess no common ground on which argument is possible. My definition of the Grand Style is certainly wider than Mr. Arnold's, whose own seems to have been framed to insist upon that 'high seriousness' of his which is no doubt a grand thing. Mine would, I think, come nearer to the Longinian 'Sublime'—the perfection of expression in every direction and kind, the commonly called great and the commonly called small, the tragic and the comic, the serious, the ironic, and even to some extent the trivial (not in the worst sense, of course). Whenever this perfection of expression acquires such force that it transmutes the subject and transports the hearer or reader, then and there the Grand Style exists, for so long, and in such a degree, as the transmutation of the one and the transportation of the other lasts. It may persist, or cease, or disappear and reappear, like a fixed or a revolving light, but there it is *in essentia* or *in potentia*. If, on the other hand, you limit the definition to the *continual* exertion of some such a transforming force, it seems to me that, in the first place, you are making an excessive and unnatural restriction, forgetful of *neque semper arcum* and other sayings of the wise, while, in the second place, as a consequence of the first error, you are preparing for yourself endless pitfalls. It is a question whether any writer, except perhaps Milton, will answer to the definition completely. Dante and Homer certainly will not—as, to give one example in each case out of a hundred, the comparison of Adam in the *Paradiso* to an animal struggling under a cloth, which has shocked so many commentators, and that passage in the *Odyssey* which shocked Longinus, will show. Further, the perpetual Grand Style of the definition which is *not* mine, can only be maintained—is only maintained by Milton himself—at the cost of an enormous *tour de force* of mannerism, which is at least questionably justifiable or artistic—which in fact itself sometimes becomes the reverse of grand. The vast region of the lighter vein must be abandoned, or clumsily handled—as it actually is by Milton when his Grand Style is once 'set'. Even in serious subjects, there must be a kind of 'second sifting' of seriousness. And, above all, there is the certainty of the arising of a spurious Grand Style—a style of mere grandiosity—a plaster imitation of the real thing, than which there has been nothing in the past, and there is likely to be nothing in the future, more detestable.

Of this there is no danger, essentially at least, under the application of that definition of the Grand Style which I prefer. It makes its appearance when it is wanted, and when the hour is come; at other times it abides apart, and possesses its strength in quietness and in confidence, not frittering it away. Of its display in this fashion I cannot remember any one in literature

—not Homer, not Dante himself, not Milton certainly—who can produce such constant, such varied, such magnificent instances as Shakespeare. Even in his novitiate, when he was making his experiments, and indeed making the tools with which to make these, this Adamastor, this King of the Waves of the vasty deep of style, never fails to come when he calls on it. We do not know the exact order of his compositions; and there is dispute about some of the probably earlier items in it. Some maintain that the *Titus Andronicus* which we have is not the *Titus* that Meres attributed to him; and some that the admitted re-writing of *Love's Labour's Lost* makes it a doubtful witness; while the date of *The Two Gentlemen of Verona* is extremely uncertain. But it would, I think, be difficult so to pack a jury of competent scholars that these plays, and the *Comedy of Errors*, should not be put in the van. And though every one of them is full of crudities, the Grand Style appears in each, as it never does appear in any other probably contemporary work, except Marlowe's, and not as it appears in Marlowe himself. The central splendour of Adriana's speech in the *Errors* (II. ii. 112 ff.); the glorious 'phrase of the ring' in the fatal discovery of the murder of Bassianus in *Titus* (II. iii. 226 ff.); the famous and incomparable veiled confession of Julia in the *Two Gentlemen* (IV. iv. 154 ff.); at least a dozen passages in *Love's Labour's Lost*—have the broad arrow—the royal mark—upon them unmistakably.

But, it is said, there is so much else—so much even of the close context of these very passages—

which has *not* the mark! And why should it have? Poetry, and most especially dramatic poetry, is a microcosm: and it may—perhaps it should, like the macrocosm—contain wood, hay, and stubble, as well as gold and silver. Again, in these plays, it is said, there are *failures* of the Grand Style—slips from it or mis-shots at it— fallings into conceit, preciousness, bombast, frigidity, what not. Is it necessary, even at this time of day, to recapitulate the classes of persons to whom, according to the adage, half-done work should not be shown? Or is there any one, not included in these classes, who really wishes that we had not got Shakespeare's half-done work? I should be sorry to think that there is—especially in this audience. But, if there be, may I suggest to him that on the calculus we are using, the fact, supposing it to be a fact, does not matter? It is not a question whether anything that is not the Grand Style exists in these plays: but whether the Grand Style itself exists there. And I profess myself unable to understand how any one can deny its presence in the passages to which I have referred, and in scores, almost hundreds, of others.

But let us come to somewhat closer quarters. What is it, in these passages themselves, which, in spite of the evident novitiate of their author, claims for them grandeur of style? It is no one thing; the sources of the Sublime in style are many—as many as the qualities and circumstances of Style itself. Whenever one of these qualities is displayed, whenever one of these circumstances is utilized, in the transmuting and transporting fashion and degree—there is the Grand Style. In the speech of Julia, above referred to,

> She hath been fairer, Madam, than she is,

the secret lies, to a great extent, in the double meaning, and in the pathetic moderation and modulation of the disguised and deserted mistress. The language is quite plain—it is an instance, one of many, which shows that poetic diction is not a *sine qua non*, though none of these shows that it can be or ought to be wholly dispensed with. But as I am, I confess, strongly and indeed irreconcilably opposed to the doctrine that the great thought *ipso facto* makes the Great Style—that the meaning is the thing—I am particularly glad to start with an instance where the secret *does* lie mainly in the meaning.

It lies there less in the passage of the *Errors*:

> For know, my love, as easy mayst thou fall
> A drop of water in the breaking gulf,
> And take unmingled thence that drop again,
> Without addition or diminishing,
> As take from me thyself, and not me too.

Here the meaning is good, is true, is pathetic—but it is not in it that the transport and the transmutation lie. They lie partly, as Longinus would assert, in the Figure—the vivid image of the breaking gulf, and the drop of water contrasted with and whelmed in it. They lie, I think, partly also in the actual verbal phrase by which that figure is conveyed. But to me they lie most in the management of the metre, the alternative check and rush of the rhythm of the now sundered, now overlapping, verses—the perfection of the entire phrase, prosodic and poetic.

The third passage, that in *Titus*, is more of a 'Passage Perilous'; for the evidence of the novitiate is here very strong:

> Upon his bloody finger he doth wear
> A precious ring that lightens all the hole,
> Which, like a taper in some monument,
> Doth shine upon the dead man's earthy cheeks
> And shows the ragged entrails of the pit.

After this it goes off into mere failure about Pyramus and the moon, and Cocytus, and other *gradus* matters. Even here, in the lines quoted, the expression is not thoroughly 'brought off'—it is the Grand Style in the rough, with the master's hand not yet in case to finish it. Yet the solemn splendour of the opening line, and the lights and shades and contrasts of dim outline and ghastly colour, have the right quality—or at least the promise of it.

When we come to such a play as *Romeo and Juliet* the command of these sources is far surer and more frequent, though it seems to be masqued or marred, to some spectators, by the accompanying comedy or farce, which is not, and is not intended to be, grand in any way. The famous 'Queen Mab' speech is not quite up to our mark—not at all because it is light in subject, but because Mercutio, pleasant as is his fancy, *does*, as Romeo says, 'talk of nothing' to some extent, or talk a little too much of his pleasant something. But the famous later scenes of the play are full of the Grand Style; and Romeo's dying speeches, after he has disposed of Paris, have it in perfection and in rare volume. If anybody denies that this is the Grand Style I should like to meet him foot to foot, he taking any passage he likes from Homer, Dante, Milton, or any one else, and to fight the question out, phrase by phrase, line by line, and total impression by total impression.

It is this increasing command of the style that transmutes the subject and transports the reader, which is so characteristic of Shakespeare; joined as it is to a perfect readiness *not* to use it when he thinks it is not required. I have pointed out that I think this somewhat misled Mr. Arnold, and has misled others. They cannot conceive Apollo without the bent bow; they think that the Grand Style is a sort of panoply which the wearer, like some adventurous knight under a vow, must never take off. Once more, I cannot help thinking this is a mistake. 'Homer and the Grand Style' is a subject which would be very interesting, and which I should not be afraid to handle; but it would be quite irrelevant to say much of it here. The Homeric grandeur, whatever it is, is quite different in species from that of Dante and Milton; and though it is more like Shakespeare's, I do not think that the difference between the two is small. But it is certain that Homer does not wear his Grand Style as a continental officer wears his uniform, while Milton does this to the utmost possible extent, and Dante to an extent extremely great. Shakespeare—who is nothing if not English, except that he is also universal—is never more English than in his preference for mufti on occasion. It seems to be this preference which has, in the eyes of some, disqualified him.

And yet no one can wear his uniform with more dignity, or assume it with such lightning quickness; while no one can keep it longer fresh on duty. The *Sonnets* are, of course, the great example of this; for with the rarest exceptions the *Sonnets*, whatever else they may be or not be, are Grand Style throughout. Their subject does not, from this point of view, matter; whether Elizabethan sonnets in general, and these sonnets at a rather extraordinary particular, present rehandlings of old stuff, or not, is of no importance. Let fifty—let five hundred, or five thousand, people have moralled, poetically or prosaically, on sunrise, noon, and sunset. When the fiftyfirst, or the five hundred and first, writes,

> Lo! in the *orient* when the *gracious* light
> Lifts up his *burning* head,

the Grand Style appears. It is nearly as impossible to describe, meticulously, the constituents of its grandeur as to describe those of the majesty of the sun itself. There is, as Dionysius of Halicarnassus was perfectly right in holding, something mysterious in the mere word-material—the contrasted sound and structure of the words 'orient', 'gracious', 'burning'. There is much more in their juxtaposition. But there is most in the whole phrase; though with the contestable exception of 'orient' and perhaps 'Lo!' there is not a single specimen of 'poetic diction' in it; most of it is in the simplest vocabulary; and the central thought and image are as common as grass or earth. But the *attitude* of the phrase is the thing; the simple dignified *attitude* which sets off, and is set off by 'orient' and 'gracious' and 'burning', as jewels set off, and are set off by, simplicity and dignity and grace combined in the human port and bearing. It is in this that Shakespeare excels all his great competitors in quantity, and differs from all but Dante in quality. In Milton there is always something that is not exactly simple; and in Homer 'perpetual epithets', compound epithets, and the like, interfere to some extent with that ever-varying yet often extraordinarily *plain* speech which we find in Shakespeare and in Dante. On the other hand, Milton is segregated from the other three by the fact that he depends less than any of them on mighty single words; it is rather (putting proper names out of the question) on the rhetorical collocation of those which he uses that he relies. The double epithets that he employs are imitations from the Greek. But Shakespeare delights in such words as 'multitudinous', 'incarnadine', 'unwedgable', just as Dante does in such as *ammassiccia* and *fiammeggiante*. And yet Shakespeare can produce the Grand Style effect with five repetitions of 'never' in a single line, or with such a renunciation of emphasis, such a miracle of negative expression, as 'The rest is Silence'. I suppose the very prodigality of his use of it, the insouciance of this prodigality, like that of

Wealthy men who care not how they give,

and above all the disconcerting way in which he

gives it when people do not expect it, and are
not prepared for it, account to some extent for
the dubiety and discomfort with which it has
been and is received, for the tendency to plead
'his time' and 'the necessities of the theatre' and
the like. For it is a great mistake to suppose that
the day of apologies for Shakespeare is over. The
form of the apology alters, but the fact remains:
and I am inclined to think that Shakespeare,
though he would certainly have been amused by
most of his modern assailants, would have been
still more amused by some of his modern apologists.
Still, the '*wil*fulness' (as his own age would
have said) of this prodigality *is* no doubt disconcerting
to some honest folk. People are uncomfortable
at being taken by surprise. They want
to be told to 'prepare to receive cavalry'; there
must be a warning-bell and a voluntary, and
ornaments and vestments, to put them into a
proper Grand Style frame of mind. Milton provides
all this, and he is recognized as a grand
stylist; Shakespeare does not, and his title is
questioned. A respectable but rather futile
gentleman like Duke Orsino is plentifully supplied
with the noblest phrase; a petulant, dishonourable,
almost worthless prince like Richard
II is supplied more plentifully still, and from a
still nobler mint. He does not grudge it to his
villains; if

    The wheel is come full circle; I am here[1]

be not in the Grand Style, I confess myself
utterly ignorant what the Grand Style is. It

[1] *King Lear*, v. iii. 174.

comes sometimes, as it were, 'promiscuously' in the vulgar sense of that term. It would, for instance, be exceedingly difficult for the most expert, or the most futile, ingenuity of the commentator to assign an exact reason for the occurrence, where it occurs, of what is perhaps the grandest example of the Grand Style in all literature—the words of Prospero to Ferdinand, when the revels are ended. An excuse is wanted to break off the pretty 'vanity of his art'; to get rid of the lovers; and to punish, in defeating it, the intentionally murderous but practically idle plot of Caliban and his mates. Anything would do; and the actual pretext is anything or nothing. But Shakespeare chooses to accompany it with a 'criticism of life'—and of more than life—so all-embracing, couched in expression of such magnificence, that one knows not where to look for its like as form and matter combined. An ordinary man, if, *per impossible*, he could have written it, would have put it at the end; an extraordinary one might have substituted it for, or added it to, the more definite announcement of abdication and change which now comes later with 'Ye elves', &c. Shakespeare puts it here.

Sometimes he will even outrage the Mrs. Grundy of criticism by almost burlesquing the Grand Style, by letting Titania, in her deluded courtship of Bottom, be not merely graceful, and fanciful, and pathetically pleading, but by making her indulge in such positive magnificence, such sheer Sublime as

The Summer still doth tend upon my state,

which the most serious poet, telling the severest tale, might be only too happy to have invented. At other times—the examples are frequent in the probably rehandled chronicle-plays—he will take another man's phrase which is not grand at all, and 'grandee' it—equip it with the Orders of the King, and the qualifications necessary to justify them—by a stroke or two of added or altered diction. Constantly it seems as though a sort of whim took him to be grand—or as if (in the words of one of his own characters who is too graceless for the strictly Grand Style, though grand enough in his own fashion) '*grandeur* lay in his way and he found it'. Some of these characters—Hamlet for one, of course, and Macbeth for another—would speak habitually in it if they had not more grace of congruity than to do so. There is no one who has it more perfectly than Antony—unless it be Cleopatra—when either chooses; and Othello at his best excels almost all others. Once more, if his last words be not in the Grand Style, where are we to look for it?

But the old *aporia*—the old curious fallacy-objection—recurs. 'These things *are* grand—but there is so much else that is *not* grand.' To this there is, once more, only the old answer to all fallacy-objections of the kind. 'Why not?' I suspect that the fallacy arises, as so many aesthetic fallacies do, from a confusion of Arts. It is sometimes forgotten that literature, especially in some of its forms, is much more of a macrocosm than any of its sister species of Imitation. The greater epic, the novel, and especially the drama, have got to face and reproduce life, character, action, circumstance, in all their varieties, foul as well as fair, trivial as well as dignified, commonplace as well as exceptional. To attempt to clothe all this in the same Grand Style, or in the Grand Style at all, is to offend against the sumptuary laws of Art itself. The so-called classical drama of modern time has made this attempt; and the wiser judgement of the best periods of criticism has decided that it has failed. Poetry at large tried to do it for a century and a half or thereabouts, and failed even more egregiously. Prose fiction never really succeeded until it cast the attempt aside. I have boldly confessed that I do not think Dante did attempt it; and that, though Milton certainly did, and achieved perhaps the only success on record, he paid for it somewhat dearly, and could not have attained what success he did attain but for the extremely exceptional nature of his subject. Further, I think that, in certain notorious passages, he actually tried to get out of the Grand Style—without succeeding in getting into anything else good. Your short poem, like your sculpture or your picture, is all the better for being Grand Style unmixed; not so your long one, and still less your drama. Thus Shakespeare himself never deserts the Grand Style in the *Sonnets*, or indeed in any of his poems, except—and then not always—songs in the plays of such a character that grandeur would be almost or wholly out of place. In his plays themselves he suits style to subject, and so alternates Grand Style with that which is not grand.

But the grandeur of its grandeur when it is grand! And the inexhaustible variety of it, and of the means whereby it is attained! I believe I was once rash enough to assert that you could not open a double page of the *Globe* edition—which means something more than two hundred lines—(excepting of course the prose passages, the plays only partially Shakespeare's and those dealing with purely comic matter) without coming on something unmistakably in the Grand Style. To justify this boast 'at the foot of the letter' would no doubt be difficult, seeing that there are something like five hundred such page-openings. But in such experiments as I have made—and they are numerous—I have very rarely drawn the cover blank, and have frequently 'found' where, from the subject and context, finding was unlikely.

This ubiquity of the Shakespearian Grand Style, as combined and contrasted with its abstinence from continuity, is one of its most notable characteristics, and is connected in the closest degree with that absence of mannerism which has been noted. The extreme difficulty of defining or even describing Shakespeare's style has been alike the theme and the despair of the commentators; it extends to, and is intensified in the case of, his *Grand* Style. The ticketing critics who were so common in classical times, and who are not unknown in modern, would be—some of the latter have been—hopelessly 'out' with him. You cannot fix on any special collocation of words like Milton's adoption and extension of the Chaucerian epithet before and after the noun; on any tricks of grammar like Milton's apposition; on any specially favourite words such as those to be found in the most diverse writers. It seems as if he had deliberately determined that no special mould, no particular tool, no *recipe* of mixture and arrangement, should be capable of being pointed out as his secret, or even as one of his secrets, of attaining grandeur. It has been remarked already that the subject, or at least the context of subject, hardly matters. But other things matter as little. Any vocabulary, any syntax, any rhetoric, will do for Shakespeare to produce his masterpieces; and it may sometimes seem as if—like conjurers very often and chemists sometimes—he had taken a sort of whimsical delight in producing his effects with the minimum of apparatus, or with apparatus of the least formal kind.

You may find curious instances of this in the very forefront of his work as it is read, though it may have been his last completed task. Take those two well-known lines of Prospero's,

In the dark backward and abysm of Time,

and

To act her earthy and abhorred commands.

Now a hasty critic may dismiss the most obvious device by which the style is raised in these as merely the old trick, familiar for generations before Shakespeare, and already almost caricatured by men like Fisher and Berners—the trick of combining native and imported elements. But there is something much more than a mere draft on the Teutonic and Romance columns of a conveniently arranged Dictionary of Synonyms. The double source *is* drawn upon; 'backward' and 'earthy' do stand to 'abysm' and 'abhorred' as the pairs so familiar in Bible and Prayer-book do to each other. But Shakespeare is not content with this grammar-school antithesis. In the first place, he varies the meaning in 'backward' and 'abysm', giving waste horizontal stretch in the one case and unplumbed depth in the other; and he also contrasts the mere sound of the words as much as possible, while deliberately adopting the form in 'ysm' for the sake of euphony. In the second he adds to the contrast of origin and sound a complete change of point of view. 'Earthy' is a quality of the commands; 'abhorred' an attitude of the mind commanded. He has tapped not one but many of the Longinian 'sources'; he has blended the products of his tapping. And yet these are mere everyday instances, the *ordinaire*, as it were, of his cellar.

Pass from the almost certainly last to one of the certainly earliest plays, the *Two Gentlemen*, and, avoiding the apex already quoted from it, taking (at whatever may be their full value) the imperfect construction, the more imperfect characterization, the superabundant evidences of the novitiate in conceit and word-play and trifling—consider for a moment one line of its second greatest passage (I. ii. 84),

> The uncertain glory of an April day.

'Quite commonplace,' says the quite commonplace reader. 'Everybody knows that April days are uncertain.' But has everybody called them so in this simplicity and consummateness of phrase? Try obvious variants:

> The fickle glory of an April day,

or 'the treacherous', or 'the passing', or a dozen others, not to mention the non-obvious ones which would have commended themselves to second- or tenth-rate writers of that day and this —far-fetched and dear-bought frigidities which will suggest themselves by the dozen. Then do the same thing with 'glory', substituting 'splendour', 'beauty', what you will. Put all the results of experiment beside the actual text, and you will, if you have a Grand Style ear, have very little difficulty in determining where the Grand Style lies—with Ariel and the bee, not beside the lamp and in the chemist's shop.

To go through all the plays, even by sample at fancy, would be impossible; but it may perhaps be permitted to me to give a few more of my *sortes Shakespearianae*. I shall avoid, as I have avoided, except by general reference, the most famous passages—for there is no need to have recourse to them, and the means by which their effects are achieved, though always different in individual, are never different in general character from those manifest in the smaller instances— if any can be called small. The most general touch of all is perhaps that already noticed—the *ambidexterity* with which the poet uses the most and the least unusual phrases and words. He has neither a studied grandiloquence nor a studied simplicity, nor does he specially affect that peculiar source of sublimity—that is to say, 'transport'—which consists in a sort of catachresis or deliberate misuse of words in secondary intentions, like that frequently adopted by Sir Thomas Browne. He will at one moment write a phrase 'to tear with thunder the wide cheeks of the air', which has the very sound-effect of which it speaks, and which has the largeness of the universe itself, with metrical accompaniments to match; and then he will pass in the same speech from this poetical magnificence to the plain downright scorn of

> This fellow had a Volscian to his mother.[1]

He will write, using the simplest words and most familiar metre,

> Fear no more the heat of the sun,
> Nor the furious winter's rages,

producing, it appears, on some people the effect of 'drivel'—certainly producing on others the effect of the most perfect and poignant poetry of ordinary life. And then, within a page or two, he will sketch a picture of war in a line and a half, with a couple of images of sound and sight that could not be beaten in effect by a paragraph, or another page:

> That when they hear the Roman horses neigh,
> Behold their quartered fires—

where the absence of superfluity, and the presence of concentration, are equally remarkable.[2]

---

[1] *Coriolanus*, v. iii. 151, 178.
[2] *Cymbeline*, IV. ii. 258, iv. 17.

For my part, if I had any doubt about Shakespeare having a hand in *Pericles*, one line would settle it—

A terrible childbed hast thou had, my dear.[1]

For even Middleton or Webster, the two who have come nearest to Shakespearian phraseology, could hardly have achieved this curious union of simplicity and the Grand Style; while Cyril Tourneur, who has been thought by some to have the touch, certainly could not have achieved it.

Nor is it less interesting to examine the passages which—not of the greatest as wholes; not containing any of the actual 'jewels five words long' which are so plentiful; not exempt, it may be, from the less grand marks of the form and pressure of the time, in conceit and euphuism and absence of restraint—still betray this Grand Style of Shakespeare's. Take, for instance, that in some ways most Shakespearian of all the plays *not* greatest—*Timon of Athens*. The central situation is, of course, dramatic enough; but it is not perhaps one which lends itself to effective dramatic treatment of the Shakespearian kind, because there is not sufficient development of character; while it *does* lend itself to that Shakespearian divagation and promiscuity of handling which, though they do not disturb some of us, seem to disturb others so much. But the play is simply drenched with the Grand Style—every rift is packed with Grand Style gold—not, it may be, refined to the point of the greatest, but gold

[1] *Pericles*, III. i. 57.

unmistakable. It peeps out of the rhetorical commonplaces of the professional cynic Apemantus:

> Like madness is the glory of this life,
> As this pomp shows to a little oil and root,

where the first verse at least is perfect.[1] Alcibiades—in Shakespeare's scheme not the Admirable Crichton of some views of him, if not of history, but only a rather good specimen of professional soldier—has vouchsafed to him that splendid cadence—

> Taught thee to make vast Neptune weep for aye
> On thy low grave, on faults forgiven. Dead
> Is noble Timon.[2]

The excellent Flavius—best of servants, but certainly not most poetical of men—is made mouthpiece of that glorious line—

> O! the fierce wretchedness that glory brings us.[3]

As for Timon himself, his misfortunes make him a Shakespeare. Even the first frantic retrospect of cursing on Athens is, till the rhyme comes at least, a Grand-Style raving. The address to 'the blessed breeding sun' is greater still; and the better known demonstration of the universality of thieving is raised by the style, despite its desperate quaintness, almost to the level of the greatest things in *Hamlet*.

The fact is, ladies and gentlemen, that this Grand Style is not easily tracked or discovered by observation, unless you give yourself up

[1] *Timon of Athens*, I. ii. 139.
[2] Ibid. v. iv. 78. [3] Ibid. IV. ii. 30.

primarily to the *feeling* of it. You cannot tell how it arises, and you will often have some difficulty in deciding why it goes. It is the truest, precisely because it is the most irresponsible, of the winds of the spirit—no trade wind or Etesian gale, but a breeze that rises and falls, if not exactly as *it* listeth—as the genius of the poet and the occasions of the subject list. We may recur once more —in the useful, not the useless, fashion of comparison, the fashion which appraises qualities, but does not ticket values—to the four names which, in Literature, have been most frequently associated with this Style. Homer has it in a form scarcely comparable with the others. If we had more early Greek epic—more especially if we had Antimachus—we should be much better judges of the Homeric Grand Style than we are. As it is, we see in it extraordinary and extraordinarily varied melody of verse and phrase, a use of Figure, especially of Simile, which is unsurpassed, and to which indeed all subsequent literary poetry is directly or indirectly indebted; and one great engine, the elaborate and mostly perpetual epithet, which is a great puzzle to cautious and widely experienced critics. For the ancients will not tell us exactly how these epithets affected them; and we ought to know, lest we make the same mistakes which, as we see, foreigners are constantly making about English, and which, no doubt, Englishmen as frequently make about foreign literature.

We are safer with Dante, for there we have practically all possible facilities of comparison. The language is still living; we know what those who have spoken and written it since thought and think about it; and we have our own independent, but in this case fully informed, judgement to be the sovereign guide. We find that there is undoubtedly a *prevalent* style in Dante: and that this is of a peculiar *gravity*, the gravest style perhaps in all literature, yet in no sense stiff or stilted, and not (to some tastes) at all affected. But it seems, to some at least, that this style is very largely influenced, and even to some considerable extent produced, by the metre—which is of an intense idiosyncrasy, and though not in the least monotonous, curiously uniform in general atmosphere—much more so indeed than the Greek hexameter, and quite infinitely more so than the English blank verse. We find, further, that Dante has no exclusive preference for lofty images or even expressions: and that though he will use the most elaborate and carefully sifted poetic-pictorial diction, his Grand Style is not so much a matter of that as of the suffused atmosphere or *aura* spoken of above. There is in fact, in the old sense of the word as applied to music, a Dantesque *mode*—pervading everything and affecting grotesque, extravagance, pedantry—(these are not *my* words, but such as others use)—almost or quite as much as the grander parts themselves. Breaking chronological order, for obvious reasons, we come to Milton, and here again we find something all-pervading. But its nature is different: and so is the nature of its pervasion. It is practically independent of metre—for the peculiarity of blank verse is that it imposes no character of its own, but takes that of its writer—'blankness' in the worst sense; the 'tumid gorgeousness' which Johnson, not without some excuse, mistook for its differentia; or a varied magnificence in the best and strictest sense of that word, which knows no limit and accepts no rule. The Miltonic style is quite above the Miltonic metre in one sense of 'above', though hardly in another; it is perceivable almost equally, in the complicated stanza of the 'Nativity', in the octo-syllables of the early middle poems, in the rhymed blank verse of *Lycidas*, in the pure blank verse of the *Paradises*, in the dialogue and the chorics of *Samson*. It admits variety; but here also, *plus ça change, plus c'est la même chose*. I do not know that we can free it from the label of affectation; though it is affectation transcendentalized and sublimed. The proof is that it cannot descend and unbend as Dante's can. But we are not talking at length of Milton here. Suffice it to say, that this undoubted uniformity, with the less universal but somewhat similar uniformity of Dante, which no doubt patterned it, and the quite different uniformity of Homer, undoubtedly helped to create the idea of a Grand Style existing almost *ab extra*, and bound to present itself separately, at demand, everywhere, for everything.

To this idea Shakespeare is certainly rebel; if a manner so absolutely aristocratic as his can even admit the suggestion of rebellion. Milton he cannot be for many reasons, including the fact that he has to go before Milton can come; Dante he does not choose to be; Shakespeare he is. And as being Shakespeare—in order, indeed, to make what we mean by Shakespeare—he uses the Grand Style as his Attendant Spirit. He says to it, 'Come', and it comes; he says to it, 'Go,' and it goes. It is not his master, as to some extent their styles were the masters both of Dante and of Milton. He does not make it his mistress, as not a few hardly lesser men have done—caressing it; doing homage to it; and never letting it out of his sight if he can help. Sometimes he seems almost wilfully and capriciously to give it its *congé*—to take up with inferior creatures for pastime. But this is a delusion. He knows that to employ a being so majestical for every purpose of a dramatic household is a profanation—that she is for the pageants and the passions, for the big wars and the happy or unhappy loves, for the actions and the agonies of pith and moment. For the rest, the handmaidens and the serving men, the clowns and the fools, the Osrics and the Poloniuses will do; though he will not grudge even to them, when it suits him, a touch of the higher language, a flash of the sublimer thought. To this you must make up your mind, if you go a Grand-Styling with Shakespeare.

There is no fear, as I said before, of drawing the covers blank. Take for our last instance that strange play—so puzzling in many ways, so offensive, I believe, to some good wits, such a mixture of almost the highest Shakespeare and almost the most ordinary University Wit—take *Troilus and Cressida*. Neglect, while to this or that extent acknowledging—for, if you cannot combine acknowledgement and neglect in this way, you may be an excellent neighbour and a very good bowler, but you are no critic—neglect the disappointment in the handling of some of the characters, the confused action, the uncomely patches. Neglect further—or rather do not neglect, but use only as a contrast and foil—the tale of bombasted blank verse and craggy conceited phrase as it seems to some. Postpone for consideration the jumble (I am here speaking throughout the language of the Advocatus Diaboli) of long-winded tirades and word-playing prose. What remains in your sieve—your crucible—your gold-washing cradle? Not merely the famous 'One touch of nature' which has been so frequently and so curiously misinterpreted. Not merely the less generally known but hardly inferior beauties of that same magnificent speech which begins—

> Time hath, my lord, a wallet at his back,

and ends—

> Made emulous missions 'mongst the Gods themselves
> And drave great Mars to faction.[1]

This singular throwing into dramatic form of the ordinary Troy-books perpetually develops Grand Style; the commonplaces of Nestor and the other chiefs break into it in the same odd fashion in which an apparently quiet wave, hardly undulating the surface a little way from shore, will break on the beach itself with a sudden burst of glittering thunder. It is extraordinary how the γνῶμαι (the 'sentences', as Greek and Latin rhetoricians would have called

[1] *Troilus and Cressida*, III. iii. 145 ff.

them) of the great debating Third Scene of the First Act stick in one's memory. The play itself is never acted; never used for those official purposes which, I fear, make other parts of Shakespeare best known to us both in youth and age; nor is it in all ways seductive to private reading. Yet the Grand Style impression is made constantly: though with that singular diversity and elusiveness of means, direct and suggested, to which attention has been drawn throughout. Take this:

> There is seen
> The baby figure of the giant mass
> Of things to come at large.[1]

That is no bad instance of what may be called the middle or average Shakespearian Grand Style—perhaps indeed it is a little below the average. It is all the better example. The poet takes, you see, the most ordinary words—the actual vocabulary of the phrase is not above even Wordsworthian proof. He takes for figure an equally ordinary antithesis—'baby' and 'giant' —though a different writer would probably have spoilt his own farther chances by using 'pygmy' or 'dwarf', instead of 'baby'. And here he gets his first hold on us; for the baby, unlike the dwarf, will grow—though whether it will grow to giant size or not, only the Future can tell. Then he thinks of something else—'figure' and 'mass' being not, like 'baby' and 'giant', contrasts of size merely, but indicating the form, the idea, that is to be impressed on the mass. And then he is not satisfied with the limited greatness

[1] Ibid. I. iii. 345.

of 'giant mass' itself; but expands and flings it out into the obscure infinity of things to come, and of things to come *at large*. You have passed in some dozen or sixteen words, artfully selected, from the definite doll of the baby figure to the vast of Space and Time.

This may seem a fanciful sermon on a more fancifully selected text; but I venture to hope that it may induce some who have not yet thought on the matter to take not uninteresting views of the Grand Style in general and of Shakespeare's Grand Style in particular. They will not find these views easily exhaustible: all the less so because all really Grand Style appeals to a certain complementary gift and faculty in the person who is to appreciate it; it is a sort of infinitely varying tally, which awaits and adjusts itself to an infinite number of counter-pieces. It abides; the counter-pieces may get themselves ready as they can and will.

ALICE MEYNELL
1850–1922

Dickens as a Man of Letters

Hearts of Controversy, 1917

It was said for many years, until the reversal that now befalls the sayings of many years had happened to this also, that Thackeray was the unkind satirist and Dickens the kind humorist. The truth seems to be that Dickens imagined more evil people than did Thackeray, but that he had an eager faith in good ones. Nothing places him so entirely out of date as his trust in human sanctity, his love of it, his hope for it, his leap at it. He saw it in a woman's face first met, and drew it to himself in a man's hand first grasped. He looked keenly for it. And if he associated minor degrees of goodness with any kind of folly or mental ineptitude, he did not so relate sanctity; though he gave it, for companion, ignorance; and joined the two, in Joe Gargery, most tenderly. We might paraphrase, in regard to these two great authors, Dr. Johnson's famous sentence: 'Marriage has many pains, but celibacy has no joys.' Dickens has many scoundrels, but Thackeray has no saints. Helen Pendennis is not holy, for she is unjust and cruel; Amelia is not holy, for she is an egoist in love; Lady Castlewood is not holy, for she too is cruel; and even Lady Jane is not holy, for she is jealous; nor is Colonel Newcome holy, for he is haughty; nor Dobbin, for he turns with a taunt upon a plain sister; nor Esmond, for he squanders his best years in love for a material beauty; and these are the best of his good people. And readers have been taught to praise the work of him who makes none perfect; one does not meet perfect people in trains or at dinner, and this seemed good cause that the novelist should be praised for his moderation; it seemed to imitate the usual measure and moderation of nature.

But Charles Dickens closed with a divine purpose divinely different. He consented to the counsels of perfection. And thus he made Joe

Gargery, not a man one might easily find in a forge; and Esther Summerson, not a girl one may easily meet at a dance; and Little Dorrit, who does not come to do a day's sewing; not that the man and the woman are inconceivable, but that they are unfortunately improbable. They are creatures created through a creating mind that worked its six days for the love of good, and never rested until the seventh, the final Sabbath. But granting that they are the counterpart, the heavenly side, of caricature, this is not to condemn them. Since when has caricature ceased to be an art good for man—an honest game between him and nature? It is a tenable opinion that frank caricature is a better incident of art than the mere exaggeration which is the more modern practice. The words mean the same thing in their origin—an overloading. But as we now generally delimit the words they differ. Caricature, when it has the grotesque inspiration, makes for laughter, and when it has the celestial, makes for admiration; in either case there is a good understanding between the author and the reader, or between the draughtsman and the spectator. We need not, for example, suppose that Ibsen sat in a room surrounded by a repeating pattern of his hair and whiskers on the wall-paper, but it makes us most exceedingly mirthful and joyous to see him thus seated in Mr. Max Beerbohm's drawing; and perhaps no girl ever went through life without harbouring a thought of self, but it is very good for us all to know that such a girl was thought of by Dickens, that he loved his thought, and that she is ultimately to be traced, through Dickens, to God.

But exaggeration establishes no good understanding between the reader and the author. It is a solemn appeal to our credulity, and we are right to resent it. It is the violence of a weakling hand—the worst manner of violence. Exaggeration is conspicuous in the newer poetry, and is so far, therefore, successful, conspicuousness being its aim. But it was also the vice of Swinburne, and was the bad example he set to the generation that thought his tunings to be the finest 'music'. For instance, in an early poem he intends to tell us how a man who loved a woman welcomed the sentence that condemned him to drown with her, bound, his impassioned breast against hers, abhorring. He might have convinced us of that welcome by one phrase of the profound exactitude of genius. But he makes his man cry out for the greatest bliss and the greatest imaginable glory to be bestowed upon the judge who pronounces the sentence. And this is merely exaggeration. One takes pleasure in rebuking the false ecstasy by a word thus prim and prosaic. The poet intended to impose upon us, and he fails; we 'withdraw our attention', as Dr. Johnson did when the conversation became foolish. In truth we do more, for we resent exaggeration if we care for our English language. For exaggeration writes relaxed, and not elastic, words and verses; and it is possible that the language suffers something, at least temporarily —during the life of a couple of generations, let us say—from the loss of elasticity and rebound brought about by such a strain. Moreover, exaggeration has always to outdo itself progressively. There should have been a Durdles to tell this Swinburne that the habit of exaggerating, like that of boasting, 'grows upon you'.

It may be added that later poetry shows us an instance of exaggeration in the work of that major poet, Mr. Lascelles Abercrombie. His violence and vehemence, his extremity, are generally signs not of weakness but of power; and yet once he reaches a breaking-point that power should never know. This is where his Judith holds herself to be so smirched and degraded by the proffer of a reverent love (she being devoted to one only, a dead man who had her heart) that thenceforth no bar is left to her entire self-sacrifice to the loathed enemy Holofernes. To this, too, the prim rebuke is the just one, a word for the mouth of governesses: 'My dear, you exaggerate.'

It may be briefly said that exaggeration takes for granted some degree of imbecility in the reader, whereas caricature takes for granted a high degree of intelligence. Dickens appeals to our intelligence in all his caricature, whether heavenly, as in Joe Gargery, or impish, as in Mrs. Micawber. The word 'caricature' that is used a thousand times to reproach him is the word that does him singular honour.

If I may define my own devotion to Dickens, it may be stated as chiefly, though not wholly, admiration of his humour, his dramatic tragedy, and his watchfulness over inanimate things and landscape. Passages of his books that are ranged otherwise than under those characters often leave me out of the range of their appeal or else definitely offend me. And this is not for the customary reason—that Dickens could not draw a gentleman, that Dickens could not draw a lady. It matters little whether he could or not. But as a fact he did draw a gentleman, and drew him excellently well, in Cousin Feenix, as Mr. Chesterton has decided. The question of the lady we may waive; if it is difficult to prove a negative, it is difficult also to present one; and to the making, or producing, or liberating, or detaching, or exalting, of the character of a lady there enter many negatives; and Dickens was an obvious and positive man. Esther Summerson is a lady, but she is so much besides that her ladyhood does not detach itself from her sainthood and her angelhood, so as to be conspicuous—if, indeed, conspicuousness may be properly predicated of the quality of a lady. It is a conventional saying that sainthood and angelhood include the quality of a lady, but that saying is not true; a lady has a great number of negatives all her own, and also some things positive that are not at all included in goodness. However this may be—and it is not important—Dickens, the genial Dickens, makes savage sport of women. Such a company of envious dames and damsels cannot be found among the persons of the satirist Thackeray. Kate Nickleby's beauty brings upon her at first sight the enmity of her workshop companions; in the innocent pages of *Pickwick* the aunt is jealous of the niece, and the niece retorts by wounding the vanity of the aunt as keenly as she may; and so forth through early books and late. He takes for granted that the women, old and young, who are not his heroines, wage this war within the sex, being disappointed by defect of nature and fortune. Dickens is master of wit, humour, and derision; and it must be confessed that his derision is abundant, and is cast upon an artificially exposed and helpless people; that is, he, a man, derides the women who miss what a man declared to be their 'whole existence'.

The advice which M. Rodin received in his youth from Constant—'Learn to see the other side; never look at forms only in extent; learn to see them always in relief'—is the contrary of the counsel proper for a reader of Dickens. That counsel should be, 'Do not insist upon seeing the immortal figures of comedy "in the round". You are to be satisfied with their face value, the face of two dimensions. It is not necessary that you should seize Mr. Pecksniff from beyond, and grasp the whole man and his destinies.' The hypocrite is a figure dreadful and tragic, a shape of horror; and Mr. Pecksniff is a hypocrite, and a bright image of heart-easing comedy. For comic fiction cannot exist without some such paradox. Without it, where would our laugh be in response to the generous genius which gives us Mr. Pecksniff's parenthesis to the mention of sirens ('Pagan, I regret to say'); and the scene in which Mr. Pecksniff, after a stormy domestic scene within, goes as it were accidentally to the door to admit the rich kinsman he wishes to propitiate? 'Then Mr. Pecksniff, gently warbling a rustic stave, put on his garden hat, seized a spade, and opened the street door, as if he thought he had, from his vineyard, heard a modest rap, but was not quite certain.' The visitor had thundered at the door while outcries of family strife had been rising in the house. ' "It is an ancient pursuit, gardening. Primitive, my dear sir; for, if I am not mistaken, Adam was the first of the calling. My Eve, I grieve to say, is no more, sir; but" (and here he pointed to his spade, and shook his head, as if he were not cheerful without an effort) "but I do a little bit of Adam still." He had by this time got them into the best parlour, where the portrait by Spiller and the bust by Spoker were.' And again, Mr. Pecksniff, hospitable at the supper table: ' "This," he said, in allusion to the party, not the wine, "is a Mingling that repays one for much disappointment and vexation. Let us be merry." Here he took a captain's biscuit. "It is a poor heart that never rejoices; and our hearts are not poor. No!" With such stimulants to merriment did he beguile the time and do the honours of the table.' Moreover it is a mournful thing and an inexplicable, that a man should be as mad as Mr. Dick. None the less is it a happy thing for any reader to watch Mr. Dick while David explains his difficulty to Traddles. Mr. Dick was to be employed in copying, but King Charles the First could not be kept out of the manuscripts; 'Mr. Dick in the meantime looking very deferentially and seriously at Traddles, and sucking his thumb.' And the amours of the gentleman in gaiters who threw the vegetable-marrows over the garden wall. Mr. F.'s aunt, again! And Augustus Moddle, our own Moddle, whom a great French critic most justly and accurately brooded over. 'Augustus, the gloomy maniac,' says Taine, 'makes us shudder.' A good medical diagnosis. Long live the logical French intellect!

Truly, Humour talks in his own language, nay, his own dialect, whereas Passion and Pity speak the universal tongue.

It is strange—it seems to me deplorable—that Dickens himself was not content to leave his wonderful hypocrite—one who should stand imperishable in comedy—in the two dimensions of his own admirable art. After he had enjoyed his own Pecksniff, tasting him with the 'strenuous tongue' of Keats's voluptuary bursting 'joy's grapes against his palate fine', Dickens most unfairly gives himself the other and incompatible joy of grasping his Pecksniff in the third dimension, seizes him 'in the round', horsewhips him out of all keeping, and finally kicks him out of a splendid art of fiction into a sorry art of 'poetical justice', a Pecksniff not only defeated but undone.

And yet Dickens's retribution upon sinners is a less fault than his reforming them. It is truly an act denoting excessive simplicity of mind in him. He never veritably allows his responsibility as a man to lapse. Men ought to be good, or else to become good, and he does violence to his own excellent art, and yields it up to his sense of morality. Ah, can we measure by years the time between that day and this? Is the fastidious,

the impartial, the non-moral novelist only the
grandchild, and not the remote posterity, of
Dickens, who would not leave Scrooge to his
egoism, or Gradgrind to his facts, or Mercy
Pecksniff to her absurdity, or Dombey to his
pride? Nay, who makes Micawber finally to
prosper? Truly, the most unpardonable thing
Dickens did in those deplorable last chapters of
his was the prosperity of Mr. Micawber. 'Of a
son in difficulties'—the perfect Micawber nature
is respected as to his origin, and then perverted
as to his end. It is a pity that Mr. Peggotty ever
came back to England with such tidings. And
our last glimpse of the emigrants had been made
joyous by the sight of the young Micawbers on
the eve of emigration; 'every child had its own
wooden spoon attached to its body by a strong
line', in preparation for Colonial life. And then
Dickens must needs go behind the gay scenes,
and tell us that the long and untiring delight
of the book was over. Mr. Micawber, in the
Colonies, was never again to make punch with
lemons, in a crisis of his fortunes, and 'resume
his peeling with a desperate air'; nor to observe
the expression of his friends' faces during Mrs.
Micawber's masterly exposition of the financial
situation or of the possibilities of the coal trade;
nor to eat walnuts out of a paper bag what time
the die was cast and all was over. Alas! nothing
was over until Mr. Micawber's pecuniary
liabilities were over, and the perfect comedy
turned into dullness, the joyous impossibility of
a figure of immortal fun into cold improbability.

There are several such late or last chapters

that one would gladly cut away: that of Mercy Pecksniff's pathos, for example; that of Mr. Dombey's installation in his daughter's home; that which undeceives us as to Mr. Boffin's antic disposition. But how true and how whole a heart it was that urged these unlucky conclusions! How shall we venture to complain? The hand that made its Pecksniff in pure wit, has it not the right to belabour him in earnest—albeit a kind of earnest that disappoints us? And Mr. Dombey is Dickens's own Dombey, and he must do what he will with that finely wrought figure of pride. But there is a little irony in the fact that Dickens leaves more than one villain to his orderly fate for whom we care little either way; it is nothing to us, whom Carker never convinced, that the train should catch him, nor that the man with the moustache and the nose, who did but weary us, should be crushed by the falling house. Here the end holds good in art, but the art was not good from the first. But then, again, neither does Bill Sikes experience a change of heart, nor Jonas Chuzzlewit; and the end of each is most excellently told.

George Meredith said that the most difficult thing to write in fiction was dialogue. But there is surely one thing at least as difficult—a thing so rarely well done that a mere reader might think it to be more difficult than dialogue; and that is the telling *what happened*. Something of the fatal languor and pre-occupation that persist beneath all the violence of our stage—our national undramatic character—is perceptible in the narrative of our literature. The things the usual modern author says are proportionately more energetically produced than those he tells. But Dickens, being simple and dramatic and capable of one thing at a time, and that thing whole, tells us what happened with a perfect speed which has neither hurry nor delays. Those who saw him act found him a fine actor, and this we might know by reading the murder in *Oliver Twist*, the murder in *Martin Chuzzlewit*, the coming of the train upon Carker, the long moment of recognition when Pip sees his guest, the convict, reveal himself in his chambers at night. The swift spirit, the hammering blow of his narrative, drive the great storm in *David Copperfield* through the poorest part of the book—Steerforth's story. There is surely no greater gale to be read of than this: from the first words, ' "Don't you think that," I said to the coachman, "a very remarkable sky?" ' to the end of a magnificent chapter. 'Flying clouds tossed up into most remarkable heaps, suggesting greater heights in the clouds than there were depths below them.... There had been a wind all day; and it was rising then with an extraordinary great sound. ... Long before we saw the sea, its spray was on our lips.... The water was out over the flat country, and every sheet and puddle lashed its banks, and had its stress of little breakers. When we came within sight of the sea, the waves on the horizon, caught at intervals above the boiling abyss, were like glimpses of another shore, with towers and buildings.... The people came to their doors all aslant, and with streaming hair.' David dreams of a cannonade.

when at last he 'fell—off a tower and down a precipice—into the depths of sleep'. In the morning, 'the wind might have lulled a little, though not more sensibly than if the cannonading I had dreamed of had been diminished by the silencing of half a dozen guns out of hundreds.' 'It went from me with a shock, like a ball from a rifle,' says David in another place, after the visit of a delirious impulse; here is the volley of departure, the shock of passion vanishing more perceptibly than it came.

The tempest in *David Copperfield* combines Dickens's dramatic tragedy of narrative with his wonderful sense of sea and land. But here are landscapes in quietness: 'There has been rain this afternoon, and a wintry shudder goes among the little pools in the cracked, uneven flag-stones. . . . Some of the leaves, in a timid rush, seek sanctuary within the low-arched cathedral door; but two men coming out resist them, and cast them out with their feet.' The autumn leaves fall thick, 'but never fast, for they come circling down with a dead lightness.' Again, 'Now the woods settle into great masses as if they were one profound tree.' And yet again, 'I held my mother in my embrace, and she held me in hers; and among the still woods in the silence of the summer day there seemed to be nothing but our two troubled minds that was not at peace.' Yet, with a thousand great felicities of diction, Dickens had no *body* of style.

Dickens, having the single and simple heart of a moralist, had also the simple eyes of a free intelligence, and the light heart. He gave his senses their way, and well did they serve him. Thus his eyes—and no more modern man in anxious search of 'impressions' was ever so simple and so masterly: 'Mr. Vholes gauntly stalked to the fire, and warmed his funereal gloves.' ' "I thank you," said Mr. Vholes, putting out his long black sleeve, to check the ringing of the bell, "not any." ' Mr. and Mrs. Tope 'are daintily sticking sprigs of holly into the carvings and sconces of the cathedral stalls, as if they were sticking them into the button-holes of the Dean and Chapter.' The two young Eurasians, brother and sister, 'had a certain air upon them of hunter and huntress; yet withal a certain air of being the objects of the chase rather than the followers.' This phrase lacks elegance—and Dickens is not often inelegant, as those who do not read him may be surprised to learn—but the impression is admirable; so is that which follows: 'An indefinable kind of pause coming and going on their whole expression, both of face and form.' Here is pure, mere impression again: 'Miss Murdstone, who was busy at her writing-desk, gave me her cold finger-nails.' Lady Tippins's hand is 'rich in knuckles'. And here is vision with great dignity: 'All beyond his figure was a vast dark curtain, in solemn movement towards one quarter of the heavens.'

With that singleness of sight—and his whole body was full of the light of it—he had also the single hearing; the scene is in the Court of Chancery on a London November day: 'Leaving this address ringing in the rafters of the roof, the very little counsel drops, and the fog knows him no more.' 'Mr. Vholes emerged into the silence he could scarcely be said to have broken, so stifled was his tone.' 'Within the grill-gate of the chancel, up the steps surmounted loomingly by the fast-darkening organ, white robes could be dimly seen, and one feeble voice, rising and falling in a cracked monotonous mutter, could at intervals be faintly heard . . . until the organ and the choir burst forth and drowned it in a sea of music. Then the sea fell, and the dying voice made another feeble effort; and then the sea rose high and beat its life out, and lashed the roof, and surged among the arches, and pierced the heights of the great tower; and then the sea was dry and all was still.' And this is how a listener overheard men talking in the cathedral hollows: 'The word "confidence", shattered by the echoes, but still capable of being pieced together, is uttered.'

With humour, derision—to each of these words we assign by custom a part in the comedy of literature; and (again) those who do not read Dickens—perhaps even those who read him a little—may acclaim him as a humorist and not know him as a wit. But that writer is a wit, whatever his humour, who tells us of a member of the Tite Barnacle family who had held a sinecure office against all protest, that 'he died with his drawn salary in his hand'. But let it be granted that Dickens the humorist is foremost and most precious. For we might well spare the phrase of wit just quoted rather than the one describing Traddles (whose hair stood up), as one who looked 'as though he had seen a cheerful ghost'. Or rather than this:

He was so wooden a man that he seemed to have taken his wooden leg naturally, and rather suggested to the fanciful observer that he might be expected—if his development received no untimely check—to be completely set up with a pair of wooden legs in about six months.

Or rather than the incident of the butcher and the beef-steak. He gently presses it, in a cabbage leaf, into Tom Pinch's pocket. ' "For meat", he said with some emotion, "must be humoured, not drove." '

A generation, between his own and the present, thought Dickens to be vulgar; if the cause of that judgement was that he wrote about people in shops, the cause is discredited now that shops are the scenes of the novelist's research. 'High life' and most wretched life have now given place to the little shop and its parlour, during a year or two. But Dr. Brown, the author of *Rab and His Friends*, thought that Dickens committed vulgarities in his diction. 'A good man was Robin' is right enough; but 'He was a good man, was Robin' is not so well, and we must own that it is Dickensian; but assuredly Dickens writes such phrases as it were dramatically, playing the cockney. I know of but two words that Dickens habitually misuses, and Charles Lamb misuses one of them precisely in Dickens's manner; it is not worth while to quote them. But for these his English is admirable; he chooses what is good and knows what is not. A little representative collection of the bad or foolish

English of his day might be made by gathering up what Dickens forebore and what he derided; for instance, Mr. Micawber's portly phrase, 'gratifying emotions of no common description', and Littimer's report that 'the young woman was partial to the sea'. This was the polite language of that time, as we conclude when we find it to be the language that Charlotte Brontë shook off; but before she shook it off she used it. Dickens, too, had something to throw off; in his earlier books there is an inflation—rounded words fill the inappropriate mouth of Bill Sikes himself—but he discarded them with a splendid laugh. They are charged upon Mr. Micawber in his own character as author. See him as he sits to hear Captain Hopkins read the petition in the debtors' prison 'from His Most Gracious Majesty's unfortunate subjects'. Mr. Micawber listened, we read, 'with a little of an author's vanity, contemplating (not severely) the spikes upon the opposite wall'. It should be remembered that when Dickens shook himself free of everything that hampered his genius he was not so much beloved or so much applauded as when he gave to his cordial readers matter for facile sentiment and for humour of the second order. His public were eager to be moved and to laugh, and he gave them Little Nell, and Sam Weller; he loved to please them, and it is evident that he pleased himself also. Mr. Micawber, Mr. Pecksniff, Mrs. Nickleby, Mrs. Chick, Mrs. Pipchin, Mr. Augustus Moddle, Mrs. Jellyby, Mrs. Plornish, are not so famous as Sam Weller and Little Nell; nor is Traddles, whose hair looked as though he had seen a cheerful ghost.

We are told of the delight of the Japanese man in a chance finding of something strange-shaped, an asymmetry that has an accidental felicity, an interest. If he finds such a grace or disproportion—whatever the interest may be—in a stone or a twig that has caught his ambiguous eye at the roadside, he carries it to his home to place it in its irregularly happy place. Dickens seems to have had a like joy in things misshapen or strangely shapen, uncommon or grotesque. He saddled even his heroes—those heroes are, perhaps, his worst work, young men at once conventional and improbable—with whimsically ugly names; while his invented names are whimsically perfect: that of Vholes for the predatory silent man in black, and that of Tope for the cathedral verger. A suggestion of dark and vague flight in Vholes; something of old floors, something respectably furtive and musty, in Tope. In Dickens, the love of lurking, unusual things, human and inanimate—he wrote of his discoveries delightedly in his letters—was hypertrophied; and it has its part in the simplest and the most fantastic of his humours, especially those that are due to his child-like eyesight; let us read, for example, of the rooks that seemed to attend upon Dr. Strong (late of Canterbury) in his Highgate garden, 'as if they had been written to about him by the Canterbury rooks and were observing him closely in consequence'; and of Master Micawber, who had a remarkable head voice—'On looking at Master Micawber again

I saw that he had a certain expression of face as if his voice were behind his eyebrows'; and of Joe in his Sunday clothes, 'a scarecrow in good circumstances'; and of the cook's cousin in the Life Guards, with such long legs that 'he looked like the afternoon shadow of somebody else'; and of Mrs. Markleham, 'who stared more like a figure-head intended for a ship to be called the Astonishment, than anything else I can think of'. But there is no reader who has not a thousand such exhilarating little sights in his memory of these pages. From the gently grotesque to the fantastic run Dickens's enchanted eyes, and in Quilp and Miss Mowcher he takes his joy in the extreme of deformity; and a spontaneous combustion was an accident much to his mind.

Dickens wrote for a world that either was exceedingly excitable and sentimental, or had the convention or tradition of great sentimental excitability. All his people, suddenly surprised, lose their presence of mind. Even when the surprise is not extraordinary their actions are wild. When Tom Pinch calls upon John Westlock in London, after no very long separation, John, welcoming him at breakfast, puts the rolls into his boots, and so forth. And this kind of distraction comes upon men and women everywhere in his books—distractions of laughter as well. All this seems artificial to-day, whereas Dickens in his best moments is the simplest, as he is the most vigilant, of men. But his public was as present to him as an actor's audience is to the actor, and I cannot think that this immediate response was good for his art. Assuredly he is not solitary. We should not wish him to be solitary as a poet is, but we may wish that now and again, even while standing applauded and acclaimed, he had appraised the applause more coolly and more justly, and within his inner mind.

Those critics who find what they call vulgarisms think they may safely go on to accuse Dickens of bad grammar. The truth is that his grammar is not only good but strong; it is far better in construction than Thackeray's, the ease of whose phrase sometimes exceeds and is slack. Lately, during the recent centenary time, a writer averred that Dickens 'might not always be parsed', but that we loved him for his, &c., &c. Dickens's page is to be parsed as strictly as any man's. It is, apart from the matter of grammar, a wonderful thing that he, with his little education, should have so excellent a diction. In a letter that records his reluctance to work during a holiday, the word 'wave' seems to me perfect: 'Imaginary butchers and bakers wave me to my desk.' In his exquisite use of the word 'establishment' in the following phrase, we find his own perfect sense of the use of words in his own day; but in the second quotation given there is a most beautiful sign of education. 'Under the weight of my wicked secret' (the little boy Pip had succoured his convict with his brother-in-law's provisions) 'I pondered whether the Church would be powerful enough to shield me ... if I divulged to that establishment.' And this is the phrase that may remind us of the eighteenth-century writers of prose, and among those writers of none so readily as of Bolingbroke: it occurs in that passage of Esther's life in which, having lost her beauty, she resolves to forgo a love unavowed. 'There was nothing to be undone; no chain for him to drag or for me to break.'

If Dickens had had the education which he had not, his English could not have been better; but if he had had the *usage du monde* which as a young man he had not, there would have been a difference. He would not, for instance, have given us the preposterous scenes in *Nicholas Nickleby* in which parts are played by Lord Frederick Verisopht, Sir Mulberry Hawke, and their friends; the scene of the hero's luncheon at a restaurant and the dreadful description of the mirrors and other splendours would not have been written. It is a very little thing to forgive to him whom we have to thank for—well, not perhaps for the 'housefull of friends' for the gift of whom a stranger, often quoted, once blessed him in the street; we may not wish for Mr. Feeder, or Major Bagstock, or Mrs. Chick, or Mrs. Pipchin, or Mr. Augustus Moddle, or Mr. F.'s aunt, or Mr. Wopsle, or Mr. Pumblechook, as an inmate of our homes. Lack of knowledge of the polite world is, I say, a very little thing to forgive to him whom we thank most chiefly for showing us these interesting people just named as inmates of the comedy homes that are not ours. We thank him because they are comedy homes, and could not be ours or any man's; that is, we thank him for his admirable art.

A. C. BRADLEY
1851—

The Reaction against Tennyson[1]

A Miscellany, 1929

WHEN he died, in 1870, Dickens was still at the height of his fame. The public idolized him, and critical readers, though they had a good deal to say against him, did not question his greatness. Some twenty years later, however, a decided change was visible, chiefly among such readers and especially among the younger men of letters. It was more than a cooling of enthusiasm: it was a strong reaction. Certain defects of the novelist were keenly felt, and all the more keenly because it seemed that his immense popularity had been largely due to them. To decry Dickens, even to protest that you could not read him, became a fashion and a mark of being up to date in taste. In this reaction two curious traits might be noticed. One was the belief that Dickens's faults were a new discovery and had never been suspected in his lifetime. The other was still stranger, and much more important. The dislike of his faults appeared often to kill the power of perceiving and enjoying his virtues. Because you could not abide the death of Paul Dombey or Little Nell, you listened to Sam Weller and Mrs. Gamp without a smile.

This was the nadir of Dickens's star. After

[1] A lecture given to members of the English Association in Birmingham, Manchester, and London.

a time it rose again. The wholesome work of reaction was finished. In the more literary sections of the public, and among men of letters, there is now a fairly general agreement about him. His defects, by no means unimportant in quality and quantity, are simply taken for granted; but his astonishing genius is fully recognized, and his almost inexhaustible creations are as keenly enjoyed as they were fifty years ago. The best critique of his works in the first decade of this century came, not from an old stager, but from Mr. Chesterton. And now, if you are unable to read Dickens and yet wish to be in the literary swim, you must either hold your tongue about him or tell lies about yourself.

This story, down to a certain stage in it, has exactly repeated itself in the case of Tennyson—a writer less astonishing in genius and much less faulty in art. At the time of his death, some five-and-twenty years ago, he was immensely popular; and of a large part of the public it may fairly be said that it did not recognize his weaknesses and even liked them. After a while, in small circles, the reaction began, and it has spread, and, so far as it has spread, is now intense. The nadir of his fame may not quite be reached, but it can hardly be far off. To care for his poetry is to be old-fashioned, and to belittle it is to be in the movement. And those curious traits of the Dickens reaction have reappeared, the first of them in a more amusing shape. The mid-Victorian, a figure amply proving the creative energy of Georgian imagination, is supposed to have been blind to Tennyson's defects, though the actual surviving mid-Victorian rarely hears a sane word about them which was not familiar to him in his youth. And—what really matters—the antipathy to these defects seems in some cases to have so atrophied the power of enjoyment that Tennyson's weakest poems and his best meet with the same indifference or contempt, and a reader will remain unmoved by lines which, if he were ignorant of their authorship, he would hail with delight.

The loss of such delight is a heavy one, and ingratitude is not a pretty vice; but otherwise the reaction against Tennyson is not, on the whole, a matter for regret. It was necessary, for one thing, in the interests of poetry itself. For the formal characteristics of his style were easily caught, and Tennysonian minor poetry, if less absurd than Byronic minor poetry, was quite as sickening; so that those who admire him most can only rejoice that no trace of his influence remains in the poetry of the present day. Besides, his popularity in the last twenty or thirty years of his life made the public unjust to other living poets, and he was over-estimated even by some good critics; and in such cases (George Eliot's is another) some reaction is both natural and wholesome. It hastens, also, that sifting process to which the works of all poets have to submit (unless, like Sappho's, they are almost all lost). The result of that process is that a part of the works is separated out and continues to be widely read or, as we say, to 'live', while the remainder passes more or less from public view and is explored only by lovers of the poet or students of literary history. This has already happened to Tennyson's immediate predecessors, and it is happening to him now. When the process is complete nobody troubles to dwell on the poet's defects, nobody is blinded by them to his merits, and it is possible to form a comparative estimate of his worth. The time for this has not yet come in Tennyson's case, and it will hardly come in my lifetime; but, if only for your entertainment, I will hazard a brief prophecy. I believe he will be considered the best poet of his own age, though not so much the best as his own age supposed; and, while I have never thought that in native endowment he was quite the equal of the best of the preceding age, yet the distance, as it seems to me, is not wide; and, as he was blessed with long life, made (like Pope) the most of his gift, and in a wonderful degree retained and even developed it to the end, I do not doubt that his place will be beside them, and expect that the surviving portion of his work will not be smaller than what survives of theirs. But I am not going to offer reasons for this forecast, or to attempt an account of his merits, and still less to try to prove them. You cannot prove the merits of Sappho's fragments or of *King Lear* (which Tolstoy thought poor stuff); and I should not dream of disputing with some one who is indifferent, say, to *The Lotos-Eaters*. The dispute would end, at best, in nothing, and, at worst, in each of us saying aloud what he only said to himself at the beginning—that his opponent, so far as poetry is concerned, should for ever hold his peace. On the other hand, the reaction, in

my view, is by no means wholly unjustified, and
I propose later, without constant reference to it,
to touch on certain features of Tennyson's poetry
which partly justify it. Only first I must refer to
what I think mere follies that appear in this
reaction; and I will begin with one or two
that are connected with his former immense
popularity.

Short poems that are very popular and so are
frequently quoted or mentioned become, as we
say, hackneyed; and then we are in danger of
thinking them commonplace. But if a poem is
very popular because it is very good, its becoming
hackneyed for us is entirely our affair. It remains
what it was, but we through our weakness cannot
get at it. Our imagination, our feelings, our ears,
act so feebly as we read it that what we read is,
in fact, not *it*, but a degraded copy of it. Now
and then the newspaper critic of a concert may
be found complaining that a Beethoven symphony is hackneyed: but a Beethoven symphony
never became hackneyed to Wagner or Brahms,
and what is really hackneyed is the critic's mind.
And so I have met people who decried as hackneyed *Break, break, break*, and *Crossing the Bar*;
and doubtless, if they cannot read these poems
freshly, they do well not to read them at all. But
as for the poems themselves, I think they are as
sure of immortality as anything in the language.

'But', some one perhaps will answer, 'they are
spoilt for me because they have been taken to
the heart of the great middle class, with its
nauseous sentiment, domestic and religious. One

of them—or a misquotation from one of them—is engraved on tombstones, and the other has now been added to *Hymns Ancient and Modern*.' Well, these uses of the poems may be fitting or unfitting; but, however that may be, one does not cease to love daffodils because the public loves them. And there are two ways of being a slave to the public. One is to be afraid to differ from it, and the other to be afraid to agree with it.

Again, the popularity of a poem may be due in part to its defects; and then those who see this sometimes make a great mistake and imagine that other poems of the author, also popular and in certain ways resembling the first, have the same defects. For example, the *May-Queen* poems used to be extremely popular, and they were so partly for a bad reason. They contain lovely lines, and stanzas that would be perfect if only the voice were not the poet's instead of the child's; but their pathos, besides being too obvious, is mingled with a sickly and even false sentiment. The same defect appears more or less in other great writers of that day. The best writers of earlier and also of later days are free from it, and it rightly offends us. But that is no excuse for talking as if the *May-Queen* poems were typical of Tennyson; and what are we to think of critics who, perceiving that *The Grandmother* also deals with rustic and domestic life, imagine that it has the same defects and is on the same level as the *May-Queen* poems? And if, again, in modernizing some of the Arthurian stories, Tennyson did them an injury, it scarcely follows without inquiry that in modernizing others he injured them too, or that it is sensible to dismiss the *Idylls of the King* in a lump with contempt.

Let us pass to matters of more weight. The root of the reaction against Tennyson among capable readers of the new generation is, we are told, that his ideas do not appeal to them—neither the more explicit ideas, sometimes called the 'philosophy', found in *In Memoriam* and elsewhere, nor the ideas or way of regarding life implicit in many other poems. This is probably true, and, if this were all, there would be little or nothing in the fact to cause surprise or regret. The statement would hold good of the ideas of Carlyle, and, with some modification, of those of Ruskin and Browning. They all permeated, more or less, the minds of several generations, and, doubtless losing something in the process, became an atmosphere surrounding the mind of the present; and an atmosphere, however wholesome, cannot well have the charm of novelty. But every generation naturally asks for novelty; and, further, the ideas and the literature of times immediately preceding its own are apt to be the least interesting of all to it, because they have less novelty for it than those of periods more distant, and may even be felt, as those more distant ideas are not, to be a prison from which it is necessary to escape. This, no doubt, is a wise provision of Nature to ensure progress, and it would be foolish to complain of it, even though its result is that the full meaning of the ideas in question is lost for a time and remains to be re-discovered when they have ceased to be familiar.

There is little I need say about the attitude of the reaction towards Tennyson's 'philosophical' ideas, but I cannot say it without interposing a word of protest. Harm has been done by those who have spoken of his 'philosophy', whether to exalt or to belittle it. He was not a philosopher, any more than Wordsworth was, or Browning, or Meredith, though he shows, I think, more signs than they do of the gift that makes a philosopher. And he, like them, is happier when he simply expressed his ideas, with the emotions that accompany them, than when he argues about them, or attempts to systematize them; happier in *The Ancient Sage* and *The Higher Pantheism* and certain passionate sections of *In Memoriam* than in certain other sections of that poem, just as Browning is happier in *Rabbi ben Ezra* or *Prospice* than in *La Saisiaz*, and Wordsworth in *Tintern Abbey* than in the most analytical passages of *The Prelude*. Coleridge might perhaps have discussed with profit, in prose, the question whether that which Wordsworth found in Nature was found there or put there; even if this question were suitable for verse at all, Wordsworth was not competent to discuss it. Neither Tennyson nor Browning offers, I believe, any argument for personal immortality that had not been stated in preciser terms and more complete connexion by philosophers; but their passion for this belief made fine poetry, and far more impressive to me than their arguments in support of it is the bare fact (whatever it may point to) that two minds so much superior to my own could make no sense of the world without it.

I come now to the 'philosophical' ideas, as distinguished from the arguments, that lay nearest to Tennyson's heart. One of them was that just mentioned. A second was the idea of human progress on the earth—the faith that man, through a process lasting for thousands or millions of years, is developing into something infinitely greater than he was at first, and even that 'the whole creation' is moving to 'some divine event'. Of this second idea I shall say nothing, because, whatever the attitude of the 'reaction' may be in regard to it, Tennyson's attitude does not appear to be a source of irritation. The third may be called the idea of God; but it would be better, I think, to call it the idea of the ultimate power, because the main source of Tennyson's interest in this idea seems to me to have lain in its bearing on the other two. The main source, that is to say, was not so much the strictly religious impulse to adore as the need to be satisfied that, since the ultimate power in the universe is clearly not man, this power,

> He, They, One, All; within, without;
> The Power in darkness whom we guess,

is of such a nature as to value highest what man at his best values highest, and therefore to ensure his progress both on earth and elsewhere. And that need, we should observe, was for Tennyson peculiarly imperative. Like his great predecessors, he may be called a poet of Nature, but with a difference. For Wordsworth and Shelley the spirit of Nature, we may roughly say,[1] is

[1] As regards Shelley the statement is not quite accurate.

wholly beautiful, good, and unhampered, while in man this same spirit is thwarted, and struggles against ugliness and evil; and so Nature is, for them, a promise and almost a pledge of man's ultimate victory. But it could not be so for Tennyson. Though he wrote *In Memoriam* before the days of Darwin, he had fully realized and keenly felt the conflict, pain, and waste in Nature; so that it presented to him not a solution, but the same problem as man's life, and required the same further guarantee. Then (to look for a moment beyond *In Memoriam*), as years went by, this need became still more insistent, because the advance of science and the theory of evolution (both of which he welcomed) had, however unjustifiably, made materialism a popular magazine-philosophy, and this philosophy again, in Tennyson's view, was in part responsible for moral phenomena which he detested. This was unfortunate for him, partly because it alarmed and exasperated him and touched some of his poetry with the spirit of ephemeral controversy, and partly because it led unwise opponents to regard him as a reactionary, and unwise admirers to make claim for him as a philosophic teacher which he never made for himself.

To return to the reaction. I quite understand that *In Memoriam*, as regards its ideas, cannot appeal to readers now as it did to thousands in the generation before mine, or even in mine or the next after mine. But why *In Memoriam* and other poems, because of these ideas, should lose all interest for those who share in the reaction, I do not understand; and still less how any one can offer the explanation that these ideas, one or all, are so alien to his own that he cannot read the poems with enjoyment or even with patience. That explanation, it seems to me, implies an altogether perverse attitude towards poetry or, for that matter, any other product of imagination.

I do not mean merely that a reader who is indifferent or hostile to the main ideas used in a poem ought to be able, in spite of this, to enjoy the beauty of its style and music. I mean that he ought to be able to adopt these ideas for the time, to identify himself imaginatively with them, to feel as his own the emotions that accompany them; and, further, that unless he has done this he cannot fully appreciate the poem or, in the full sense of the word, read it. If, as I read Browning's *Cavalier Tunes*, my Roundhead sympathies prevent my feeling like a Cavalier, how can I read the *Tunes* with any gusto; and, read without gusto, are they themselves? Are the Jolly Beggars to me what they are in the poem, if I refuse to be a Jolly Beggar for the moment and insist on remaining a member of a Charity Organization Committee? And if this holds of poems like these, equally, or if possible even more, it holds of a poem like *In Memoriam*, which is concerned not with a past political conflict or a minor form of free enjoyment, but with something which has been, is, and always must be, the centre of men's doubts, fears, hopes, or convictions about themselves and the world, and which, in a variety of shapes, may even be said to form the ultimate subject of all great philosophies and religions and of most of the greatest poems. In *In Memoriam* it takes a particular shape. There is a large and beautiful soul—for all who know it, a pre-eminently large and beautiful soul; for them, therefore, something of the highest value: and suddenly, with all its promise unfulfilled, it appears to vanish like the rainbow of a minute, and therefore to have no more value than the rainbow for the ultimate power. Can this really be so? Again: this power, as Job believes, is the friend of the man who tries to do its will; yet Job, who knows—and, for the author of the poem, truly knows—that, imperfect as he is, he has tried with all his heart to do that will, is treated like a defiant rebel: how can this be? Again: God is perfect goodness and power; how is it, then, that Satan and his host exist, and that man, who was made in God's image, has lost his Paradise; and how, once more, that countless images of God appear to walk their way to Purgatory or to Hell? And, whether visibly or no, the same mystery haunts all great tragedy and even great works not tragic. Was ever soul nobler than Antigone's or Othello's; yet what becomes of them? And if Don Quixote's soul was no less noble, why was it the prey of delusions and a butt for vulgar insult? Well, then, when I read the *Book of Job*, the *Divine Comedy*, or the *Antigone*, surely I do not say, 'These ideas about God or Zeus or Heaven and Hell are not my ideas and clash with mine, and therefore I cannot enter into them'. On the contrary, I do enter into them and feel in them the same problem and the same passion that belong to my own ideas, truer perhaps than they, but unlikely perhaps to be the unveiled truth. And if I did anything else, what would you call me? A man with no literary education; or else a man with a literary education, but—stupid.

We may pass now from what I have called mere follies of the reaction to consider characteristics of Tennyson's poetry which, at any rate in some degree, seem to justify it. And I will begin with the moral content or spirit of the poetry.

This, we hear it said, is conventional. If that charge meant, as it ought to mean, that Tennyson's morality was a thing of use and wont, taken up without personal conviction from the social atmosphere around him, it would be ridiculous. He was himself about as unconventional as a decent citizen can be, and the moral ideas in his poetry are plainly matters of intense conviction. But it is true that there is nothing startling in them, and little that would even be arresting apart from the poems themselves. Here he resembles Dickens and Thackeray rather than Browning and Meredith. Further, the ideas or, let me say, the virtues that he cares about most are mainly of one type: self-control, self-sacrifice, faithfulness, loyalty to law and to obligations personal and social, patriotism, and the like. They are not, with Tennyson, ascetic virtues; but, if we use the slippery antithesis of order and progress, we may call them the virtues of order.[1]

[1] Tennyson would have objected to this. 'Progress' for him meant moving upward, working out the beast, the slave of mere instinct and impulse; and those virtues are fundamental forms of this working out.

The 'moral' of the *Lotos-Eaters* (if under protest we use the word) is that the law of life is labour, and that to reject it is to lose all that makes life worth living and to imagine gods as idle and selfish as yourself. The *Palace of Art* tells us that the self-centred uncreative enjoyment of beauty is poison to the soul; the *Vision of Sin*, that abandonment to sensual excitement leads to cynicism and incapacity to enjoy anything at all; *Love and Duty*, that, where these clash, love, even at its best, must give way. The pursuit of the Beatific Vision, we hear in the *Holy Grail*, is for a Galahad or a Percivale here and there; and the Vision comes to Bors, who could not care to see it unless Lancelot might see it too; but wellnigh all the Knights, and even the King himself, are here on earth, not to spend their force in seeking it, but to right human wrongs.

The poems which enshrine these ideas certainly do not lack originality, and the significance of the ideas themselves is not easily exhausted; but of course they do not arrest the reader's attention in at all the same degree as the ideas contained in not a few poems by Browning, Arnold, or Rossetti. Nor do they resemble ideas which are popular now, or at least were popular three years ago. The idea, for instance, that the business of life is to develop one's individuality is foreign to Tennyson, and he would not have been sympathetic towards it, I imagine, even in the rare cases where there is much individuality to develop. Again, there is the view of life as an adventure. It may not be a profound view, but unquestionably there are virtues of adventure, and in Tennyson's poetry they hardly get their due. He is not, indeed, unsympathetic here, but he feels strongly the perils of the adventurous temper. 'God help me', cries his sailor-boy,

> God help me! save I take my part
>   Of danger on the roaring sea,
> A devil rises in my heart
>   Far worse than any death to me.

The sailor-lad worked his devil out, or used it up, in that way; and if Tennyson had written the poem later, he would probably have sent him into the Navy. The poor wild youth in *Rizpah* came to a bad end, and Tennyson makes the mother say:

> The king should have made him a soldier; he would have been one of the best.

It is hard, he seems to tell us, for such spirits to find their place in the social order, and yet, if they cannot do so, they are apt to make havoc of their own lives and the lives of others. There are other poems of Tennyson's, no doubt, which breathe the spirit of adventure in a much higher sense of that word: *Ulysses*, for example, or *Merlin and the Gleam*. And the first of these is one of his very best, and the second one of his latest and most personally characteristic. But (though this does not injure the poem) the 'idea' in *Ulysses* is adopted from Dante; and neither the adventure in the other poem, nor yet that portrayed in *In Memoriam*, is of the kind that would appeal to the reaction or soften its heart to Tennyson.

There seems to be a notion that Tennyson was from the first popular. In reality it was long before he became so. After the volumes of 1842, no doubt, he was generally regarded by literary readers as the first of living poets; but even those volumes did not make him popular, nor yet did *The Princess*, or *In Memoriam*, or the *Maud* volume. It was the four *Idylls of the King* published in 1859 that opened to him the heart of the public and began that immense popularity which he never saw diminished. On the other hand, FitzGerald was disappointed with every volume that appeared after 1842, and held that Tennyson never fulfilled the promise of early days; those very *Idylls* of 1859 were a rock of offence to admirers like Swinburne and Meredith; and, to the reaction, the whole collection of *Idylls*, his most ambitious work, is probably the most obnoxious. Without considering the reaction in particular, I may connect with these facts some further remarks on Tennyson's limitations.

In one respect FitzGerald was, surely, quite wrong. It is true—or at any rate I do not deny—that after 1842 Tennyson wrote nothing *of the same kind* that was equal to the *Lady of Shalott*, or the *Lotos-Eaters*, or even *Mariana*; but in most, perhaps in all, of the non-dramatic volumes after 1842 there was, I should say, something of *another* kind quite equal to those poems, and I doubt if Meredith or Swinburne would have questioned this, or if any critic of repute would question it now. And yet most lovers of

Tennyson's poetry, while sure that FitzGerald was so far wrong, still vaguely feel, I think, that the extraordinary promise of the early poems was never quite fulfilled. This fact seems puzzling, but the explanation seems to be that, rationally or not, we expect a man who writes first-rate short poems in his earlier life to write long ones at least as good in later years; and Tennyson failed to do this, none of his long poems being equal, as a whole, to the best of his short ones, early and late. Well, that would hold good of some other nineteenth-century poets, and I have tried elsewhere to point out general reasons for the fact. But what were the more special reasons in the case of Tennyson?

Let us take the *Idylls of the King*. They swarm with beautiful passages. Some of them, taken separately, I for my part continue to read with undiminished pleasure. But the whole, beyond doubt, fails to satisfy. There are various causes of the failure, affecting various readers in different degrees. Some readers are most displeased with certain defects of style, to which I will return. Some object most to Tennyson's morality; others to the element of allegory; others to his departure from the spirit of the old stories, or at any rate to his degradation of heroes like Tristram or Gawain. I feel all these objections more or less; and at the same time I do not think a poem can be too moral if its morality is sufficiently original or deep, and I do not care how much allegory it contains, or how freely it treats its material, if the result is successful. In poetry, at all events, the end justifies the means.

But in the morality and the allegorical meaning of the *Idylls* there is not much that is new, and what is new does not appear to deepen much the old. It fails to do so, I think, because Tennyson had not in any marked degree that universal interest in human nature, that penetrating insight into it, or that power of portraying it in uniquely individual forms, which belonged in different degrees to Shakespeare and to Browning. On what may be called the metaphysical or mystical side his mind was not simple, but in regard to human character it was. He could express perfectly certain feelings and moods, even passionate ones. He could depict admirably, in later years, such typical figures as the Grandmother and the Northern Farmer. But that is not enough for a long and wholly serious narrative, and it could not suffice for the *Idylls*, where the characters were to be modernized, and where, if the story was to have the effect of tragedy, it was especially important that the leading characters should be intensely imagined and thoroughly individual. This they are far from being. Guinevere is the most shadowy, and Lancelot the least; but Lancelot is not more individual than many heroes in novels of the second rank, and, although he is meant to be a *large* character, large as Othello and Antony are large, somehow he is not so. Arthur, again, in Tennyson's early *Morte d'Arthur*, is what he should be, because neither his relation to the lovers nor his semi-allegorical character comes in. But in the *Idylls* both come in, and the position is hopeless. He has in some measure to represent conscience; and then he is no person, and the relation of the lovers to him ceases to be personal. And yet he must be a person, a noble friend and a loving husband; and then we cannot give to the lovers the degree of sympathy which a tragic story demands. The result of all this is, to me, that, apart from the numberless beautiful passages in the *Idylls*, and apart from the *Passing of Arthur*, Tennyson succeeds most where the story makes but slight demands on the side of character (as in *Enid* and *Elaine*), and where the character interest is united with the mystical (as in the *Holy Grail*).

In *In Memoriam* this weakness of Tennyson's naturally does not appear. In *Maud* it is plain enough, but is not of much consequence. It matters little that neither Maud herself nor her brother is an individual, as each would have been if Browning had treated the subject. The hero, too, answers Tennyson's purpose sufficiently; but in his case the weakness in question is not quite unimportant, and one feels there is something amiss. This hero, like the speakers in the two *Locksley Hall* poems, drew down on Tennyson both anger and ridicule. The anger was mainly due to his attitude, real or supposed, towards war, and I pass it by. But what is the cause of the ridicule? The hero in Maud, it is said, is a poor hysterical creature. 'Well,' one answers, 'he was meant to be, and why should he not be? He excites enough sympathy for the purpose, and he is not the hero of a great tragedy like *Hamlet*.' And yet this answer does not suffice. For one thing it is doubtful if Tennyson was aware how poor a creature the hero was. It is the same case as that of Stephen Guest in the *Mill on the Floss*, and that of Ladislaw in *Middlemarch*. Some say that Maggie and Dorothea could not have been fascinated by such beings. I am sorry to say that I think this false; only I suspect that George Eliot herself was not heart-whole towards them. That is one thing; and another is this. When people took all the railing in *Maud* and the *Locksley Hall* poems for Tennyson's own railing, he justly protested. But, while they were clearly wrong in law, were they wholly wrong in fact? He once told his neighbour at a dinner-party that all the Tennysons were afflicted with black bile, and he dilated on this affliction with sufficient eloquence. Had it not something to do with the railing in those poems, and is it not this that we feel? And is not railing in literature a mistake? We may remember that the practice of railing distinguished two other great writers of that time, Carlyle and Ruskin, and that it diminished their influence. It has died out now: partly for good reasons, partly perhaps for the worst—that there is no prophet left in Israel.

In spite, however, of these defects, it remains true that, among the longer works, *Maud* and *In Memoriam* have the great advantage of not requiring original or intense conceptions of character. They have another. Though long, they are lyrical; and, if it would be absurd to class Tennyson with Herrick or Burns as simply or essentially a lyrical poet, one may still think that his style is most constantly and perfectly right when he is using lyrical forms. In particular, it is then, except in some of the earliest pieces, least open to the charge of elaborateness. This charge has been brought against Tennyson by good judges; most readers now feel, perhaps, that there is some ground for it; and I must refer to it briefly. As with other charges, so with this, it is necessary to distinguish. Tennyson rarely, perhaps never, 'pipes but as the linnets sing'. He does not attain, if he ever attempts, the artless air of the best songs of Burns or of some of the Elizabethans. Nor again has his style, even in his simpler lyrics, the bare trenchant force which Wordsworth, and Byron occasionally, could command. But 'elaborate' is surely not the appropriate word to apply to 'Break, break, break' or *Crossing the Bar*, to *Rizpah* or the *Northern Farmer*, to *Boadicea* or *The Revenge*, or even to 'Tears, idle tears' or 'The splendour falls',—and how easy it would be to extend this list of examples! In other and equally characteristic lyrical pieces—for instance, the *Dream of Fair Women*—the style is enriched, and may fairly be called elaborate. But then the word need bear no tinge of blame; it need not imply artifice, glossy polish, or irrelevant jewellery. And this holds good of many non-lyrical poems, such as *Oenone* or *Lucretius*. On the other hand, a good deal of the poetry, and especially, I think, of the narrative poetry, *is* elaborate either in a way or in a degree that is faulty. The defect is patent in cases where Tennyson makes most effort to be direct and plain (as in *Dora*, or again in *Enoch Arden* and in some of the English Idylls parodied by Calverley).[1] If again one turns from the *Idylls of the King*, I will not say to Chaucer, but to Morris or even to Arnold, one has at once a sense of relief and refreshment; and in the later *Idylls*, especially when the poet has to deal with matter that does not inspire him, one is conscious of effort and artifice and often of the mannerism to which they led. Now such defects (though they are not absent from *In Memoriam*) are much rarer in the lyrical verse, and therefore—to return to my point—it was an advantage to *In Memoriam* and *Maud* that they are lyrical. And *Maud*, on this side, is the superior. The stanza used in *In Memoriam* suits the poem admirably; but *Maud* has a much larger variety of metrical shapes, movements, and velocities; and the form of 'lyrical monodrama', where only one person of the drama speaks, but speaks always in a lyric, was perfectly adapted to the poet's genius. It seems to have been his own invention, and it has seldom been used since.[2]

[1] See Arnold's lectures *On Translating Homer*, Popular edition, pp. 161 ff.; and again Swinburne's *Essays and Studies* (1875), where Tennyson is frequently criticized without being named. If the 'reactionary' would consult these books he would understand why the surviving mid-Victorian fails to learn much from the reaction. I may add, what Swinburne would have confirmed, that, as Tennyson advanced in age, the lyrical verse, and in some degree the other verse, of the wonderful old poet freed itself more and more from the defects discussed above. And I take the opportunity to add further that, if I have made no mention in this lecture of Tennyson's dramas, it is not because I fail to admire and enjoy most of them, but merely because no one would base on them his claim to stand in the company of his immediate predecessors.

[2] I could not discuss in the lecture the merits and defects

Maud illustrates another characteristic of Tennyson's—one that we cannot wish away, but at the same time a source of danger. You know the distinction drawn between two strains in the Romantic Movement: the first, the more strictly 'romantic', best represented by Coleridge and Keats, with its love of picture and colour, the marvellous or mysterious, the far-away in time or place; the other, sometimes called 'naturalistic', of which Wordsworth, writing of the peasants around him, was the great exponent. Tennyson united these strains more completely than any of his predecessors. His poetic instinct, I think, impelled him most strongly in the more romantic direction. What first made his reputation in small circles, and still in the 'fifties most fascinated Rossetti and Morris, is to be found mainly in such poems as *Mariana*, the *Lady of Shalott*, the *Lotos-Eaters*, the *Dream of Fair Women*, *Morte d'Arthur*. But from the first he wrote also poems, usually much less good, dealing directly with the

of *In Memoriam*, and I can add here only a brief note. The questionings and arguments in that poem, like the more emotional sections, are subsidiary to its main subject, which is identical with that of *Maud*—the development of a soul through love, loss, and the conquest of loss. The treatment of this subject is very much deeper in *In Memoriam* than in *Maud*. On this side, indeed, *In Memoriam* seems to me, in point of originality and depth, much superior to any other long poem by Tennyson; and that its superiority here has not *poetic* value I cannot for a moment admit. That it is very defective as an 'organism' (which it does not claim to be) is obvious; and it has other defects. Perhaps my view, or feeling, may be indicated by the formula that it is the 'greatest' of the long poems, and *Maud* the 'best'.

life of his own time; and, though we have only internal evidence to go upon, it seems to me that he must have formed the conviction (often expressed by others in later days) that a poet ought to speak to his generation about itself. Therefore he wrote the English Idylls, and later he wrote *Maud*, and fixed the date of the events in the time of the Crimean War. Therefore, also, in writing of subjects of the other kind, he almost always modernized them. The old stories of Arthur's death and of the Sleeping Beauty enchanted him; but when he re-told them he added Prologues and Epilogues which show his intention to modernize; and his Lotos-Eaters and Ulysses were certainly not meant to be those of Homer. It was not till he came to write the *Idylls of the King* that the danger of this tendency became pressing, but in an inverted form it may be seen perhaps in *The Princess*, where he tries to put a present-day or future-day problem into surroundings that belong to no earthly place or time.

In his poems of contemporary life Tennyson enlarged considerably the range of the social subject-matter used by his great predecessors. I can only give one example. With a little exaggeration one may say the Englishwoman belonging to 'the nobility and gentry'—a person whom Shakespeare introduced often enough, usually under a foreign name—had for some time wellnigh vanished from serious poetry; for Crabbe did not often soar above the lower-middle class. Tennyson brought her back. He is reproached with doing so; but to do so was, in principle, a merit. His intention was not always well carried out, and I confess that I do not desire a closer acquaintance with Adeline or Lilian. But, to take two out of many instances, I think the stanzas *To Mary Boyle* one of the most perfect things he ever wrote, and an example of a kind of verse in which no contemporary approached him; and the stanzas beginning 'Come into the garden' were addressed to a girl leaving a ball-room 'in gloss of satin and glimmer of pearls', and their rhythm (Verrall told us) is meant to recall that of a polka. The weakness of character-drawing in *Maud* cannot affect those stanzas, or 'I have led her home', or 'O that 'twere possible'. When they are forgotten, *Romeo and Juliet* will be forgotten too.

After all this balancing and distinguishing, it would be a relief to me, as well as to you, if I ended with mere praise of what is greatest and highest in Tennyson's poetry. That I cannot do, but I will end with praise of a minor merit, which I think as indisputable as any poetical merit can be. It appears, though not solely, in his treatment of Nature. As regards that particular treatment of Nature which we associate with the name of Wordsworth, I should not think of comparing Tennyson either with Wordsworth or with Shelley: but I believe he is unsurpassed, and I suspect he is unequalled, among English poets in two things—one, the accuracy and delicacy of his perceptions; and the other, the felicity of his translation into language of that which he perceives. The first of these things is not specially distinctive of a poet; the second, though not by itself enough to make a poet great, is *the* distinction of a poet from other artists. Poetry is an art of language; and the born poet, of whatever size, is a person who has a peculiar gift for translating his experiences—whatever he sees, hears, feels, imagines, thinks—into metrical language, a special necessity in his nature to do this, and a unique joy in doing it well. The universe, we may say, is for him an invitation or a challenge to such expression. Well, just now we are concerned with sense-experiences, and especially those that come from Nature; and I repeat that here Tennyson seems to me unsurpassed and perhaps unequalled among our poets in the accuracy and delicacy of his perceptions, and in the felicity of his translation into language of that which he perceives.[1] As to the latter you may perhaps recall Ruskin's emphatic statement: 'Tennyson's "Rivulet" [he means *The Brook*] is far beyond anything I ever did, or could have done, in beauty of description.' As to the former you will certainly remember how attention was called in *Cranford* to the line,

More black than ash-buds in the front of March,

and how, since then, this line has been quoted *ad nauseam* as though it were something exceptional. In reality it is an example, and not a remarkable one, of something ubiquitous in Tennyson. If a man who had derived great happiness from the observation of nature were stricken with blind-

[1] Since this lecture was given, two excellent papers by Mr. Morton Luce on *Nature in Tennyson* (Birds and Trees) have appeared in the *British Review* (1915).

ness or confined for the rest of his life to a sick-room, and if he were condemned to lose his recollection of all poets but one, Tennyson's is the poetry he should choose to keep. There, for example, he could follow the progress of spring, from the beginning when

> Once more the Heavenly Power
> Makes all things new,
> And domes the red-plowed hills
> With loving blue;

when rosy plumelets tuft the larch, and a million emeralds break from the ruby-budded lime, and the ruddy-hearted blossom-flakes flutter down from the elm in tens of thousands; when the satin-shining palms appear on sallows in the windy gleams, and, later, a gust strikes the yew and puffs the swaying branches into smoke, and all the wood stands in a mist of green, till, later still, as you cross the wood you pass through a green gloom. Or, again, Tennyson will bring back to him the coming of the storm; its green malignant light near the horizon; then the ragged rims of thunder brooding low, with shadow-streaks of rain; and then the blasts that blow the poplar white and lash with storm the streaming pane; the stammering cracks and claps, the bellowing of the tempest, and at last the sounds of its retreat into the distance, moaning and calling out of other lands. Or, if he has loved the sea, with Tennyson he may still watch, on a windless day, the crisping ripples on the beach, and tender curving lines of creamy spray; or, on a windy one, crisp foam-flakes scudding along the level sand; or may recall from memories of the open sea a huge wave, green-glimmering towards the summit, with all its stormy crests that smoke against the skies. It will be just the same with him if he thinks of sunrise and sunset; of the nightingale or the thrush (whose voice has so become speech in *The Throstle* that, as he remembers it, he will laugh for amusement and joy); or of the mother-dog with her blind and shuddering puppies, or the rabbit fondling his own harmless face. And, as our invalid lies awake through the night in his sick-room, he may remember Tennyson when the grandfather clocks in rooms beneath throb thunder through the floors, and may remember Tennyson again as the dawn approaches and the casement slowly grows a glimmering square.

These are a few examples of what I mean, out of hundreds. Well, my friend of the reaction will not find in the poetic virtue shown in them the deepest and highest that poetry can reach or that this poet can reach; but he will not belittle it if he loves nature and knows what poetry is. Let him enjoy it, if he can enjoy nothing else in Tennyson. And if he enjoys and reveres science too (from a closer acquaintance, I hope, than mine), perhaps he will consider favourably the last claim that I urge on behalf of this poet. We live, and civilized man must continue to live, in an age of science. But, with the partial exception of Shelley, Tennyson is the only one of our great poets whose attitude towards the sciences of Nature was what a modern poet's attitude ought to be; the only one whose words constantly come to your mind as you read, if you can get no farther, your manual of astronomy[1] or geology; the only one to whose habitual way of seeing, imagining, or thinking, it makes any real difference that Laplace, or for that matter Copernicus, ever lived. He gazed too, without flinching, on aspects of Nature which Wordsworth did not face; and in this also the poetry of the future must surely follow him. One may hope that courage and faithfulness like his will not prevent it, as it prevented him, from sharing Wordsworth's intuition of

> A central peace, subsisting at the heart
> Of endless agitation.

But, however that may be, when we have again a poetry of Nature equal to Wordsworth's, it will have to be, in his own phrase, 'the inspired expression that is in the countenance of all science', and it will look back with gratitude to Tennyson.

GEORGE MOORE
1852–1933

George Eliot

Conversations in Ebury Street, 1924

MAID. Mr. Freeman, sir.
FREEMAN. I am afraid I am interrupting.
MOORE. You are welcome to interrupt my reading. I am always willing to lay aside a book to talk.

[1] Readers who may be interested in Tennyson's very numerous astronomical passages will find a full treatment

FREEMAN. To anybody?

MOORE. I prefer a man of wit; but since I am confessing myself I will disclose all. I would lay aside the wisest book to talk to a stupid woman.

FREEMAN. Or man?

MOORE. Yes; or man, for I have lost my taste for reading, and there are few greater misfortunes. We cannot always be talking, we cannot always be at the theatre, we cannot always be listening to music or visiting exhibitions of pictures; and to lose one's taste for reading is really like losing one's taste for bread.

FREEMAN. But I find you reading.

MOORE. Reading with a purpose, which is a very different thing from reading for pleasure. I am reading one of George Eliot's novels.

FREEMAN. Reading George Eliot, and for a purpose! I should not have been surprised if I had found you reading Jane Austen or the Brontës, but *Daniel Deronda*!

MOORE. *Silas Marner*, the story I am reading, is less purposeful. Ah, if she had been less purposeful!

FREEMAN. Yet in spite of her purposes, which are manifold, you find something to admire?

MOORE. The book has only just come from the library. I am in the first pages and am surprised to find that she has a better conception of what a story should be than most English writers. Her first book, *Scenes from Clerical Life*, had one story in it that has haunted me ever since.

of the subject by Mr. C. T. Whitmell in the *Journal and Transactions of the Leeds Astronomical Society for 1906*.

FREEMAN. You do not intend to write something like it?

MOORE. My dear Mr. Freeman!

FREEMAN. Forgive me. You intend to write an essay about her?

MOORE. An essay I must write about somebody, for I am short of copy. You remember that I withdrew *Impressions and Opinions* from the list of books that Liveright is publishing in America.

FREEMAN. Yes, and almost regretted your decision. Mr. Arthur Symons, your first critic, speaks of *Impressions and Opinions* as your best book.

MOORE. Arthur Symons speaks out of vague memories. If he were to open the book again he would see at once that it lacked unity of subject and language.

FREEMAN. Pater's definition of style: unity of subject, language, and something else. I have forgotten.

MOORE. So have I. In the 'eighties I collected much that I had written for various newspapers, for it seemed enough to flaunt ideas on all subjects.

FREEMAN. So the new book which will replace *Impressions and Opinions* will be a unity?

MOORE. To have made my meaning clear I should have said that if we are artists we must spend our lives in a continual striving after perfection, though in so doing we lose something we have already won. You asked me if I am writing an essay. No; I am weary of essays, and I don't write them well;

perhaps that's the reason why I am weary of them.

FREEMAN. And the name of the new book?

MOORE. *Conversations in Ebury Street.*

FREEMAN. Ah, I like the title. But why in Ebury Street? Why not simply *Conversations*? Too Landorian, and you would discriminate. Since Landor nobody has attempted conversations, and after the long interval it has come to you to revive a form in which criticism can be conducted more agreeably than in the essay.

MOORE. My admiration for Landor is without limit; I place him above Shakespeare, and to imitate him would be honour enough for me. But it was not Landor that prompted me to go and do likewise; the form rose out of what I had to say quite naturally. I was tempted, I know not why, but I was tempted to examine the novels that had come down to us from Defoe one after the other, to compare them to our poetry and to find them deficient in seriousness. This I could not do in an essay; the constant change of subject would have been irksome: to me at least it would have been. Of course, I might not have thought of the dialogue if I had not known Landor; and perhaps Landor would not have thought of the dialogue if he had not read Plato.

FREEMAN. Who is your interlocutor in the present instance?

MOORE. You are, as the manuscript on the table tells: Maid. *Mr. Freeman, sir.* Freeman. *I am afraid I am interrupting——*

FREEMAN. So you have begun the conversation?

MOORE. Yes; I have sketched some pages.

FREEMAN. Pray read them to me.

MOORE. The sheets on the table are only a beginning. I am at the stage of feeling my way into the subject, and the conversation may already have taken a wrong turn.

FREEMAN. So we discuss George Eliot together?

MOORE. George Eliot and Mr. Thomas Hardy are contrasted, or will be, in the dialogue that I am meditating.

FREEMAN. They are contrasted in the *Confessions*, and very violently.

MOORE. Has it come to be held as a crime to do else than to voice public opinion? to strike up with the little boy going down the street whistling gleefully in defiance of time and tune?

FREEMAN. Public opinion changes slowly, but it changes. Lord Byron and George Eliot are examples of how public opinion sees black where it once saw white, and to find an example in our time we have only to remember Tennyson. No doubt public opinion will change regarding Thomas Hardy, but I doubt the wisdom of treating the public like a whistling boy——

MOORE. Ordering his breeches to be taken down and you to hoist him? Of course, if you don't like the subject I shall abandon it at once; but will you tell me why?

FREEMAN. It seems to me that I have already given a reason. But if you want another, here it is. You have just told me that you are willing always to lay aside a book to talk, a thing which you are doing now, forgetful that George Eliot is a voluminous writer, and of the length of *Middlemarch*, which I think you will find difficult to finish before the winter. And then there is *Romola*, another long book.

MOORE. A book that I read at a time when I considered seriously the claims of Lord Leighton to be a great painter.

FREEMAN. He supplied the illustrations.

MOORE. And a better choice of an illustrator could not have been made. Both were workers in wax. *Daniel Deronda* I have never opened, and I shudder at the name of *Felix Holt*, a very leaden book that I stopped in the middle of long, long ago. You are quite right; I shall not be able to re-read all George Eliot. But that is not a reason why I should abandon my subject. I have read George Eliot, and if I send the book on the table back to the library at once I shall be able to speak to you out of my memories of her, which will be more agreeable than to read *Felix Holt* and ask you to dinner to argue about a defunct literature in which neither of us is in the least interested. So true is this that I am beginning to regret having opened the book on the table; my mind is already taking a bias.

FREEMAN. In her favour?

MOORE. Somewhat. You were going to ask me?

FREEMAN. It was certainly in my mind to ask you if your memories of George Eliot are enough for the dialogue you propose to write.

MOORE. You have come from her writings later than I have. Be my examiner.

FREEMAN. Tell me about *Silas Marner*.

MOORE. *Silas Marner* is an old man, a miser, who discovers a foundling at his door, boy or girl, I have forgotten which. He must have heard the child cry and risen from his bed, for he found the child by the light of the lantern. I am sure of that; I remember the lantern. Or am I inventing?

FREEMAN. I see that you still keep some faint memory of the story.

MOORE. I can speak more precisely of some of the others.

FREEMAN. Of *Middlemarch*?

MOORE. Of *Middlemarch* I remember the delight with which I read each volume, and there were six or eight in the edition that I came upon in my grandfather's library in Moore Hall when I was twelve or thirteen, mayhap fourteen. You may have caught sight of the portrait of an old gentleman on the wall of the lobby as you came upstairs—my grandfather the historian who in his preface to his history of the French Revolution (I give the preface in *Ave*), speaks with delightful resignation and humility of his failure to obtain recognition.

FREEMAN. Whosoever sees the portrait cannot but be attracted. A more characteristic portrait I have never seen.

MOORE. The portrait may be accepted as a commentary on the little confession which his pen ran into without his knowing that he was telling his secret—wherefore an admirable confession. He stops short almost in the middle of a sentence, and I can see him in my thoughts staring at the lake, associating it in some dim way with his own loneliness.

FREEMAN. Was the manuscript lost?

MOORE. Nothing was saved.

FREEMAN. I am sorry I did not see Moore Hall before I wrote my book.

MOORE. For no reason, at least for none that we can discover, some places are fixed deeper in our memories than others and become with time more real than the realities we live among. My grandfather's library is one of these spiritual realities, and with what strange intensity do I see the old gentleman's portrait over the chimney-piece, the wire-netted bookcases, the round table, the telescope, the view of the lake winding sadly mile after mile by low shores. And the hours that I spent reading *Middlemarch* can be recalled at will, and none more easily than the moment of disappointment when I returned the book to the shelves.

FREEMAN. Every man remembers his first intimations that life is not permanent. You read *Middlemarch*——

MOORE. My memories of *Adam Bede* are more explicit, and I can still hear the tone of the young squire's words when the parson tries to dissuade him—from what, I have forgotten; probably from walking out with Hetty; and I can recall how the story lost its humanity for me when the dairy-maid was taken by the police and tried for murder of her child, for the story of a crime is never a good story.

Some years ago I read *The Mill on the Floss*, a well-modulated narrative, with the aunts of Maggie Tulliver, each in her house, and her habits, and Maggie Tulliver going to meet a cripple or a hunchback in a pine wood. A delightful, intellectual companionship this was, one that George Eliot's readers thought should continue and end in marriage; but George Eliot knew better than her readers how life is made, and she chose that Maggie's bodily instincts should be awakened by a commonplace young man, who takes her away somewhere in a boat or a barge; I have forgotten which, but remember very well my delight when the young man seized Maggie's bare arm and kissed it, a very natural act, one which a girl would expect who was eloping with a young man, and my stifled disappointment when Maggie returned home despite the young man's apologies, tears and promises of amendment.

FREEMAN. You remember the flood, with Maggie and Tom Tulliver in a boat?

MOORE. Yes, and I have nothing to say against the end; it's harmless, it's almost good. But I am thinking now of the passing of all this literature, as well built as the mill itself, for George Eliot constructed well and solidly; her prose is rich and well balanced. But these qualities were not enough to save her from the whirling, bubbling flood of Time; her books have gone down like the mill. Lighter things have floated; hers have sunk out of sight; and I would see a reason for the sudden overthrow of one who in her day was looked upon as almost Shakespeare's equal.

FREEMAN. You have known many more old Victorians than I have, but I doubt——

MOORE. Doubt not, for I heard Professor Tyrrell, a great scholar, whose Latin and Greek verse was as perfect as such things can be, speak the words that you have just heard me speak: Almost Shakespeare's equal.

FREEMAN. Whereby we may deduce the moral that learning is insufficient.

MOORE. We may, indeed. But I would look into the soul and see why this woman's mind has passed into a dust hardly less anonymous than her body's.

FREEMAN. The bent of her mind was towards philosophy rather than imaginative literature.

MOORE. And it was George Henry Lewes who drew her attention to prose narrative as an outlet for her genius. Even genius is dependent on accident. The accident is always going by; talent misses it, but genius avails itself of it instantly, and George Eliot availed herself of her chance. But that is a side issue; we are seeking the reason why she should have passed into such sudden oblivion whilst others, the Brontës, should remain.

FREEMAN. You admit that her prose is rich and well balanced, and I agree with you. But there is no pleasure in it.

MOORE. You are quite right; there is very little pleasure in it. But why is there no pleasure in it?

FREEMAN. Something in her character, perhaps.

MOORE. Let us then seek her failure in her character. I know she met George Henry Lewes and that is about all I do know of her. Whence came she? Was she a townswoman or a countrywoman? Did she come from the north or the south or the east or the west? Whom did she know before she met Lewes? Was he her first lover, her second, her third? Tell me all you know about her.

FREEMAN. Her name was Marian Evans, and she came from Warwickshire.

MOORE. From the middle of England, like Shakespeare. Balzac, too, came from the middle of France.

FREEMAN. Her father was a land agent to Mr. Francis Newdigate, a Warwickshire squire.

MOORE. And she was sent to school. But to what school?

FREEMAN. That I can't tell you, but without doubt to some school in the neighbourhood, perhaps in Warwick. Do you know Warwick?

MOORE. Yes. In my boyhood Warwick was a lovely old English town full of gardens and gables, and associated with the Middle Ages—Warwick Castle, with a bad picture of a man in a cave shown to travelling folk, the very town in which there would be a fine, large, handsome school for young ladies. Birmingham is over the border, but no more than twenty miles away, and she may have been educated in Birmingham.

FREEMAN. I can tell you that at her mother's death she was recalled from school to look after her father's house. I have always heard that the change was welcomed by her, for even in her teens she resented direction in her studies. At Arbury Farm she applied herself to the French and Italian languages, and I think music was a hobby of hers.

MOORE. I shouldn't have suspected music from her writing. But Nature is ever capricious. Tell me more.

FREEMAN. At Arbury Farm she refused to go to church and nearly quarrelled with her father, and afterwards she began to write for the *Westminster Review*.

MOORE. I am beginning to understand. And after the publication of two or three articles the editor wrote asking her to call at the office when she came to London; and in London she made the acquaintance of John Stuart Mill, Herbert Spencer, the inevitable Harriet Martineau and the desirable George Henry. Can you give me the date when she left Arbury Farm?

FREEMAN. I will inquire the matter out in the library.

MOORE. I am beginning to understand. She came up to London to participate in the discovery that pleasure was a mistake, almost a vulgarity, and to hear the beautiful eighteenth century spoken of as the mischievous and shameful century. We have always been under the domination of France, spiritually, and having worshipped beauty must needs follow France into ugliness. I would tell you who began the new cult if I could; there must have been somebody before Courbet, who spoke about truth of effect and local colour. Be this as it may, he was committed to it, and Troyon still more so, and these were followed by Millet, who took it upon himself to explain the miserable lot of the peasant; and whosoever saw it, remembers *L'Homme à la Houe*, a detestable object, but which so stirred the loose bowels of compassion that the very world was certain something must be done to relieve the monotony of the peasant's lot. Philanthropy and realism entered art arm in arm; and it is believed that Rosa Bonheur never wore a crinoline, preferring to walk about in breeches and a blouse. She wore clogs and led a life more laborious than that of the carthorses she painted. Rosa Bonheur—how well the name goes with her pictures! The syllables tramp just like the great grey cart-horse that the peasant rides into the middle of the fair. Rosa Bonheur—was there ever a more cynical name? She only just escaped Rose. Rose Bonheur—a woman in whose life a rose never flourished, and who repudiated happiness! Do tell me, and quickly, when Marian Evans changed her name to *George Eliot*.

FREEMAN. But you do not believe that the character of a human being is modified by a name, inherited or assumed? You said just now that Rosa Bonheur's name was in direct contradiction to her character.

MOORE. The name tramps like a cart-horse, and I cannot believe she would have painted the same pictures if her name had been plain Rose. But Rosa Bonheur is a side issue; we are speaking of George Eliot. Tell me when she changed the name of Marian Evans, a splendid name, and how well it goes with Arbury Farm! I can see myself in my imagination directing an envelope: Miss Marian Evans, Arbury Farm, Warwickshire. Can you tell me when she changed her name?

FREEMAN. I have no exact information. Have you an encyclopaedia?

MOORE. An encyclopaedia in this house! No.

FREEMAN. We may assume for the moment that her first book, the translation of Strauss's *Life of Jesus*, was published under the name of *George Eliot*.

MOORE. Why should we assume that?

FREEMAN. I have told you that her father was much distressed by her refusal to go to church——

MOORE. Had I been her father, I should have said: Marian, I will allow you to omit church if in return you will choose some other name than *George Eliot*.

FREEMAN. What name would you suggest to her?

MOORE. *Oliver Brunskill*.

FREEMAN. There's not much beauty in that name.

MOORE. We mustn't seek beauty in names—character. Do you think my writings would have been the same if I had adopted *Annie Grey* as my pseudonym? George Henry Lewes, her guide and bugle-call (it was he who first suggested that she should turn her hand to fiction), should have said, when they were debating the pseudonym necessary for *Scenes from Clerical Life*: I do not urge you, Marian, to choose *Annie Grey*—indeed, I urge you not to choose it; and we can imagine Marian answering: But why, dear George, are you averse from the name *George Eliot*? It is so uncompromising.

FREEMAN. And what answer would you set down for George Henry Lewes?

MOORE. A name too faintly genteel for you, Marian. The phrase might have risen up in his mind *as genteel as an omnibus*, but he would not have spoken it, and continued: Hardly a man's name, hardly a woman's, without any sex on it. The word *sex* would have frightened Marian, and she would have answered that the name was chosen before she knew him as a suitable name to go on the title page of a translation of Strauss's *Life of Jesus*. But why continue it? George Henry would have interposed. *Scenes from Clerical Life*, by Marian Evans, to which Marian would have answered drily: I have to consider my father.

FREEMAN. I do not know if the translation was made at Arbury Farm or when she went to London.

MOORE. It can't be helped. In London she adopted the morality of her circle: morality without God, a fantastic theory if ever there was one. Even with God's help men and women stray into the primrose path; how then can we expect them to remain in the strait and narrow way if there be no promise of reward or punishment? an altogether impracticable morality, as is proved indeed by Marian herself who went to live with a married man and wrote under his roof *Scenes from Clerical Life* and other admonitory works, thereby hanging herself out like a banner from the roof on which is inscribed the magic word: Excelsior!

FREEMAN. Lewes was her single transgression from the moral law.

MOORE. Our information on the subject is too slight to warrant literary investigation, and further transgressions, could they be proved against her, would weaken my argument.

FREEMAN. You think then that the foundations of her style are to be discovered in Lewes?

MOORE. Not in Lewes's writing, but in the double life she was leading.

FREEMAN. You trace George Eliot's style to a conflict between theory and conduct, and I think you are on surer ground than you were in that fantastic theory that the name we bring into the world or that we assume is accountable for all our acts and thoughts.

MOORE. Encouraged by your sympathy I will venture a little further into a theology which some will regard as casuistical, saying that if she had transgressed oftener her style would no longer be the same. You see, she may have gone to live with Lewes for doctrinal reasons (indeed, it almost looks as if she had), false reasons, of course. But if further transgressions could be urged against her we might assume that she was pursuing happiness, and happiness being in her mind would have found an outlet in her works. You see, my dear Mr. Freeman, a woman who transgresses frequently, escapes the Christian conscience, and we acquit her of the sin against the Holy Ghost, a sin that the Pagan and the Christian worlds look upon with equal detestation. I flatter myself that I stand shoulder to shoulder with Canterbury in all that concerns this sin, except its unforgivable nature.

FREEMAN. If a man or a woman cannot accept Christian doctrine you would advocate that he or she should lead a licentious life, escaping thereby from setting a bad example?

MOORE. I would not have you fall into the makeshift argument of the preacher, who would have us look upon Antiquity as a degrading past of which the least said the better.

FREEMAN. Antiquity affords the highest instances of morality.

MOORE. As I have said, Antiquity and Christianity hold one sin in equal detestation and I think I am guilty of no paradox if I say that her style is the outcome of the moral conflict in which she found herself involved; but redeemed by Paganism or by Christianity (if there be redemption in the Christian creed for the soul guilty of the sin against the Holy Ghost), she might have written—well it's impossible to say how she might have written, but cretainly more delightfully than she has written.

FREEMAN. You would distinguish between a moral man and a moralist, and I think you are right. And I would add that the moralist is seldom happy.

MOORE. If she had been a happy woman her happiness would have crept into her writings, as I have said, for what is in the mind finds its way on to the page, an almost needless amplification of your criticism that the moralist is seldom happy. Indeed, an essay might be written by some philosopher, poet, painter and critic, who would discern in Velazquez an icy spirit who saw no more in his fellows than subjects for portraits or pictures. The critic of whom I am thinking would cry, on turning from Velazquez to Rubens: A happy man! His paintings tell the tale. He meditated no doctrine, and to be free accepted Catholicism outwardly, thereby getting his freedom to wander among nymphs and satyrs without receiving reproofs from Spain. Among modern writers your enemy Stevenson——

FREEMAN. My enemy? No. If, as some people think, I have criticized Stevenson harshly it is because he seems to be taking a place in public estimation higher than he deserves, getting a great deal that was due to Pater. Moreover, the happiness that he expressed seems to me a very superficial kind of happiness; the cudgelling of a little donkey in the Cevennes!

MOORE. At once you bring in a morality which casts a gloom upon the radiant pages of *Travels with a Donkey*.

FREEMAN. He did not keep religion out of his writings; he remained a sour Protestant. He could not visit the monks without commenting, and adversely, on the mode of life they chose to adopt, and in the *Inland Voyage* he is also ready to advance the claims of Protestantism against those of Rome; and in his essay on

Villon he never ceases to thank God that he was not himself like Villon. No; I think you would have done better to have left Stevenson out of this argument. Morris would have supplied you with a better example, for men fight and love and wander in his poems as they do in Homer.

MOORE. The visible world was enough for the Greek and the English poet, and all that you say in praise of Morris I will applaud, hat in hand. A greater poet than Stevenson, I grant you; still— Let us not wrangle, however, but agree that ancient literature was happier than modern. Homer's fighting, though heavy-handed, is always light-hearted. The wanderings of Odysseus are untouched by melancholy, and Virgil, too, and Horace are free from this bane.

FREEMAN. Your chronicle runs too fast, for we have come to imperial Rome, overlooking Sicily.

MOORE. Yes; you are quite right. I had forgotten Sicily, and thank you for reminding me. How the very name of Theocritus brings up before our eyes sunny hill-sides, with shepherds gathering under tamarisk trees, and for single ornament a torrent dashing over the face of the high rock. More real, more true are these than George Eliot's Norfolk hinds. The shepherds and shepherdesses have come down to us from more than two thousand years, gaining in every generation, it would seem, a new and more intense life. Battus is clearer to us now than he was, perhaps, to his creator, certainly more real than Tom Tulliver is to me, or his sister Maggie. And the incident of the thorn that Corydon plucked from Battus's foot under the ankle we would not exchange for the story of the flood.

FREEMAN. I would certainly not give up Amaryllis for Maggie Tulliver.

MOORE. All her walks with the cripple in the pine wood are not worth the verses in which we read that Battus goes to Amaryllis's cave to plead his love, saying that if she refuses him he will die at her feet. He says some lovely things to her: *Lo, ten apples I bring thee, plucked from that very place where thou didst bid me pluck them, and others to-morrow I will bring thee. Ah, regard my heart's deep sorrow! ah, would I were that humming bee, and to thy cave might come dipping beneath the fern that hides thee, and the ivy leaves!*

FREEMAN. In such words as these we reach immortality.

MOORE. *Ah, lovely as thou art to look upon, ah, heart of stone, ah, dark-browed maiden, embrace me, thy true goatherd, that I may kiss thee, and even in empty kisses there is a sweet delight!* In the simple words *even in empty kisses there is a sweet delight*, he reaches to the very heart of the sensual instinct. The unfortunate goatherd continues to plead, but for the moment I am at the end of my memories.

FREEMAN. Theocritus records not the answers of Amaryllis; not a word do we hear her speak. And in the next Idyl Battus and Corydon, two neatherds, meet, and after some random banter their talk turns on the death of Amaryllis.

MOORE. *Ah, gracious Amaryllis! Thee alone even in death will we ne'er forget. Dear to me as my goats wert thou, and thou art dead! Alas, too cruel a spirit hath my lot in his keeping.* That is all we know of Amaryllis, and the scene of this great love grief is described in an anecdote—the plucking out of a thorn that has run into Battus's foot under the ankle. Battus's sighs for Amaryllis were the first, but they were not the last. The world has continued ever since to sigh for Amaryllis. Is it her name that has given her an immortality that has endured for more than two thousand years? and given immortality to a hind like Battus? for we like him when he says: *I will sing no more, but dead will I lie where I fall, and here may the wolves devour me.* This rough goatherd was a true lover. Why are these hinds and shepherdesses immortal, Mr. Freeman? Why are they real? Why are they enough? Because his Idyls tell of happy days and men and women who lead happy lives, following their flocks and their instincts. It would be hard to find an unhappy day in his pages, not even when two fishermen wake up in their broken hut with nothing before them but another toilsome day in search of food, two old men at the end of their lives who will soon be unable to put forth again. Theocritus brings into his story a dream. Tell me, says one old man, the vision of the night; nay, tell all to thy friend. And the fisherman tells of the dream in which he hooked a fish with golden scales, and the great difficulty he had to bring it on shore. You remember?

FREEMAN. Yes; and the answer to forget the dream and *seek the fish of flesh, lest thou die of famine with all thy dreams of gold!*

MOORE. Even the genius of Wordsworth could not redeem him from the curse of morality, and had we to choose between *The Leech-gatherer* and the fisherman, we should choose the earlier story.

FREEMAN. You can usually give reasons for your preferences.

MOORE. Happy days are remembered always; moralities are doleful. I had a subject—— But you were going to say?

FREEMAN. I was going to remind you of a story in verse by George Eliot of a girl who loved a king, and who for the king's sake refused to marry her lover; but the king, hearing of her broken faith, sent for her and kept her in his court till she began to perceive that he was only a man like another——

MOORE. And the Victorian returns the poor girl to her betrothed, attired in all the prejudices and conventions of 1860. How very admirable!

FREEMAN. You don't think that the intimacy of the king would have checked the girl's admiration of him and turned it back to its source, the young man she had discarded?

MOORE. Not unless the king had possessed himself of the girl's affections and wearied of them; then, of course, she might have picked up the thread she had dropped.

FREEMAN. Is not your view very cynical?

MOORE. George Eliot's view is the cynical: the robbing a girl of her illusions and the imposition instead of Christian conventions. Ah! here is Mabel bringing in the tea. You'll stay and have a cup of tea with me, won't you?

WILLIAM PATON KER
1855–1923
Pope
The Art of Poetry, 1923.

For many years past, ever since the publication of Joseph Warton's *Essay on the Writings and Genius of Pope*, the poetry of Pope has been judged indirectly and with deference to opinions, cavils, and misgivings about him; even Dr. Johnson does not ignore 'the question that has been put', whether Pope is a poet. Warton's Essay, the controversies of Bowles and Byron, are apt to come between the reader and his author. Pope is valued not exactly as he is, but as he is thought about. He is judged through 'second intentions': a phrase which in another place than this might appear to be pedantic, but in Oxford, the proper home and seat of Queen Entelechy and the old logic of the schools, to speak of 'second intentions' is surely allowable:

—still
Doth the old instinct bring back the old names!

The estimate of Pope's poetry, more than of any

other poet, is made through the judgement of other people. Swinburne is one of the few who disregard the stale problem; in his essay on Dryden and Pope (disguised under the title *A Century of English Poetry*) he goes on proudly and happily, enjoying and praising, in spite of the temptation to touch on Matthew Arnold, who makes Dryden and Pope into 'classics of our prose', or on Mark Pattison, whose sentence is that 'Pope had no thought, no mind, no ideas, but he had the art of rhymed language in a degree in which no English poet before or since has possessed it'. But let us leave *secundas intentiones in vacuo* to the chimera whose food they probably are. Let the authors speak. And this is what you hear (for example) from the author of *Absalom and Achitophel*:

> The Jews, a headstrong moody murm'ring race
> As ever tried the extent and stretch of grace,
> God's pamper'd people whom debauch'd with ease
> No king could govern nor no God could please:
> (Gods they had tried of ev'ry shape and size
> That godsmiths could produce or priests devise)
> And when no rule, no precedent was found
> Of men by laws less circumscrib'd and bound,
> They led their wild desires to rocks and caves,
> And thought that all but savages were slaves.

Is there anything equal to that in Pope, the pupil of Dryden, the master of rhymed language? What shall we try?

> The skilful Nymph reviews her force with care:
> Let spades be trumps, she said, and trumps they were.
>   Now move to war her sable Matadores,
> In show like leaders of the swarthy Moors.

Spadillio first, unconquerable Lord!
Led off two captive trumps and swept the board.
As many more *Manillio* forced to yield
And march'd a victor from the verdant field.
Him *Basto* followed, but his fate more hard
Gain'd but one trump and one Plebeian card.
With his broad sabre next, a chief in years,
The hoary Majesty of Spades appears,
Puts forth one manly leg, to sight reveal'd;
The rest his many colour'd robe conceal'd.
The rebel Knave who dares his prince engage,
Proves the just victim of his royal rage;
Ev'n mighty *Pam*, that Kings and Queens o'erthrew
And mow'd down armies in the fights of Lu,
Sad chance of war! now destitute of aid
Falls undistinguish'd by the victor spade!

Who doubts that the *Rape of the Lock* is Pope's most perfect work? It is one of the few things wholly without a flaw: is it vain and futile to ask where the music comes from and what it is worth with all its perfection?

It is not easy to understand without some pieces of ancient learning. There is pedantry in it, or what seems so to us who do not take the Heroic Poem as seriously as Milton, Dryden, and Pope; and unless you think seriously about the Epic, the Heroic Poem, you cannot think rightly of the *Rape of the Lock*, an Heroi-Comical Poem. This descriptive epithet is part of the tradition: it is used by Tassoni and Boileau. Pope was haunted by the orthodox critical doctrine of the Epic Poem. Like Milton and Dryden, he had the epic ambition; he wrote *Alcander Prince of Rhodes* when he was a boy; he made the plan of *Brutus*, an epic, when he was older. He saw the absurdity of the formalists such as the Reverend Father Le Bossu; he wrote for Steele's *Guardian* the comic receipt to make an epic poem which was incorporated in Martinus Scriblerus on the Art of Sinking in Poetry. But his preface to the *Iliad* goes over, seriously, the same divisions of the subject: Fable, Characters, Machines, Allegory. His plan of *Brutus* follows the receipt; the fable is taken from Geoffrey of Monmouth, the machines are guardian angels of kingdoms, such as Dryden had recommended. He puts the old allegories into his Homer. The revised version of the *Rape of the Lock*, the very successful 'machinery' of sylphs and gnomes, is something more than play; it is parody of one of the most important things in life for Pope, and his heroi-comical expedient, his most excellent lively burlesque substitute for the Olympians of Homer, is valued by him for its epic quality and its faithfulness to the epic idea. Pope makes his story out of no elements that are ungraceful; he aims at beauty, and the *Rape of the Lock*, a poem with no substance at all, is nothing but grace; the astral body of an heroic poem, pure form, an echo of divine music, how thin and clear!

This heroi-comical poem, if it is his finest and most absolute work, still does not fully give all his range, all his power: and Pope himself did not reckon it as letting him off the task of true heroic poetry. He went on to Homer; the first volume published in 1715 gives his opinion in the Preface: fifteen years after Dryden's Preface to his Fables and no less remarkable for its freedom of speech and its unlikeness to the poetry which it precedes. Both Dryden and Pope in their prose say things which their verse cannot say, and declare themselves, express themselves, more freely. Dryden's comparison of Chaucer and Ovid tells you more of Dryden's mind and temper than his paraphrase of the Knight's Tale; Pope's description of Homer tells you something of Pope which you do not find explicitly in his verse. Here let me say with the greatest respect for Matthew Arnold that his description of Dryden and Pope as 'classics of our prose' is a double sin in criticism, because it confuses the kinds in two ways; ignoring their poetry and their prose alike. For of course they are classics of our prose, when they write prose. Pope as a prose writer comes between Dryden and Johnson, less large in his periods than the older man, less formal than the younger. All three have the same strength of admiration, the same glorious delight when they meet with great poets. And this is Pope's theory of Homer:

It is to the strength of this amazing invention we are to attribute that unequalled fire and rapture which is so forcible in Homer that no man of a true poetical spirit is master of himself while he reads him. What he writes is of the most animated nature imaginable; everything moves, everything lives and is put in action. If a council be called or a battle fought, you are not coldly informed of what was said or done as from a third person; the reader is hurried out of himself by the force of the poet's imagination, and turns in one place to a hearer, in another to a spectator. The course of his verses resembles that of the army he describes

οἱ δ' ἄρ' ἴσαν, ὡσεί τε πυρὶ χθὼν πᾶσα νέμοιτο.

They pour along like a fire that sweeps the whole earth before it. It is however remarkable that his fancy, which is everywhere vigorous, is not discovered immediately at the beginning of his poem in its fullest splendour; it grows in the progress, both upon himself and others, and becomes on fire like a chariot wheel by its own rapidity. Exact disposition, just thought, correct elocution, polished numbers, may have been found in a thousand, but this poetical fire, this *vivida vis animi*, in a very few. Even in works where all those are imperfect or neglected, this can overpower criticism and make us admire even while we disapprove. Nay, where this appears, though attended with absurdities, it brightens all the rubbish about it, till we see nothing but its own splendour. This *fire* is discerned in Virgil, but discerned as through a glass, reflected from Homer, more shining than fierce, but everywhere equal and constant: in Lucan and Statius it bursts out in sudden short and interrupted flashes: in Milton it glows like a furnace kept up to an uncommon ardour by the force of art: in Shakespeare it strikes before we are aware, like an accidental fire from heaven: but in Homer, and in him only, it burns everywhere clearly, and everywhere irresistibly.

Fire is Pope's element: Pope returns to 'the *fire* of the poem' later in the same preface: this is what he says of Chapman: 'that which is to be allowed him, and which very much contributed to cover his defects, is a daring fiery spirit that animates his translation, which is something like what we might imagine Homer himself would have writ before he arrived to years of discretion'. Of course Pope believed that he himself possessed a daring fiery spirit; and, that being so, his ideal of verse ought not to be an ideal of glaze and polish, 'fix'd as in a frost'; his ideal of verse is not very different from Dryden's. Is his practice different? It is not exactly the same, certainly. An essay by an old friend of mine, Mr. Armine Kent of Balliol, on the *Crime of Alexander Pope*, shows what is implied in Cowper's complaint that Pope's musical finesse had made poetry a mechanic art for his imitators. Kent was a great admirer of Pope, and his charge is delivered only against the mechanical warblers who copied him. Did Pope himself in his own practice spoil the old heroic couplet and make it too complete, too separate, too epigrammatic? We may answer this by saying that Pope had many different aims and varieties of style. He certainly knew how to work in mosaic, and Swift describes him so engaged:

> Each atom by another struck
> All shapes and motions tries,
> Till in a lump together stuck
> Behold a poem rise.

Sometimes it pleased him to put together independent couplets and make a string of pointed sentences out of them; but nevertheless his fiery spirit would not allow great arguments to be broken up into separate verses and couplets; and in fact he carries on long periods with nearly the same success as Dryden—does not that come out in Belinda's game?—is not that a well-sustained heroic battle? While on the other hand Dryden's strength and eloquence carry with them the same talent for epigram as Pope's. Dryden's brilliance in this respect is not denied by any one; what is less generally recognized is

Pope's power of keeping up an argument or a story so that it grows in effect and overrides the single couplets. Neither Dryden nor Pope has always the same wave-length; both of them are sometimes choppy, and in both of them you often find the short waves carried on the back of a long swell.

Pope in his *Iliad* took some trouble to escape monotony. He has calendared his experiments in the *Poetical Index* under the head 'Versification expressing in the sound the thing describ'd'. The interest of this Index and those passages is of course that they show how seriously Pope believed in his own teaching about the sound and the sense, in the *Essay on Criticism*. They also show how he could break the traditional rules of the couplet in order to carry on his story. The regular couplet had been no sooner fixed than it was challenged. Prior in his *Solomon* claimed the freedom of running on the sense: Pope says nothing about this, as Prior does, in his preface, but his verse can be remarkably unlike the ordinary fashion. Here is a quotation from the twenty-third Book of the *Iliad*—a passage which is noted in the Index for three imitations: 'the rattling and jumping of carts over a rough and rocky way', 'a sudden fall', and 'the rattling and crashing of trees falling'.

> Thus while he spoke, each Eye grew big with Tears:
> And now the rosy-finger'd Morn appears,
> Shews every mournful Face with Tears o'erspread,
> And glares on the pale Visage of the Dead.
> But *Agamemnon*, as the Rites demand,
> With Mules and Waggons sends a chosen Band;

To load the Timber and the Pile to rear,
A Charge consign'd to Merion's faithful Care.
With proper Instruments they take the Road,
Axes to cut, and Ropes to sling the Load.
First march the heavy Mules, securely slow,
O'er Hills, o'er Dales, o'er Crags, o'er Rocks, they go:
Jumping high o'er the Shrubs of the rough Ground,
Rattle the clatt'ring bars, and the shockt Axles bound.
But when arriv'd at *Ida's* spreading Woods,
(Fair *Ida*, water'd with descending Floods)
Loud sounds the Axe, rebounding Strokes on Strokes;
On all sides round the Forest hurles her Oaks
Headlong. Deep-echoing groan the Thickets brown;
Then rustling, crackling, crashing, thunder down.
The Wood the *Grecians* cleave, prepar'd to burn;
And the slow Mules the same rough Road return.

Now we see the meaning of that couplet quoted by Spence from Pope's martyred epic of *Alcander*:

Shields, helms, and swords all jangle as they hang
And sound formidinous with angry clang.

Why did Atterbury allow or advise Pope to burn *Alcander*? It must have been a spirited story: if it was not otherwise like *Endymion*, at any rate it had, like *Endymion*, an under-sea adventure; the swords that jangle as they hang are portents of romance. Shall we mourn for *Alcander*? At any rate Alcander Prince of Rhodes has escaped the danger of a dissertation, and the schools have lost a subject: they are not expected to *Compare Pope and Keats in a submarine light, and allude to Beowulf in this connexion*. Is it fanciful to think that the sea, of which he knew little or nothing, had great power over the mind of Pope?

He steer'd securely and discover'd far
Let by the light of the Maeonian star.

Aristotle is thought of as a voyager. Brutus in the story as Pope had sketched it puts out, like Dante's Ulysses, through the Pillars of Hercules to the Atlantic; he sails to Norway and the Orkneys, and probably to Iceland, before he undertakes the settlement of Britain. I return to Pope's Homer.

Coleridge speaks of Pope's Homer as the chief source of the conventional pseudo-poetic diction which drew Wordsworth's attack. Coleridge, the inventor of 'pantisocracy' and 'esemplastic', author of 'defecates to a pure transparency', is not unfair to Pope's original work; on the contrary he recognizes and praises the excellence and ease of his style when he is writing for himself. He is probably unjust to Pope's Homer. Sir Walter Raleigh makes Milton the chief model of pseudo-poetic diction: and Pope would not disagree with this; in his postscript to the *Odyssey* he speaks of the imitators of Milton and how they overdo their archaism. This essay of Pope's is worth reading if only as an answer to Wordsworth and Coleridge: it says clearly what Wordsworth was always more or less meaning to say in his argument about the language of poetry. Pope himself thought well of this essay; better, he said, than the preface to the *Iliad*, where he was too much on the high horse. It gives a true reading of the *Odyssey* as including everything in human life; it gives a fine description of the poet's style and language as they change with the mood and matter of the story and the dialogue. The *Odyssey* is not for him a stiff formal classical composition: it is as various as Shakespeare.

There is a real beauty in an easy, pure, perspicuous description even of a *low action*. There are numerous instances of this both in *Homer* and *Virgil*; and perhaps those natural passages are not the least pleasing of their works. It is often the same in History, where the representations of common, or even domestic things, in clear, plain, and natural words, are frequently found to make the liveliest impression on the reader.

The question is, how far a Poet, in pursuing the description or image of an action, can attach himself to *little circumstances*, without vulgarity or trifling? what particulars are proper, and enliven the image; or what are impertinent, and clog it? In this matter Painting is to be consulted, and the whole regard had to those circumstances which contribute to form a full, and yet not a confused, idea of a thing.

Homer in his lowest narrations or speeches is ever easy, flowing, copious, clear, and harmonious. He shows not less *invention*, in assembling the humbler, than the greater, thoughts and images; nor less *judgment*, in proportioning the style and the versification to these than to the other. Let it be remember'd that the same Genius that soar'd the highest, and from whom the greatest models of the *Sublime* are derived, was also he who stoop'd the lowest, and gave to the simple *Narrative* its utmost perfection. Which of these was the harder task to *Homer* himself, I cannot pretend to determine; but to his Translator I can affirm (however unequal all his imitations must be) that of the latter has been much the more difficult.

Whoever expects here the same pomp of verse, and the same ornaments of diction, as in the Iliad; he will, and he ought to be disappointed. Were the original otherwise, it had been an offence against nature; and were the translation so, it were an offence against *Homer*, which is the same thing.

Some use has been made to this end, of the style of

Milton. A just and moderate mixture of old words may have an effect like the working old Abbey stones into a building, which I have sometimes seen to give a kind of venerable air, and yet not destroy the neatness, elegance, and equality requisite to a new work; I mean without rendering it too unfamiliar, or remote from the present purity of writing, or from that ease and smoothness which ought always to accompany Narration or Dialogue. In reading a style judiciously antiquated, one finds a pleasure not unlike that of travelling on an old *Roman* way; but then the road must be as *good*, as the way is *antient*; the style must be such in which we may evenly proceed, without being put to short stops by sudden abruptnesses, or puzzled by frequent turnings and transpositions: No Man delights in furrows and stumbling-blocks: And let our love to Antiquity be ever so great, a fine ruin is one thing, and heap of rubbish another. The imitators of *Milton*, like most other imitators, are not *Copies* but *Caricatura's* of their original; they are a hundred times more obsolete and cramp than he, and equally so in all places; Whereas it should have been observed of *Milton*, that he is not lavish of his exotick words and phrases every where alike, but employs them much more where the subject is marvellous, vast and strange, as in the scenes of Heaven, Hell, Chaos, &c. than where it is turned to the natural and agreeable, as in the pictures of Paradise, the loves of our first parents, the entertainments of Angels, and the like. In general, this unusual style better serves to awaken our ideas in the descriptions and in the imaging and picturesque parts, than it agrees with the lower sort of narrations, the character of which is simplicity and purity. *Milton* has several of the latter, where we find not an antiquated, affected, or uncouth word, for some hundred lines together; as in his fifth book, the latter part of the eighth, the former of the tenth and eleventh books, and in the narration of

Michael in the Twelfth. I wonder indeed that he, who ventur'd (contrary to the practice of all other Epic Poets) to imitate *Homer's* Lownesses in the *Narrative*, should not also have copied his plainness and perspicuity in the *Dramatic* parts: Since in his speeches (where clearness above all is necessary) there is frequently such transposition and forced construction, that the very sense is not to be discovered without a second or third reading: and in this certainly he ought to be no example.

Now what are Pope's original poems worth, if they are not this same variety? 'The narrow sound of Satire', if I may use a phrase and figure of Swinburne's, opens out to a large sea; the beauty of his satiric poetry is its reflection of the whole world, not steadily, or as the great masters render it in Epic or Tragedy, but with all the lights of the greater modes represented here and there—so that anywhere you may be caught away, for a moment, to different regions.

The postscript to the *Odyssey* explains Pope's ideal of poetic expression, and this is what he actually obtains in his own poetry.

He is a master of point and epigram; but this is not what makes his success. Other writers have done as well in separate pieces. There is nothing better in one way than Prior's address to Boileau:

> I grant, old friend, old foe (for such we are
> Alternate as the chance of peace and war)—

the very spirit of the old courtesy, so notable in the wars and intervals of war through the eighteenth century, here mingled with irony, but not so as to detract from the grace of the gesture.

For satirical art in direct attack no one can do much better than Johnson's imitation of Juvenal, giving the London equivalent of the Roman poets reciting in the Dog-days:

> Here falling houses thunder on your head,
> And here a female atheist talks you dead.

Or one might quote, for point and malice, that single couplet of Gray on the ecclesiastical history of Britain:

> When love had taught a monarch to be wise
> And gospel light first dawn'd from Bullen's eyes.

For another mood Tickell in his lament for Addison—a poem honoured by Swift—has drawn from the heroic couplet its deepest music:

> Never to mansions where the mighty rest
> Since their foundation came a nobler guest.

As deep as this and as solemn, Johnson on *The Vanity of Human Wishes*:

> How few there are whom hours like these await
> Who set unclouded in the gulfs of Fate—

From Goldsmith, from Akenside's *Epistle to Curio*, from *The New Morality* in the *Anti-Jacobin*, it would be easy enough to quote single couplets that are not 'distained' by any jewel of Pope's; and Pope's superiority is not merely in his larger store of such things. The beauty of Pope's verse is its living variety; the wave changes its colour, you might say, as the sun or the cloud takes it, as it runs green over the sands, or blue over the deep water. You never can be certain from the subject what the language and the tune will be like; and the advantage of Satire, which is not the highest order of Poetry, is that it can at any moment take the reflection of epic or tragedy. The *Dunciad*, a mock heroic poem more villainous than any of the old ribald travesties of Homer or Virgil, ends in the way we know, beyond all praise:

> Lo! thy dread empire CHAOS is restor'd:
> Light dies before thy uncreating word:
> Thy hand, great Anarch, lets the curtain fall—

while before you come to this magnificence you find the couplet which Pope thought the most musical of all his verse:

> Lo! where Maeotis sleeps, and hardly flows
> The freezing Tanais through a waste of snows.

It does not need the grand style to bring out the strength of Pope; it is shown in a touch here and there, in the effect of a seemingly light and ordinary phrase:

> Like Journals, Odes, *and such forgotten things*
> As Eusden, Philips, Settle writ of Kings.

The phrase comes again in *Sordello*:

> To clear away with such forgotten things
> As are an eyesore to the morn,

and it may be through Browning's repetition that we notice it more readily in Pope.

The old device of *Alcander*, the 'angry clang', reappears in the description of Blackmore:

> What! like Sir Richard, rumbling, rough and fierce,
> With ARMS and GEORGE and BRUNSWICK crowd the verse;

Rend with tremendous sound your ears asunder
With Gun, Drum, Trumpet, Blunderbuss and
  Thunder;
Or nobly wild, with Budgel's fire and force,
Paint Angels trembling round his falling horse.

A different sort of phrasing in the *Essay on Man*, Epistle IV, at the beginning. Before I read it may I say that I think the *Essay on Man* is too much neglected: taken as a curiosity, part of the history of English thought in the eighteenth century, an example of popular philosophy 'in the best of all possible worlds'. Some of it is difficult, the sentences, like the reasoning, clogged; some of it is too merely rhetorical:

The lamb thy riot dooms to bleed to-day;

some of it is sinking in poetry:

Why has not man a microscopic eye?
For this plain reason, man is not a fly—

though this slip is pretty well recovered in what follows. But the Essay contains some of the best of Pope's poetry; the passage on Fame, and this, in a different way:

Oh Happiness! our being's end and aim!
Good, Pleasure, Ease, Content, whate'er thy name,
That something still which prompts the eternal sigh
For which we bear to live, or dare to die,
Which still so near us, yet beyond us lies,
O'erlook'd, seen double, by the fool, and wise.
Plant of celestial seed! if dropt below
Say in what mortal soil thou deign'st to grow:
Fair op'ning to some Court's propitious shine,
Or deep with di'monds in the flaming mine?
Twin'd with the wreaths Parnassian laurels yield
Or reap'd in iron harvests of the field?
Where grows? where grows it not?

Something of Pope's style may be learned from a reference to 'iron harvest' as he had used the phrase in his *Statius*:

> How with the serpent's teeth he sow'd the soil,
> And reap'd an iron harvest of his toil.

Here it is no more than a conceit; the import, the value, is different in the *Essay on Man*.

I will not quote the passage about his friends in the *Epistle to Arbuthnot*, but I will ask you to remember what Charles Lamb thought of it, and how he read it at that evening party a hundred years ago which is described by Hazlitt in the essay *Of Persons we would wish to have seen*, which is, throughout, Hazlitt's truest recollection of Charles Lamb, as the essay *My First Acquaintance with Poets* is nothing but Coleridge. But I must repeat the opening of the *Epistle to Arbuthnot*, for it has long appeared to me, if not the best of Pope at any rate the most expressive of all his confessions.

> Shut, shut the door, good John! fatigu'd I said:
> Tie up the knocker, say I'm sick, I'm dead.
> The Dog-star rages! nay, 'tis past a doubt,
> All Bedlam, or Parnassus, is let out:
> Fire in each eye, and papers in each hand,
> They rave, recite, and madden round the land.
>   What walls can guard me, or what shades can hide?
> They pierce my thickets, thro' my grot they glide.
> By land, by water, they renew the charge;
> They stop the chariot and they board the barge.
> No place is sacred, not the Church is free;
> Ev'n Sunday shines no Sabbath-day to me.
> Then from the Mint walks forth the Man of rhyme,
> Happy to catch me, just at Dinner-time.

Is there a Parson, much bemus'd in beer,
A maudlin Poetess, a rhyming Peer,
A Clerk, foredoom'd his father's soul to cross
Who pens a Stanza when he should *engross*?
Is there who lock'd from ink and paper scrawls
With desp'rate charcoal round his darken'd walls?
All fly to *Twit'nam*, and in humble strain
Apply to me, to keep them mad or vain.
Arthur, whose giddy son neglects the laws,
Imputes to me and my damn'd works the cause;
Poor *Cornus* sees his frantic wife elope,
And curses wit, and poetry, and Pope.

Nothing of Pope's poetry and not the whole of it all together represents fully what he thought and admired. Spenser was one of his favourite poets, all his life long; his praise of Shakespeare goes far beyond the limits of his own poetry.

I will conclude by saying of *Shakespeare*, that with all his faults, and with all the irregularity of his *Drama*, one may look upon his works, in comparison of those that are more finish'd and regular, as upon an ancient majestick piece of *Gothick* Architecture, compar'd with a neat Modern building: The latter is more elegant and glaring, but the former is more strong and more solemn. It must be allow'd that in one of these there are materials enough to make many of the other. It has much the greater variety, and much the nobler apartments; tho' we are often conducted to them by dark, odd and uncouth passages. Nor does the Whole fail to strike us with greater reverence, tho' many of the Parts are childish, ill-plac'd, and unequal to its grandeur.

Pope's poetical work is not the whole of his life. Nor is it, as we are often inclined to think, the dominant force in the poetry of his own time. It is one among many, and his success does not establish a ruling tradition, except for the mechanic warblers. Already in the time of Dryden there were signs of novelty coming on: Atterbury (or the author of the Life of Waller, 1690) recommends blank verse—and Thomson takes the advice. Young competes with Pope in Satire and leaves this for an original policy of his own in the *Night Thoughts*. Prior commanded lyrical forms of Satire unfamiliar to Pope.

> Now let us look for Louis' feather,
> That used to shine so like a star:
> The generals could not get together,
> Wanting that influence great in war.
> O Poet! thou hadst been discreeter,
> Hanging the Monarch's hat so high,
> If thou had'st dubb'd thy star a meteor,
> That did but blaze, and rove, and die!

Gay's address to Pope on the completion of the *Iliad*—'Mr. Pope's welcome from Greece'—is a fresh invention, in the light octaves of Italian burlesque poetry, such as had never been tried in English before, such as the English of Gay's time left unrepeated, to be taken up long after by Frere and Byron:

> Cheer up, my friend, thy dangers now are o'er;
>   Methinks—nay sure, the rising coasts appear;
> Hark, how the guns salute from either shore,
>   As thy trim vessel cuts the Thames so fair:
> Shouts answering shouts from Kent and Essex roar,
>   And bells break loud from ev'ry gust of air:
> Bonfires do blaze, and bones and cleavers ring,
> As at the coming of some mighty king.

It is no depreciation of Pope to recognize that

there were other fashions of poetry available in his day. On the contrary, it was a superstitious and exclusive admiration and following of Pope that so long prevented and to this day prevents a right understanding of his varieties of mood and phrase. Dr. Johnson knew better: this is his description of 'an intelligence perpetually on the wing, excursive, vigorous, and diligent, eager to pursue knowledge, and attentive to retain it'.

Of this intellectual character, the constituent and fundamental principle was good sense, a prompt and intuitive perception of consonance and propriety. He saw immediately of his own conceptions what was to be chosen and what to be rejected, and in the works of others what was to be shunned and what was to be copied.

But good sense alone is a sedate and quiescent quality, which manages its possessions well but does not increase them; it collects few materials for its own operations, and preserves safety but never gains supremacy. Pope had likewise genius; a mind active, ambitious and adventurous, always investigating, always aspiring; in its widest searches still longing to go forward, in its highest flights still wishing to be higher; always imagining something greater than it knows, always endeavouring more than it can do.

Dr. Johnson, who found the right words exactly for the terror and beauty of the Isle of Skye, for the religion of Iona, seems here to have read truly the mind of another Adventurer.

A. C. BENSON
1862–1925

Theodore Watts-Dunton

Life and Letters, Dec. 1932

I HAD met Watts-Dunton once or twice previously at luncheon with Gosse, and again at the Cornish's house at Eton. At Gosse's he seems to me, as I search among rather dim recollections of the occasion, to have been a small dusky man, with an air of demure importance. I fancy it was a literary luncheon-party, peopled by not very significant individuals, all horribly afraid of each other, afraid of committing themselves to any commonplace statement, and most afraid of Gosse's hovering and pouncing wit, which had on these occasions a rather strident and excited quality, framed on some strangely devised model of petulance and childish archness, and quite decisively adapted to cause anxiety and discomfort in the guests. At the Cornish's, Watts-Dunton is a more distinct figure, because I sate next to him, and he was himself obviously disconcerted by Mrs. Cornish's ironical appeals to him to settle literary questions and generally to enlighten and guide us in our search for artistic certainties. Mrs. Cornish was in great majesty on that day, and managed to convey to me in some way that she considered the presence of Watts-Dunton, in the character of a literary celebrity, to be an affront and an intrusion; though I suppose she had invited him!

But for literature, as represented and interpreted by Watts-Dunton, she certainly contrived to indicate a lofty disdain.

Yet the man was curious and stimulating to me. He had been the chosen friend and guardian of Rossetti in the dark years, and I was just beginning to study Rossetti as a subject for a biography; he had since then taken on the hardly less dreadful charge of Swinburne, whom he kept, it was supposed, almost under lock and key. Moreover, it was understood that Watts-Dunton, through the *Athenæum*, wielded a strong and peremptory influence in literary matters, and could make or mar reputations. He seemed to me, I remember, to my great relief, a mild and not unfriendly man, courteous and gentle, with no suggestiveness of fineness of talk, with a weary and jaded air, and wholly without personal distinction. I had prepared, I fancy, some foolish compliment to his greatness, which I must have contrived to impart to him, because he proved suddenly accessible, and even grateful for recognition, and gave me a cordial invitation to come and see him at some unspecified date.

When I found myself finally embarked on the Rossetti book, I wrote deferentially to him, and was treated with much epistolary ceremony in return, receiving several courteous letters, written by a secretary, arranging the precise details of my visit. Accordingly, on April 4th, 1902 I got off from Eton about noon, on a dark and gloomy day, and reached Putney at 1.15. I knew that he lived near the station, but I was surprised at the common suburban air of the street, full of omnibuses and cabs, and was expecting to find some more quiet and dignified retreat, when I suddenly discovered the house—The Pines, as it was strangely called—a very ordinary yellow-brick, bow-windowed affair, with a few shrubs in a tiny front garden. The house inside was redolent of cooking, dark, somewhat dusty and neglected-looking, but with a solid bourgeois sort of comfort, the walls much crowded with pictures, among which I noticed many designs and studies by Rossetti, in pen-and-ink or chalk. I was shown into a little sitting-room, looking out on the back. The view was a pleasant surprise, because the adjacent houses opened away on either side, leaving a long prospect of small gardens, with many orchard trees in bloom. In the little villa-garden belonging to the house itself there was a yew hedge and a rather smoke-stained statue of a nymph, and the background was pleasantly screened by some more distant elms.

Mr. Watts-Dunton came in and greeted me with much cordiality: 'What a big fellow you are!' he said playfully. I was equally surprised by his size: I had not remembered he was so very minute a man. He was oddly dressed, in a waistcoat and trousers of some greenish stuff, and with a large, heavy, blue frock-coat, obviously too big for him, his little fingers only just protruding from its massive cuffs. He was bald, his remaining hair grown thick and long, and with a huge damp-looking moustache, concealing a small secretive chin, in full retreat. He seemed to have lost his teeth since I had seen him, and altogether appeared to me a very old man, though healthily bronzed, his hands firm and small. While we stood talking, the door being open, the front door clicked and was shut again, and some unseen person half-rushed, half-flitted up the stairs, and began (it seemed from the sounds) to jump and dance overhead.

'There is Swinburne!' said Watts-Dunton. 'He has come in from his walk—we will go and see him.' We went up the thickly-carpeted stairs, and found a door, with a pair of elastic-sided boots thrown down beside it. Watts-Dunton went quickly in, and I followed. It was a large, comfortable room, crammed with books, the bookcases full, books on the table, a great sofa stacked with books. A fire was burning, by which stood a little man who turned sharply round as we entered. He was entirely unlike what I had expected. Swinburne looked like a little rather faded don, a large head and dome-like forehead, quite bald, small watery uncertain eyes, a little red aquiline nose, and a ragged reddish beard grown in irregular wisps. He looked supremely shy, but received me with great courtesy, bowing, drumming impatiently on the ground with his feet, and uttering strange little whistling noises. He seemed very deaf and blinking. He bowed me to a chair: 'Will you sit?' He shook hands with me across the sofa and, for some reason obscure to me, seemed to feel safer if he were entrenched behind it. On the fender lay a pair of brown rough socks. Watts-Dunton said to me in a low tone: 'He has just come in from one of his long walks,' and then, observing the socks, he took them up with an air of disgust and threw them behind the coal-scuttle. Swinburne darted out after them, and I saw that his feet were bare. He picked up the socks, and making a gesture with the other hand, said: 'Hold, they are drying!' and then carefully replaced them. Watts-Dunton said something about their being scorched. Swinburne sate down with his feet under his chair, and then proceeded, with odd little noises, to draw the socks on to his feet. 'He seems to be changing his things,' said Watts-Dunton. He clearly was. Swinburne said nothing, but continued to whistle and drum. Then he rose and bowed me out of the door, while he opened his window. I went down with Watts-Dunton to a dining-room below, a big comfortable room, but equally overcrowded with books and pictures. Watts-Dunton sate with his back to the window, I on his left and Swinburne opposite me. We had an excellent meal, a sort of midday dinner, soup, chicken, various sweets, plovers' eggs. Swinburne had a small bottle of beer, which he drank carefully as though husbanding it. He seemed tremulous and clumsy with his hands, and was often in difficulties with his plate. At first Swinburne said nothing, but gazed out of the window with a mild blue eye, or examined me curiously, exhibiting much confusion when he met my gaze, and looking sharply away with many little whistles and finger-taps on the table. Watts-Dunton and I talked gravely. He mumbled his food a good deal, his little chin disappearing totally under the heavy fringing moustache, often dripping and clotted with soups and sauces. When he thought that Swinburne was sufficiently refreshed, he drew him into the talk. I was wholly unable to make Swinburne hear a word, and he often inquired mournfully of Watts-Dunton: 'What does Mr. Benson say?' Watts-Dunton, speaking clearly and distinctly, had no difficulty in being audible to him. But Swinburne, once launched, was full of talk. He spoke of Hawthorne and said that the *Scarlet Letter* was a great book, but that the development of any book, after such a first chapter, 'must be a bother!' 'I want more catastrophe for my money!' he added, and smiled at me. Then he talked about Elizabethan plays, and said of *Elizabeth Arden* that it was as great as Shakespeare's, but greater than *Romeo and Juliet* or the early plays. 'Here is an extraordinary fact,' he added, 'that if it is *not* by Shakespeare, we have a dramatist living at the same time who could create and embody a perfectly natural, stainless, and supreme woman!'

He listened to Watts-Dunton with great and serious attention. Swinburne had said that the *Bride of Lammermoor* was a *perfect* story, and Watts-Dunton spoke of the necessity, when Scott became bookish, of translating him into patois. 'Very beautiful and just!' said Swinburne. 'I have never heard that said before, and it is just! You must put that down; it must be said publicly and firmly.'

Watts-Dunton quoted some dictum of Rossetti's about Chatterton. Swinburne smiled, and said to him: 'I have often heard you say that, but' (turning to me) 'there is no truth in it, Mr. Benson! Gabriel had no opinions on Chatterton and many kindred subjects. Our friend here had only to say a thing to him, and it was absolutely adopted and fixed in the firmament.' He looked triumphantly round. Watts-Dunton smiled, and stroked Swinburne's little pink hand, which lay on the table. Swinburne smiled a pleased schoolboy smile.

Luncheon being over, Watts-Dunton said that he and I had matters to discuss. Swinburne, who was now quite revived and no longer shy, looked concerned, and drawing near said: 'Mr. Benson may come and sit a little in my room first?' So we went up very ceremoniously. He began pulling down books and talking about them quite delightfully; as he became more assured, he began to discourse more rhetorically and in long elaborate sentences of eulogy or disdain. He had a high, thin, resonant voice with a fine thrill in it, but occasionally his voice went off into a curious squeak; once he went into a corner furtively and drank medicine from a glass. There was an odd fragrant bookish scent about the room, which clung, I noticed, to his own clothes. He had on an old black morning coat with tails, a light homespun waistcoat and trousers, slippers, a low white collar with a made-up tie, all very shabby, and he was evidently quite unconscious of his appearance. He talked a little about Eton, but when Watts-Dunton endeavoured again to lead me away, Swinburne said: 'There is time, surely, just to show Mr. Benson one of these fine scenes?' 'Well, *one* scene,' said Watts-Dunton firmly; 'we have much business to get through—you choose and read it to him.'

Swinburne took the book I was holding—the Arden play—and read very finely and dramatically, his voice rising high and shrill, with a moving tremulo. All the time his little feet drummed under the chair, and he kept up a brisk battery of taps on the table. At one point he said rather roguishly to Watts-Dunton: 'Do you think Mr. Benson will be shocked if I show him that?', indicating a line with his finger. Watts-Dunton glanced, and said: 'No, of course not!' So he read it—a little bit of schoolboy coarseness—and giggled decorously. Then at last I was led away. Swinburne shook hands very cordially, with a shy winning smile in his pale eyes. 'You must come again!' he said. 'I suppose you were at Eton about my time?' 'My dear fellow,' said Watts-Dunton, 'Mr. Benson's a *young* man!' 'Of course, of course!' said the bard. As we went down, Watts-Dunton said to me: 'Now Swinburne must be alone—he must get a good siesta; he is such an excitable fellow, like a schoolboy; unfailing animal spirits, always pleased with everything; but he has to take care!'

I gathered that Swinburne was about sixty-six and Watts-Dunton about seventy-two. What was pleasant was to see how they paid each other such fine compliments, and showed such distinguished consideration; nothing bluff or abrupt about them.

I suppose that the secret of Watts-Dunton's

influence with both Rossetti and Swinburne is that they were sensitive, lazy, helpless creatures, hating trouble of any kind, and that Watts-Dunton was willing to shelter them in every way and arrange everything for them, and to be at the same time sedulous, gentle and complimentary: moreover, he was intelligent, critical, and appreciative, and sensitive enough himself to require and evoke some sympathy.

Watts-Dunton's egotism came out strongly in our subsequent conversation. I became aware of many little provincialisms: first, he drops an 'h' occasionally, he says 'proad' for 'proud', 'cload' for 'cloud', 'roaned' for 'round'. He talked a little about Rossetti, but told me very little I did not know. The difficulty was that he was for ever recurring to himself. I became aware that I was in the company of an extremely ambitious, sensitive, anxious, and timid man. He was afraid, I found, of criticism, of enmity, of ridicule; at the same time I gathered that he felt himself in the very front rank—a novelist, a poet, a biographer, a critic. 'Good God,' he suddenly said to me, tremulous with passion and alarm, 'the world's a great whispering-gallery: all is known and discussed!' He spoke of his own peculiar strength of character. He said that as a child dogs never bit him, cattle fled before him; that when he was at school—he was careful to add that it was a large and fashionable private school—he dominated all the boys, adding that it was wholly unconscious influence, never deliberately aimed at or exerted, that no boy ever got a hamper without bringing it to him for him to choose what he liked best, how they would have carried him about all day long on their shoulders if he had desired it, and how no edict of any master would have prevailed if he had given contrary orders. He added that he was the only one of Rossetti's circle who had not been dominated by Rossetti.

At one time he sighed heavily and said that he had not done in literature what he felt he was entitled to have done, but that detraction was both malignant and powerful.

He said with a forced air: 'However, I am content. In the friendship of Rossetti and of Swinburne I find my consolation.'

He diverged upon Swinburne again. 'He is a mere boy still and must be treated like one—a mere schoolboy, full of hasty impulses and generous thoughts, like April showers. His mental power grows stronger every year—every intelligent man's does—and he is now a pure and simple improvisatore. The need for thought and toil exists no more for him.' He added, very decisively: 'Swinburne has been censored for the sensuous element in his poetry—not unfairly. But, believe me, he has no animal nature at all: he is a mere bookman and a mere schoolboy. The sensuous element in his poetry was entirely due to Rossetti's dominating influence.'

We sate long together; he sipped whiskey and water and smoked a cigarette, sometimes reclining in a chair, sometimes coming and standing in front of me. I sate in a great carved chair of Rossetti's, facing the light. Finally he loaded me with books of his, writing my name in them, some pictures, and an autograph of Rossetti's. He said: 'Come and see me again—at any time—don't *write* to me; my correspondence is the curse of my life—I have often thirty letters by the post, and keep two secretaries employed. I have a dozen letters a day about *Aylwin* alone!'

I went off much touched by the kindness of the two men; but what remained in my mind was a sense of the real genius of Swinburne's mind, the air of intellectual fervour in which he seemed to live habitually and without effort, and his complete abstraction from all ordinary considerations. He was like a man living in a dream of art, and without any ripple or murmur of the world penetrating his solitary paradise. All his enmities and jealousies and ambitions seemed to have faded, and left him like a dry flame consuming the pure oil of art.

On the other hand, Watts-Dunton seemed to me precisely the opposite. I thought him a man of mediocre power and no inspiration. *Aylwin* is a positively grotesque book, a childish, clumsy falsetto romance; the poetry purely imitative. As a critic I expect he is laborious, and well-informed; but he lives, not in art or in emotion, but in professional literature; and I doubt if he has any real *enjoyment* of art at all. It is simply a ladder to climb to power. I believe him to be a man who is at the same time afraid of life, and deeply covetous of security and recognition and influence. He seemed to me all the time to be holding a fear at arm's length, a fear of the world, of criticism, a fear, deepest of all, that his own powers were of a second-rate order, and that this might somehow be dreadfully revealed to him. A man of closely calculated and terrified pose, feeding on illusions, dismayed by the truth, with a certain natural kindliness the moment that he feels himself recognized and not menaced. Not exactly an unhappy man, for he is busy and laborious, and his health must be remarkably strong; but essentially a hollow man, morbidly sensitive, and afraid to face the truth. After writing the above passage, much of which is taken verbatim from my Diary, written at the time of my visit, I had a good many talks with Edmund Gosse about Watts-Dunton. It is clear that Watts-Dunton was a very jealous man, especially with regard to Swinburne, and wished to establish an indefeasible right to the literary and emotional possession of Swinburne. Gosse had for some years been the associate and friend of Swinburne, and I do not doubt that Watts-Dunton resented this. Gosse described to me a visit which his son Philip paid to The Pines on Swinburne's invitation. He said that Philip found Watts-Dunton and Swinburne sitting out together, each furnished with a copy of *Aylwin*, which they were engaged in studying; and before Philip went away, Watts-Dunton, with an air of secrecy, took him into a small study, and opened a drawer full of MS. tied up in packets, which he said was the original MS. of *Aylwin*, and added that he thought that Philip would be interested in seeing it.

Later on, after Swinburne's death, Gosse told me curious stories of the dispersal, at high prices, to America and elsewhere, of the Swinburne MSS., and further said that he had evidence that Watts-Dunton had torn out of books presented by himself to Swinburne, the pages which bore Gosse's autograph inscriptions, with the idea, he thought, of obliterating as far as possible any evidence that Gosse and Swinburne had formerly been friends.

Since then I have read the *Life of Watts-Dunton* in two volumes, a book which will have done more to destroy the reputation of Watts-Dunton, both as a man and as a writer, than I could have thought possible. It exhibits Watts-Dunton in the light of a pretentious egotist, bent upon communicating an atmosphere of mystery and romance to a most trumpery and commonplace life. What is most remarkable about the book is that it betrays and emphasizes the fact that Watts-Dunton wrote an almost typically provincial style of English, crammed with cumbrous periphrases, and with an inveterate fondness for commonplace and threadbare phrases. There is not a single fragment quoted, from letters, conversations, or public writings, which has the least beauty or distinction of expression. It would appear that Watts-Dunton had a genuine love of literature, that he had read widely and studied carefully the poetry of the nineteenth century; but even here his judgements are curiously amateurish, personal, and partial. Whether he had really thought out any theory of poetry or arrived at any interesting conclusions on the subject, it is difficult to say, because of the heavy and clumsy treatment which he had made his own. The book frankly abandons his claims to be considered a novelist or a poet. He seems to have said loftily that he never wrote poetry except under the stress of urgent inspiration; yet his sonnets, on which he set great store, are vapid and laborious constructions in the style of Rossetti. But his critical writings are dull and confused, and there is total absence in them of any freshness or power of illumination.

The *Life* also shows his extreme dilatoriness. He seems to have always been behindhand with his work, and the despair of editors; while there is something pathetic about the endless revision and retouching which he seems to have given, both to an early novel which he never published, and to the intolerable *Aylwin*. 'A month more of revision,' he cried, when the MS. of *Aylwin* was at last wrested from his unwilling hands, 'and what a book I could have made of it!'

Further, the record of his life shows from end to end an intense ambition to win fame as a writer, coupled with a morbid diffidence, and a terror, amounting to an obsession, for any sort of critical disapproval. He never seems to have brought himself to write anything of a biographical kind about either Rossetti or Swinburne, while he seems to have deliberately hunted all biographers out of the field, and to have sate firmly on the top of his memories and manuscripts. I think that what made him relent in the case of my own monograph about Rossetti was that he felt that such a book was inevitable, particularly as William Rossetti had published such a mass of letters and biographical material about his brother. He was disarmed, I believe, by my deference, and by my frank recognition of him as the one and supreme arbiter of Rossetti's fortunes.

What is undoubtedly surprising is that Rossetti should have subjected himself so much to Watts-Dunton's domination, and still more that Swinburne should have entertained so lofty a notion of Watts-Dunton's critical powers. What had happened was that Watts-Dunton had made himself necessary to these two men. In the first place his legal knowledge was useful to them; and in the second place he accepted with great loyalty the difficult and disagreeable task of standing between the world and those two men of high genius and confessed frailty. Whatever his motive was, he undoubtedly acquitted himself very conscientiously. He was neither censorious nor peremptory with them. He minimized as far as he could their failings and self-indulgences. He gave them both a sense of security, and he openly declared his appreciation of their genius. Moreover, though a dreary writer, he was a man of real intelligence; he could discuss literary questions sympathetically and critically, while his own extreme sensitiveness led him to interpret their sensitiveness skilfully, and to avoid occasions of offence. Then, too, he was a man who had a real capacity for affection, in spite of his egotism, or perhaps because of it. He desired to be understood and reassured; and though it is difficult to feel about

Watts-Dunton that his affections and admirations were perfectly disinterested, yet he undoubtedly rendered his two great friends sincere and faithful service. What I believe lay behind all his own labour and devotion was a deep and instinctive need to create a romantic atmosphere about his own life, and the care of these two erratic men of genius perhaps ministered to this sense of romance more than anything else could have done.

There is something singularly dreary about the picture of his later years. We see the old man, day after day, rising to breakfast at seven, and employing the services of two secretaries until late in the evening in answering letters of admirers about *Aylwin*, disposing of Swinburne's manuscripts, wrestling with endless real or imaginary legal difficulties. It is the picture of a man going down to the grave in the grip of an immense illusion of influence, fame, detraction, romance, mystery; delaying, procrastinating, beating off the doubts which assailed him, fighting hard for his imagined supremacy, determined to pile up about himself a fortress of honour and glory and self-respect. Whether he knew that it was all a colossal and vulgar failure, can hardly be discerned; but if effort and determination are worthy of reward, then we need not grudge to Watts-Dunton his attainment of a singular literary notoriety. He certainly became a notable fact, as the friend and associate of two men of genius, and as the distributor at one time of literary favours, on a remarkably slender outfit of literary taste, and as the master of a style excelling in prolixity, dilution, conventionality and general dreariness—the apotheosis, in fact, of the provincial amateur.

SIR EDMUND CHAMBERS
1866–1954

Matthew Arnold

Warton Lecture on English Poetry, 1932

MATTHEW ARNOLD is now, I suppose, like most of his contemporaries, a natural target for the shafts of post-war criticism. I have read a book about him, the writer of which appears to have taken his inspiration from the insolent grace of Mr. Lytton Strachey, and to have succeeded admirably in catching the insolence. I shall say no more about it. In this company, I hope that I speak to many impenitent Victorians like myself, who still find in that bygone verse the cool refreshment which it breathed upon its first readers, in days which seemed to Matthew Arnold feverish enough, although they were far less feverish than our own. *Virgilium vidi tantum.* I have a boyhood's image of an Olympian figure, moving somewhat aloof on the outskirts of an Ambleside garden-party; and it was in the week in which I first came up as a freshman that Arnold paid his last visit to Oxford, staying with Thomas Fowler of genial memory in my own college of Corpus, and took his last walk in the happy coombes of Hinksey.

The chronology of the poems is rather difficult. It appears to have been Arnold's habit to let things lie aside for some time after they were written, and even when they had been published to drop and revive them, and arrange and rearrange them according to the shifting moods of his critical taste. The Rugby and Oxford prize poems he never admitted to the canon, but the earliest pieces therein contained must have come soon after the Newdigate of 1843. One of them was the sonnet on Shakespeare, of which an autograph copy is dated 1844. The lines *To a Gipsy Child* were written on a visit to the Isle of Man in 1845. Both of these appeared in Arnold's first volume, named from *The Strayed Reveller*, of 1849. This probably only had a small circulation, and before the year was out, Arnold wrote that he had 'got absolutely to dislike it'. A second volume of 1852, which included *Tristram and Iseult*, was withdrawn out of dissatisfaction with its title-poem, *Empedocles on Etna*. Most of the contents of both volumes were gradually reissued, with other work, old and new, in small gatherings of 1853, 1854, 1855, and 1857. The *New Poems* of 1867 gave the vintage of another decade. A fairly complete collection of 1869 restored some things that had been lost. But its order was only tentative, and that of the current editions dates from a recast of 1877. Here most of the pieces from the volume of 1849 and a few from those of 1852 and 1853 are relegated to a category of *Early Poems*, and as the rest of the classification is by 'kinds' of poetry, a good deal of cross-division is entailed. The critical estimate of a life-work of poetry depends so much on chronology that it would not be unreasonable for a writer who arrives at a collective edition, while following what arrangement he thinks fit, to label each piece with its date. As it is, one cannot I think, in the case of Arnold, rely upon the propinquity of poems, at any stage of publication, as evidence either of a common date or of common inspiration. An exception must of course be made for a few which are brought together in groups under comprehensive headings.

In those groups we are met on the threshold by the enigmatic figure of Marguerite. There are nine poems which were definitely written around Marguerite. All but one name her, in text or title, and about that one there can be no doubt. Eight of them were gradually issued from 1849 to 1857; one, *The Terrace at Berne*, which appeared in 1867, was professedly an epilogue, written after an interval of ten years. All nine, at one time or another, found a place in the group called *Switzerland*, which was differently composed in 1853, 1854, 1869, and 1877. Two, *A Memory Picture* and *A Dream*, are now separated from the rest, and put among the *Early Poems*. These nine poems, taken by themselves, sufficiently shadow out a story. It is one of an attraction passing into a passion, of doubt and reluctance from the beginning, of a growing sense of incompatibility on both sides, of a parting which, for a time at least, presented itself as a tragedy, a tragedy inevitable because it was based on character:

> A God, a God their severance ruled!
> And bade betwixt their shores to be
> The unplumb'd, salt, estranging sea.

The poet is left with a bitter sense of isolation, which he takes as a law of existence for him, and perhaps in some measure for all men. As he turns away, a consciousness of his own nature and vocation, which has beset him throughout, brings into the utterance of his 'vainly throbbing heart' an undertone akin to relief. A sterner life than that of his alluring dream has long been his lot:

> Farewell!—and thou, thou lonely heart,
> Which never yet without remorse
> Even for a moment didst depart
> From thy remote and spherèd course
> To haunt the place where passions reign—
> Back to thy solitude again!
>
> Back! with the conscious thrill of shame
> Which Luna felt, that summer-night,
> Flash through her pure immortal frame,
> When she forsook the starry height
> To hang over Endymion's sleep
> Upon the pine-grown Latmian steep.
>
> Yet she, chaste queen, had never proved
> How vain a thing is mortal love,
> Wandering in Heaven, far removed.
> But thou hast long had place to prove
> This truth—to prove and make thine own:
> 'Thou hast been, shalt be, art, alone.'

> Or, if not quite alone, yet they
> Which touch thee are unmating things—
> Oceans and clouds and night and day;
> Lorn autumns and triumphant springs;
> And life, and others' joy and pain,
> And love, if love, of happier men.
>
> Of happier men—for they, at least,
> Have *dream'd* two human hearts might blend
> In one, and were through faith released
> From isolation without end
> Prolong'd; nor knew, although no less
> Alone than thou, their loneliness.

Many of the earlier poems, besides *Switzerland*, must be put, wholly or in part, to the account of Marguerite. I think we are bound to give her the five which were gathered into the group called *Faded Leaves* in 1855. And there are several others in the volume of 1852 and a few even in that of 1849 which either directly concern her, or at least, like *The New Sirens*, echo the spiritual issues which his relations with her raised in Arnold's mind. There are hints of her, beyond the name Margaret, in *The Forsaken Merman*, and again in *Tristram and Iseult*, both in the main theme and in the Merlin and Vivian story at the end. I do not dissent from Professor Garrod when he calls the volume of 1852 'Marguerite's book, the book of forsaken or separated lovers'. But I think that he is inclined to press the point rather far. She is not the only woman in the book. I cannot find her reflected in Urania, who has seen through the hearts of men, and whose

> Lovely eyes maintain
> Their pure, unwavering deep disdain.

There was mockery in Marguerite's eyes, but it was the mockery of tenderness, not of disdain. And it is surely fantastic to suppose that a morbid imagination of her death inspired the *Lines Written on a Death-Bed*, to which one would certainly have to add the *Requiescat* of 1853. This was the death-bed of a tired woman, who had known fear and shame, and whose face bore the ravages of time. But Marguerite is ever fresh and young, and her feet flit lightly down the flowery track. It is true that Arnold did once, in *The Terrace at Berne*, long after she had passed out of his life, have the thought that she might be dead, but only to reject it:

> Could from earth's ways that figure slight
> Be lost, and I not feel 'twas so?
> Of that fresh voice the gay delight
> Fail from earth's air, and I not know?
>
> Or shall I find thee still, but changed,
> But not the Marguerite of thy prime?
> With all thy being re-arranged,
> Pass'd through the crucible of time;
>
> With spirit vanish'd, beauty waned,
> And hardly yet a glance, a tone,
> A gesture—anything—retain'd
> Of all that was my Marguerite's own?

I have written as if Marguerite were a real woman, and I find it hard to believe that it is not so. I am aware of the tradition handed down in Arnold's family that he had declared her to be imaginary; and no doubt one must give full value to any statement made by a middle-aged poet in reply to the questionings of his daughters about the object of his early love lyrics. And no doubt, too, imagination has played its part. But the poems do at least leave the impression of a very definite and vivid personality, with many details which are not essential to the emotional theme, and give an air of verisimilitude. Marguerite was a daughter of France. She was literate enough to lend Arnold a volume of the *Letters of Ortis*, a sentimental romance by the Italian poet Ugo Foscolo. She dwelt in a steep street by the Aar, near the 'roof'd bridge that spans the stream' and the twin lakes. It is clearly Thun. She had a housemate, Olivia; the names may of course have been altered. She had a slight figure, an arch smile, an exquisite voice, a 'pale sweet-rounded cheek'. A kerchief commonly enwound her hair. Several of these intimate touches recur again and again. They do not suggest a figure of drama. The only possible inconsistency is in colouring. In *Parting* Marguerite has 'soft, ash-colour'd hair'—*blond cendré* one supposes, rather than the black of Tennyson's ashbuds in March. Her eyes are normally blue. But in *Absence* a 'stranger's eyes of grey' recall them, and in *Separation*, one of the *Faded Leaves* group, there is a wish that she may be wholly forgotten, and at some future meeting,

> Who, let me say, is this stranger regards me,
> With the grey eyes, and the lovely brown hair?

Between brown and ash-coloured, however, we need not dispute, and although eyes are a point on which lovers ought to be clear, it is not always so. Perhaps we may call in aid another of the *Faded Leaves* poems, which has—

> Eyes too expressive to be blue,
> Too lovely to be grey.

Even so Swinburne writes of—

> Those eyes the greenest of things blue,
> The bluest of things grey.

There can have been no mystery about Marguerite in the Arnold family at the time, although personal references have been rather carefully cut out of such of the poet's letters as have yet been published. *Absence*, however, was read to one of his sisters just after it was composed, and Arnold reminds her, a quarter of a century later, how she had been touched by it.

As to the date of the Marguerite episode, we cannot at present be quite certain. The only poem which names her in the 1849 volume is *A Memory Picture*, the first of the *Switzerland* series, and that is written in a lighter tone than the rest. But here is also to be found *The Voice*:

> So sad, and with so wild a start
> To this deep-sober'd heart,
> So anxiously and painfully,
> So drearily and doubtfully,
> And oh, with such intolerable change
> Of thought, such contrast strange,
> O unforgotten voice, the accents come,
> Like wanderers from the world's extremity,
> Unto their ancient home!

> In vain, all, all in vain,
> They beat upon mine ear again,
> Those melancholy tones so sweet and still.
> Those lute-like tones which in the bygone year
> Did steal into mine ear—
> Blew such a thrilling summons to my will,
> Yet could not shake it;
> Made my tost heart its very life-blood spill,
> Yet could not break it.

I agree with Professor Garrod that this can only be one voice, the voice of Marguerite in *The Terrace at Berne*, her voice in *Parting*:

> But on the stairs what voice is this I hear,
> Buoyant as morning, and as morning clear?
> Say, has some wet bird-haunted English lawn
> Lent it the music of its trees at dawn?
> Or was it from some sun-flecked mountain-brook
> That the sweet voice its upland clearness took?

And if so, the closing lines of *The Voice* seem to make it clear that the episode was already over when that poem came to be printed in 1849. A date in 1848 is just possible, but one in 1847 or earlier is more likely. I ought to add that I have quoted a revised text of 1877. That of 1849 has, among variants of a more literary character, 'long-distant years' for 'the bygone year', and 'long sober'd heart' for 'deep-sober'd heart'. I do not much believe in 'long distant years' which would take us back to Arnold's boyhood. It is conceivable that there was some *camouflage* in 1849, and that in these points the text of 1877 is the original one. The Berne poem ought to help in the dating, but I am not sure that it does. In the collection of 1869 it stood at the end of the *Switzerland* group, with a note that it was 'composed ten years after the preceding'. Arnold was at Berne in 1865, and the last of the earlier *Switzerland* poems was printed in 1855. But the words of the poem itself would suggest that the lapse of ten years had been since the parting. Arnold's letters record several visits to Switzerland towards the end of the 'fifties, but none that clearly took him to Berne. I think that 1857 is a possibility, because he then wrote of 'two or three things I have in hand, which I cannot finish till I have again breathed and smelt Swiss air'. But Berne would have entailed some alteration of his planned itinerary.

I make no apology for being curious about Marguerite. The first love of a poet can never be without interest, or without significance. But I do not want to inquire too closely how much in the lyrics she evoked is a literal transcript from experience, and how much grew up round that experience when it was in fact over. These are delicate things to handle.

Tread softly, because you tread on my dreams.

If I am right as to the dates, there was time between 1849 and 1852 for the 'shaping spirit of imagination' to have play. Certainly the parting with a blue-eyed girl became for Matthew Arnold something more than itself, a parting with the whole world of passionate romance which he put behind him. The Marguerite poems are not merely poems of isolation, but of renunciation, of self-dedication. There had been a κάθαρσις. He turned back to his 'spherèd course', to the rigorous teachers who had seized his youth, to

> The dragon-warder'd fountains
> Where the springs of knowledge are,

and incidentally to the routine, which he often found irksome, of the Education Office. But these early poems have a lyric plangency, which is not quite the note of those that followed.

Poetry, indeed, he did not lay aside, but for a time it took a more impersonal form, on classical models which were always dear to him. By 1853 he was at work upon *Sohrab and Rustum*, which appeared later in the year with the famous preface, in which Arnold laid down that 'the eternal objects of Poetry, among all nations, and at all times' are 'actions; human actions; possessing an inherent interest in themselves, and which are to be communicated in an interesting manner by the art of the Poet'. This was consonant enough with his own mood when it was written. But it is a curious limitation of the scope of high poetry, the criterion of which, on the side of impulse, as distinct from craftsmanship, is surely to be found, not in the nature of its subject-matter, but in the quality of the emotional excitement which that subject-matter, whether a human action or some simple fact of observation, or feeling, or reflection, has roused in the mind of the poet. Matthew Arnold has said many sound things about poets and poems, and in particular about poetic diction, but I do not think he was ever at his best in attempting to expound the fundamental basis of poetic activity. He comes nearer to the truth in a much later essay, at the point where, after exalting Wordsworth over other poets because he deals with more of life, and deals with it, as a whole, more powerfully than they do, he is suddenly taken back at finding himself in apparent agreement with the logical but eminently prosaic mind of Leslie Stephen. Wordsworth's poetry was great, according to Leslie Stephen, because his philosophy was sound. 'No,' says Arnold, 'Wordsworth's poetry is great because of the extraordinary power with which Wordsworth feels the joy offered to us in nature, the joy offered to us in the simple primary affections and duties; and because of the extraordinary power with which, in case after case, he shows us this joy, and renders it so as to make us share it.' But I am not here to discuss Matthew Arnold as a critic. He wrote *Sohrab and Rustum*, with 'more pleasure than anything I have done yet'. And it is a noble poem, the fruit of his constant preoccupation with Homer, whose works, he says, for one or two years, were seldom out of his hands. But it is no mere transcript from Homer. It is Homeric in its large utterance, its forthrightness, its constant use of expanded similes; un-Homeric and modern in its concentration on a theme of family relationship such as Homer only lightly touches, in the more conscious elaboration of its decorative passages, and above all in the enveloping presence of the river Oxus, which is a recurrent note throughout, and culminates in the magnificent *finale*, too familiar for me to quote, where the father and the son are left alone on the darkling plain, and the Oxus, regardless and serene, moves onward to the Aral sea. *Sohrab and Rustum* was followed by *Balder Dead*, of which Arnold remained proud, thinking that it had 'a natural propriety of rhythm and diction', which he found in Virgil, and did not, in after thought, altogether find in *Sohrab and Rustum*. The verse has dignity, no doubt, and there are some good similes, and one very beautiful and characteristic one, in which the touch of a brother in the dark is

> As a spray of honeysuckle flowers
> Brushes across a tired traveller's face
> Who shuffles through the deep dew-moistened dust,
> On a May evening, in the darken'd lanes,
> And starts him, that he thinks a ghost went by.

But few will put the poem, as a whole, on a level with its predecessor. Its theme, indeed, hardly satisfies Matthew Arnold's own requirements for poetic narrative. Here is no excellent human action, where the shadowy figures of a priestly mythology are impelled by unintelligible motives to inconclusive ends.

During the next decade, Arnold's poems came slowly, although, as gathered in the volume of 1867, they form a substantial body, of unimpaired poetic quality. They close, indeed, with the *Thyrsis* of 1866, which is perhaps his finest single work. But educational duties pressed upon him throughout, and in 1857 the Professorship of Poetry turned his thoughts to prose. Probably his poetic impulse never flowed easily. Over *Thyrsis* itself he brooded long. Clough, on whom it was in part written, died in 1861.

Arnold had meant to begin it at Oxford in the spring of 1863, but was prevented by 'a detestable cold wind'. He could do no more, he wrote, than accumulate stores for it. In the same letter he notes the fritillaries in the meadows by the Thames. All the images in *Thyrsis*, he said later, were from actual observation. The cuckoo, however, was heard, not at Hinksey, but at Woodford, in Epping Forest, during 1864. The poem, therefore, took at least two or three years in the making. There is much evidence that at all times in this decade Arnold found the writing of poetry difficult. Another letter, of 1858, is in the nature of an *apologia* for *Merope*. It was motived by the temptation 'if you cannot bear anything not *very good*, to transfer your operations to a region where form is everything'. A kind of perfection might thus be approached. But to attain perfection in thought and feeling, as well as in form, seemed to him impossible, 'unless one can devote one's whole life to poetry', as Wordsworth, Shelley, Byron, and Tennyson were able to do. Probably Matthew Arnold was carrying too great a load of competing activities. But I do not myself believe in the doctrine of a complete dedication to poetry. Poetry is, after all, the reflex of life, and life, if its reflex is to be of value, must be lived for itself. It is remarkable how much of the world's greatest poetry has in fact been written by men who largely spent themselves in normal occupations, and, on the other hand, how dilute the poetry of life-long poets has often become. Wordsworth is an outstanding example of this. It is no part of my object to attempt a comparison between the best work of Matthew Arnold and that of his six greatest contemporaries. Personal taste and emotional sympathy inevitably play too great a part in any such estimate. But one may fairly maintain that the *proportion* of work which endures is greater in the case of Matthew Arnold than in that of any one of them. Nevertheless it is true that in middle life he came more and more to feel poetry slipping away from him, and that for this his preoccupations were at least in part responsible. More than once he resolved to lay critical writings aside and return to the Muses. 'The period between forty and fifty', he wrote in 1861, 'is not a bad ten years of one's life for poetry, if one resolutely uses it, but it is a time in which, if one does not use it, one dries up and becomes prosaic.' One does, no doubt. But his hopes were not to be realized. Forty saw him plunged in educational controversy, and on the eve of those long inquiries into the conditions of foreign schools, which were destined to have so profound an ultimate influence upon the development of education in this country. And these in their turn were followed by the remarkable essays on the trend of English civilization, social and religious, which have done more than we always realize to determine our modern apprehension of spiritual values. Matthew Arnold's poetic activity practically closed with the volume of 1867. Even so, twenty years was a reasonable span. As it happens, it was just that of Shakespeare's poetic life, and of Spenser's. The Destinies gave Shelley no more than twelve, and Keats no more than five. Wordsworth's poetic life, rightly measured, was about ten. Perhaps Arnold recognized the inevitable, when he issued his collection of 1869. It was not quite complete. One of the omitted poems was *The Voice*, in which he detected a tone of falsetto. I do not myself feel that there is much falsetto, if by that is meant the kind of thing which you get in *Maud* and *Locksley Hall*, and some other of the less successful attempts of Tennyson. But Arnold was always fastidious. One or two other poems were more or less re-written. The texts of the rest do not differ substantially from the earlier ones. But there was a good deal of touching up, generally for the better, in small details of craftsmanship. Clashes of sound and repetition of epithets were eliminated. Arnold, like meaner men, was occasionally worried by the difficulty of securing the right alternation of 'that' and 'which'. And there are some amusing alterations due to the increased knowledge of field botany which he acquired in his later years. The original blue convolvulus on the stubble field of *The Scholar Gipsy* becomes a pink one. The reaping scene of *Bacchanalia* is turned into a mowing scene, because the dog-rose is over before harvest time. The 'green fern' of *Tristram and Iseult* gives place to 'last year's fern', because that is what you really get in April. Another example of Arnold's desire for literal fidelity of visual rendering is also to be found in *The Scholar Gipsy*. Instead of 'the slow punt swings round' he put 'the punt's rope chops round'. It is less elegant, but the punt at Bablock-hythe is so fixed as to make a moving bridge which cannot swing round. Arnold lived for nearly twenty years after the collection of 1869 was issued. Even to the end he was still occasionally wondering, rather wistfully, whether he should ever do anything more in poetry. 'It is something', he adds, 'to have been of use in prose.' And so, indeed, it is. The occasional pieces, mostly elegies on household pets, of these later years, although gracefully turned, do not amount to much. But I must own that I should like to know what became of the *Lucretius*, which Arnold long had by him, and evidently never finished. It must be the 'tragedy of the time of the Roman Republic', which he was full of in 1855, but did not expect to have ready before 1857. In 1866 he was perturbed by hearing that Tennyson was at work on the story of Lucretius, and thought that a common friend must have suggested the subject. He had himself been occupied with it for twenty years. He meant to go on, but could not publish before the following year. A month later four lines from *Lucretius, an unpublished Tragedy*, were prefixed to *Thyrsis* as it first appeared in *Macmillan's Magazine*. They are not reprinted in the *Collected Poems*, and I will quote them:

> Thus yesterday, to-day, to-morrow come,
> They hustle one another and they pass;
> But all our hustling morrows only make
> The smooth to-day of God.

Writing to F. T. Palgrave in 1879, Arnold again named *Lucretius*, as one of the things which he would like to do in poetry before he died, and of which lines and bits had long been done. The subjects of the others were St. Alexius and the journey of Achilles after death to the island of Leuce. 'But', he adds, 'we accomplish what we can, not what we will.'

I turn to another aspect of Matthew Arnold's poetry. The elegiac temper pervades it from beginning to end, and it is perhaps this, rather than the exaltation of the early lyric, or the deep harmony of *Sohrab and Rustum*, which seems to the modern reader his peculiar characteristic. The elegy, as is common with elegy, often has an idyllic setting. *The Scholar Gipsy* and *Thyrsis* we all know, but let me quote in illustration from two shorter poems. The first is *Resignation*, which is early:

> He sees the gentle stir of birth
> When morning purifies the earth;
> He leans upon a gate and sees
> The pastures, and the quiet trees.
> Low, woody hill, with gracious bound,
> Folds the still valley almost round;
> The cuckoo, loud on some high lawn,
> Is answer'd from the depth of dawn;
> In the hedge straggling to the stream,
> Pale, dew-drench'd, half-shut roses gleam;
> But, where the farther side slopes down,
> He sees the drowsy new-waked clown
> In his white quaint-embroider'd frock
> Make, whistling, tow'rd his mist-wreathed flock—
> Slowly, behind his heavy tread,
> The wet, flower'd grass heaves up its head.
> Lean'd on his gate, he gazes—tears
> Are in his eyes, and in his ears
> The murmur of a thousand years.

The second is *Bacchanalia*, which is late:

> The evening comes, the fields are still.
> The tinkle of the thirsty rill,
> Unheard all day, ascends again;
> Deserted is the half-mown plain,
> Silent the swaths! the ringing wain,
> The mower's cry, the dog's alarms,
> All housed within the sleeping farms!
> The business of the day is done,
> The last-left haymaker is gone.
> And from the thyme upon the height,
> And from the elder-blossom white
> And pale dog-roses in the hedge,
> And from the mint-plant in the sedge,
> In puffs of balm the night-air blows
> The perfume which the day forgoes.

For such writing I will venture to borrow the phrase of a poetess who herself wrote no poetry, 'It calls home the heart to quietness'. The country dear to Matthew Arnold was very quiet country. Hinksey and Cumnor, the haunts of his youth and mine, to which he always returned on his visits to Oxford, were not what are called beauty spots. They were merely uplands of ancient pasture, down some of which, by the time of *Thyrsis*, the ploughboy's team had already gone; with a bit of woodland, a wide outlook over Oxford itself and the surrounding valleys, and little footpaths running from farm to farm beneath high hedges. You may taste such quietness in any part of England still, if you care to leave the roadways. Arnold has other scenery as well; that of the Lake Country, that of a Surrey common, with its hollies, in *Tristram and Iseult*, that of the lower Alps, where the yellow gentian flames on the way to

> Jaman, delicately tall,
> Above his sun-warm'd firs;

that of Sicily in *Empedocles on Etna*, with its classical reminiscences. It is all quiet. From all alike he draws the cool refreshment of which I have already spoken. You will find, if you run through the poems, that 'cool' is his favourite epithet. Above all he loves the coolest things in the world, the dew at morning and in the evening, and the moon. How many of his best things are drenched in moonlight! The Merman creeps to shore,

> When clear falls the moonlight,
> When spring-tides are low.

In *The Youth of Nature*,
> The lake,
> Lovely and soft as a dream,
> Swims in the sheen of the moon.

The Scholar Gipsy has its 'moon-blanched green', *Dover Beach* its 'moon-blanch'd land', *A Summer Night* its 'moon-blanch'd street'; and both this and *A Southern Night* recall an unforgotten experience in which the moon had its part:

> And to my mind the thought
> Is on a sudden brought
> Of a past night, and a far different scene.
> Headlands stood out into the moonlit deep
> As clearly as at noon;
> The spring-tide's brimming flow
> Heaved dazzlingly between;
> Houses, with long white sweep,

Girdled the glistening bay;
Behind, through the soft air
The blue haze-cradled mountains spread away,
The night was far more fair—
But the same restless pacings to and fro,
And the same vainly throbbing heart was there,
And the same bright, calm moon.

The moon, again, shines on Tristram's deathbed, and through the clerestory windows of *The Church at Brou*. The Oxus flows through the hushed Chorasmian waste 'under the solitary moon'. Apollo and the Muses in *Empedocles* roam through the 'moon-silver'd inlets' of Thisbe vale. The nightingale of *Philomela* sings in the moonlit cedar. The full moon lights the 'groups under the dreaming garden-trees' in *Thyrsis*. The quietness of Arnold's vision is enhanced by the quality of his verse; its simplicity, lucidity, and straightforwardness; its literalness, I think he would have said; the sparing use of aureate words, or of far-fetched words, which are all the more effective when they come; the avoidance of inversions, and the general directness of syntax, which gives full value to the delicacies of a varied rhythm, and makes it, of all verse that I know, the easiest to read aloud. Here are some at least of the characteristics which Arnold found in Homer and did not find in some of Homer's translators. But it was only in *Sohrab and Rustum* and *Balder* that he essayed the Homeric grandeur. The diction of *Thyrsis*, he says, was modelled on that of Theocritus. He felt that it was 'a very quiet poem'.

As a poet of natural beauty Matthew Arnold

is the direct inheritor of Wordsworth. He acknowledges the derivation more than once; in *The Youth of Nature* and in the *Memorial Verses*:

> He laid us as we lay at birth
> On the cool flowery lap of earth,
> Smiles broke from us and we had ease;
> The hills were round us, and the breeze
> Went o'er the sun-lit fields again;
> Our foreheads felt the wind and rain.
> Our youth return'd; for there was shed
> On spirits that had long been dead,
> Spirits dried up and closely furl'd,
> The freshness of the early world.

And like Wordsworth, the Wordsworth of 'The world is too much with us', he contrasts the quiet of nature with the disquietude of man,

> This iron time
> Of doubts, disputes, distractions, fears,

the 'benumbing round', the 'faded, ignoble lives of worldlings, the

> Strange disease of modern life,
> With its sick hurry, its divided aims.

He looks upon

> The long heart-wasting show,
> Wherein earth's great ones are disquieted.

Man is 'the eternal trifler':

> We see all sights from pole to pole,
> And glance, and nod, and bustle by,
> And never once possess our soul
> Before we die.

The thought is more habitual than in Wordsworth. And indeed the parallel between Wordsworth and Arnold must not be pushed too far. They differed both in temper and in conviction. We have seen that what Arnold felt most clearly in Wordsworth's reaction to nature and life was joy. But the poet of *Resignation*, written around those fells of Watendlath which Wordsworth knew so well, has another outlook. He too, as he leans on his gate in the misty morning, sees the whole of life unroll before him, just as Wordsworth might have done. But for him it is a life

> Whose secret is not joy, but peace.

And again:

> Yet, Fausta, the mute turf we tread,
> The solemn hills around us spread,
> This stream which falls incessantly,
> The strange-scrawled rocks, the lonely sky,
> If I might lend their life a voice,
> Seem to bear rather than rejoice.

Nor were the spiritual implications in Wordsworth's matured poetry of nature such as Arnold could accept. Content as a boy to take 'the harvest of a quiet eye', or at the most, in retrospect at least, shot through from time to time with dim intimations of unknown modes of being, Wordsworth found his way to a conviction, based on mystic intuition rather than logical reasoning, of a universal harmony in things. The life of man is bound up with the life of nature, and together they are the vehicle of a power that informs them both. This doctrine finds its clearest expression in the lines on *Tintern Abbey*. Ultimately Wordsworth gave it a more specifically Christian turn.

> I have felt
> A presence that disturbs me with the joy
> Of elevated thoughts: a sense sublime
> Of something far more deeply interfused,
> Whose dwelling is the light of setting suns,
> And the round ocean, and the living air,
> And the blue sky, and in the mind of man:
> A motion and a spirit, that impels
> All thinking things, all objects of all thought,
> And rolls through all things.

This philosophic optimism, if the term is not too intellectual a one to use, was never Matthew Arnold's. His rigorous teachers had purged his faith, and shown him 'the high, white star of Truth', and in that clear and searching light he could see no certainty of such a harmony. His prevailing elegiac mood is one of disequilibrium. He can arrive at no coherent vision of the scheme of things entire. Nature follows the course of nature, and man follows the course of man. Between these there may be contacts. Man may learn endurance as well as peace from nature, when

> With joy the stars perform their shining,
> And the sea its long moon-silver'd roll.

It is the lesson of the sonnet on *Toil and Tranquillity*, which once stood at the head of his first volume. The 'sleepless ministers' of nature are the 'labourers that shall not fail, when man is gone'. But what assurance is there that even the reasonable strivings of men serve a divine end? We strive to little purpose:

> Unbreachable the fort
> Of the long-battered world uplifts its wall.

And we strive blindly:

> We are here as on a darkling plain
> Swept with confused alarms of struggle and flight,
> Where ignorant armies clash by night.

Once again the sense of isolation is strong upon him. At the best we are 'in some unknown Power's employ'. Arnold stood too near his lost faith to become a contented pagan. He feels as one adrift from his moorings. He envies the Scholar Gipsy, in his single-eyed chase, year after year, of a constant aim,

> Still nursing the unconquerable hope,
> Still clutching the inviolable shade.

He envies the calm security of the Carthusian in his cell, regardless of the banners and the bugles of the outer world:

> Like these, on earth I wait forlorn.
> Their faith, my tears, the world deride—
> I come to shed them at their side.

But the 'cloister-floor of humid stone' is not for him; and indeed he would have been ill at ease on it.

> The Sea of Faith
> Was once, too, at the full, and round earth's shore
> Lay like the folds of a bright girdle furl'd.
> But now I only hear
> Its melancholy, long, withdrawing roar,
> Retreating, to the breath
> Of the night-wind, down the vast edges drear
> And naked shingles of the world.

It is possible to lay too much emphasis upon this side of Arnold's poetry. That is an error of perspective into which, I think, some of his critics have fallen. After all, the elegies only represent one factor in a complex personality, reacting from strenuous days of unfaltering devotion to the service of what is best in humanity. Arnold was no Obermann, sadly watching the irretrievable flux of things from the door of his high chalet on the green slopes of Jaman. The pulse of living in him was too strong for that stern withdrawal and its 'hourly varied anodynes'. To that 'unstrung will' and 'broken heart' he bade farewell, with much else, when he returned to his 'spherèd course'. A visit to Glion brought an hour of recollection:

> An eremite with thee, in thought
> Once more I slip my chain.

But although Obermann had been 'the master of my wandering youth', he had then been 'left for many a year'. One must not expect to find consistency in the moods of a poet. Often enough, natural beauty seems to be for Arnold a mere *refrigerium*. But it is not always so. There is at least meliorism, if not optimism, at the end of *Obermann Once More*, as the dawn breaks over the Valais; and again in *The Future*, where the river of Time, in 'wider, statelier' flow, may yet strike peace to the soul of humanity,

> As the stars come out, and the night-wind
> Brings up the stream
> Murmurs and scents of the infinite sea.

Nor is the tonic strain of 'unresting, unhasting' endeavour a rare one. It is something more than mere acceptance; rather the spirit of morality suffused by emotion which Arnold found in Marcus Aurelius, 'a spirit not so much of gladness and elation, as of gentleness and sweetness; a delicate and tender sentiment, which is less than joy and more than resignation'. It informs, very notably, the musings over the example of Arnold's own father in *Rugby Chapel*. The testament of Empedocles to Pausanias does not show the poet's thought at its clearest, or give it its finest expression, but here too is such consolation as a stoic may take. Life has a bounty for man, if he will only be moderate in his demands on it:

> Is it so small a thing
> To have enjoy'd the sun,
> To have lived light in the spring,
> To have loved, to have thought, to have done;
> To have advanced true friends, and beat down baffling foes?
>
> I say: Fear not! Life still
> Leaves human effort scope.
> But, since life teems with ill,
> Nurse no extravagant hope:
> Because thou must not dream, thou need'st not then despair.

And this is echoed, long after, in the sincerity and simplicity of *A Wish*. The poet would have no doctor at his death-bed, and no 'brother-doctor of the soul', no whispering crowded room, no air of ceremony.

> Bring none of these; but let me be,
> While all around in silence lies,
> Moved to the window near, and see
> Once more, before my dying eyes,

Bathed in the sacred dews of morn
The wide aerial landscape spread—
The world which was ere I was born,
The world which lasts when I am dead;

Which never was the friend of *one*,
Nor promised love it could not give,
But lit for all its generous sun,
And lived itself, and made us live.

There let me gaze, till I become
In soul, with what I gaze on, wed!
To feel the universe my home;
To have before my mind—instead

Of the sick room, the mortal strife,
The turmoil for a little breath—
The pure eternal course of life,
Not human combatings with death!

Thus feeling, gazing, might I grow
Compos'd, refresh'd, ennobled, clear;
Then willing let my spirit go
To work or wait elsewhere or here!

The wish was only half fulfilled. It is a little ironical, and more than a little pathetic, that Matthew Arnold, the apostle of quiet, died running to catch a tram.

Matthew Arnold's tree, the 'lone sky-pointing' elm of *Thyrsis*, fell in one of the great gales of December 1929. It is not quite certain where it stood. The late A. D. Godley wrote a paper in which he traced very conclusively the course which Arnold must have taken on the footpath from Childsworth Farm to the neighbourhood of Cumnor Hurst, and came to the decision that the elm must have been that on the top of the Hurst. I believe it myself to have been one which was reached a little farther along the same line of walk. It was a noble tree, which stood, 'bare on its lonely ridge', in the great field between Chawley Farm and Cumnor Village, a good deal lower than the Hurst, but with the same double prospect of the Berkshire Downs and the Upper Thames Valley. And it was solitary, whereas the tree on the Hurst was close to the ring of firs which gives its main character to that eminence. It matters little now, since both trees fell in that same night of wreck. Cumnor still keeps its incommunicable secret. In the grassy harvest of the Eynsham water meadows the fritillaries blow no longer. And now we must believe that the Scholar Gipsy has ceased to roam those slopes. His quest was bound up with the life of the tree. Already there are spots near Cumnor which he could not wish to haunt. And I gather that the bridle-track from Appleton, down which the troop of Oxford hunters came in *Thyrsis*, is marked out by the industrial masters of our destiny for a range of electric pylons. When I last trod the Childsworth footpath its serenity was undisturbed. A single wayfarer was crossing it towards an opening in 'the high wood'. He stooped, and may have been a scholar. But he was not the Scholar Gipsy, for he was pushing a bicycle. Immortal, like mortal things, touch the mind in their perishing.

MAX BEERBOHM
1872–

Ouida

More, 1899

THE Democracy of Letters will exasperate or divert you, according to your temperament. Me it diverts merely. It does no harm to literature. Good books are still written, good critics still criticize, in the old, quiet way; and, if the good books are criticized chiefly by innumerable fools hired to review an imponderable amount of trash, I do not really see that it matters at all. The trash itself is studied, now and again, by good critics and so becomes a spring-board for good criticism, and it were unfair as it were useless, therefore, to shield good books from the consideration of ordinary reviewers. You may call it monstrous that a good writer should be at the mercy of such persons, but I doubt whether the good writer is himself aggrieved. He needs no mercy. And, as a matter of fact, the menaces hurled by the ordinary reviewers, whenever something new or strange confronts them, are very vain words indeed, and may at any moment be merged in clumsy compliments. A good critic—and by that term I mean a cultured man with brains and a temperament—may at any moment come by, and, if he praise, the ordinary reviewers, most receptive of all creatures, will praise also. I was glancing lately through a little book of essays, written by a lady. At the end of the book were printed press-notices about a volume of this lady's book of verse. Among these gems, and coruscating beyond the rest, was one graven with the name of Mr. William Sharp: 'In its class I know no nobler or more beautiful sonnet than "Renouncement"; and I have so considered it ever since the day when Rossetti (who knew it by heart), repeating it to me, added that it was one of the three finest sonnets ever written by women.' Such a confession as Mr. William Sharp's is not to be found in the ordinary press-notice, but that is merely because the ordinary reviewer is of a less simple and sunny disposition than our friend, and speaks not save as one having his own authority. Nevertheless he is in no wise more clever than Mr. Sharp (or Captain Sumph), and very likely he did not ever know Rossetti. Whether Mr. Sharp liked this sonnet before he met it under high auspices, is a point which may never be made clear, but there can be no doubt that the method of the ordinary reviewer is to curse what he does not understand, until it be explained to him. The element of comedy becomes yet stronger if the reviewers be subsequently assured that the explanation was all wrong. Who shall forget the chorus of adulation that rent the welkin for the essays of this very lady whose sonnet Mr. Sharp 'so considered'? Two great writers had greatly praised her. I, humble person, mildly suggested that their praise had been excessive, and gave some good reasons for my opinion. Since then, the chorus has been palpably less loud, marred even by discordant voices. I do not pride myself particularly on this effect; I record it only because it gives a little instance of a great law.

Simpler, more striking, and more important, as an instance of reviewers' emptiness, is the position of Ouida, the latest of whose long novels, *The Massarenes*, had what is technically termed 'a cordial reception'—a reception strangely different from that accorded to her novels thitherto. Ouida's novels have always, I believe, sold well. They contain qualities which have gained for them some measure of Corellian success. Probably that is why, for so many years, no good critic took the trouble to praise them. The good critic, with a fastidiousness which is perhaps a fault, often neglects those who can look after themselves; the very fact of popularity—he is not infallible—often repels him; he prefers to champion the deserving weak. And so, for many years, the critics, unreproved, were ridiculing a writer who had many qualities obvious to ridicule, many gifts that lifted her beyond their reach. At length it occurred to a critic of distinction, Mr. G. S. Street, to write an 'Appreciation of Ouida', which appeared in the *Yellow Book*. It was a shy, self-conscious essay, written somewhat in the tone of a young man defending the moral character of a barmaid who has bewitched him, but, for all its blushing diffidence, it was a very gentlemanly piece of work, and it was full of true and delicate criticism. I myself wrote, later, in praise of Ouida, and I believe that, at about the same time, Mr. Stephen Crane wrote an appreciation of his own in an American magazine. In a word, three intelligent persons had cracked their whips—enough to have called the hounds off. Nay more, the furious pack had been turned suddenly into a flock of nice sheep. It was pretty to see them gambling and frisking and bleating around *The Massarenes*.

Ouida is not, and never was, an artist. That, strangely enough, is one reason why she had been so little appreciated by the reviewers. The artist presents his ideas in the finest, strictest form, paring, whittling, polishing. In reading his finished work, none but a few persons note his artistic skill, or take pleasure in it for its own sake. Yet it is this very skill of his which enables the reviewers to read his work with pleasure. To a few persons, artistic skill is in itself delightful, insomuch that they tend to overrate its importance, neglecting the matter for the form. Art, in a writer, is not everything. Indeed, it implies a certain limitation. If a list of consciously artistic writers were drawn up, one would find that most of them were lacking in great force of intellect or of emotion; that their intellects were restricted, their emotions not very strong. Writers of enormous vitality never are artistic: they cannot pause, they must always be moving swiftly forward. Mr. Meredith, the only living novelist in England who rivals Ouida in sheer vitality, packs tight all his pages with wit, philosophy, poetry, and psychological analysis. His obscurity, like that of Carlyle and Browning, is due less to extreme subtlety than to the plethoric abundance of his ideas. He cannot stop to express himself. If he could, he might be more popular. The rhapsodies of Mr. Swinburne, again, are so overwhelmingly exuberant in their expression that no ordinary reader can cope with them; the ordinary reader is stunned by them before he is impressed. When he lays down the book and regains consciousness, he has forgotten entirely what it was all about. On the other hand reticence, economy, selection, and all the artistic means may be carried too far. Too much art is, of course, as great an obstacle as too little art; and Pater, in his excessive care for words, is as obscure to most people as are Carlyle and Browning, in their carelessness. It is to him who takes the mean of these two extremes, to that author who expresses himself simply, without unnecessary expansion or congestion, that appreciation is most readily and spontaneously granted.

Well! For my own part, I am a dilettante, a *petit maître*. I love best in literature delicate and elaborate ingenuities of form and style. But my preference does not keep me from paying due homage to Titanic force, and delighting, now and again, in its manifestation. I wonder at Ouida's novels, and I wonder still more at Ouida. I am staggered when I think of that lurid sequence of books and short stories and essays which she has poured forth so swiftly, with such irresistible *élan*. What manner of woman can Ouida be? A woman who writes well never writes much. Even Sappho spent her whole life in writing and re-writing some exquisite, isolated verses, which, with feminine tact, she handed down to posterity as mere fragments of her work. In our own day, there are some ladies who write a large number of long books, but I am sure that the 'sexual novel' or the 'political novel', as wrought by them, must be as easy to write as it is hard to read. Ouida is essentially feminine, as much *une femme des femmes* as Jane Austen or 'John Oliver Hobbes', and it is indeed remarkable that she should yet be endowed with force and energy so exuberant and indefatigable. All her books are amazing in their sustained vitality. Vitality is, indeed, the most patent, potent, factor in her work. Her pen is more inexhaustibly prolific than the pen of any other writer; it gathers new strength of its every dip into the ink-pot. Ouida need not, and could not, husband her unique endowments, and a man might as well shake his head over the daily rising of the indefatigable sun, or preach Malthusianism in a rabbit-warren, as counsel Ouida to write less. Her every page is a riot of unpolished epigrams and unpolished poetry of vision, with a hundred discursions and redundancies. She cannot say a thing once; she must repeat it again and again, and, with every repetition, so it seems to me, she says it with greater force and charm. Her style is a veritable cascade, in comparison with which the waters come down at Lodore as tamely as they come down at Shanklin. And, all the while, I never lose interest in her story, constructed with that sound professional knowledge, which the romancers of this later generation, with their vague and halting modes, would probably regard as old-fashioned. Ouida grips me with her every plot, and—I can believe even in her characters. True, they are not real, when I think of them in cold blood. They are abstractions, like the figures in early Greek tragedies and epics before psychology was thought of—things of black or white, or colourless things to illustrate the working of destiny, elemental puppets for pity or awe. Ouida does not pretend to the finer shades of civilized psychology. Her men and women of Mayfair are shadows, as I see when I am not under the direct spell of her writing, and she reproduces real life only when she is dealing with childish or half-savage natures—Cigarette the *vivandière*, Redempta the gipsy, Italian peasants, dogs and horses. She cares for the romance and beauty and terror of life, not for its delicate shades and inner secrets. Her books are, in the true sense of the word, romances, though they are not written in Wardour Street. The picturesqueness of modern life, transfigured by imagination, embellished by fancy, that is her *forte*. She involves her stock-figures—the pure girl, the wicked woman, the adorable hero, and the rest—in a series of splendid adventures. She makes her protagonist a guardsman that she may describe, as she alone can, steeplechases and fox-hunts and horses running away with phaetons. Or she makes him a diplomat, like Strathmore, or a great tenor, like Corèze, or a Queen's messenger, like Erceldoune, or something else—anything so that it be lurid and susceptible of romance. She ranges hither and thither over all countries, snatching at all languages, realizing all scenes. Her information is as wide as Macaulay's, and her slips in local colour are but the result of a careless omniscience.

That she should have referred to 'the pointing of the *digito monstrari*', and headed one of her chapters with the words 'Thalassis! Thalassis!' and made the Queen present at a Levée, and thrown one or two false side-lights on the Oxford Eights Week, may seem very terrible to the dullards who think that criticism consists in spotting mistakes. But the fact remains that Ouida uses her great information with extraordinary effect. Her delight in beautiful things has been accounted to her for vulgarity by those who think that a writer 'should take material luxury for granted'. But such people forget, or are unable to appreciate, the difference between the perfunctory faking of description, as practised by the average novelist—as who should say 'soft carpets', 'choice wines', 'priceless Tintorettos'—and description which is the result of true vision. No writer was ever more finely endowed than Ouida with the love and knowledge of all kinds of beauty in art and nature. There is nothing vulgar in having a sense of beauty—so long as you have it. Ouida's descriptions of boudoirs in palaces are no more vulgar nor less beautiful than her descriptions of lakes and mountains.

With their fair, silken moustachios and their glengarries and their velvet jackets, Ouida's guardsmen, pegs for luxury and romance, are vastly stimulating. I should like to have peered through the cloud of 'Turkish' that did always involve them, and have seen Lord Laulerois tossing aside a pile of millefleurs-scented notes and quaffing curaçoa, as he pondered the chances of Peach-Bloom for the Guards' Steeplechase, or the last mad caprice of Léla Liette! Too languid, as he lay there on his divan, to raise the vinaigrette to his nostrils, he was one who had served his country through more than one campaign on the boiling plains of the Sahara; he who, in the palace of a *nouveau riche*, had refused the bedchamber assigned to him, on the plea that he could not sleep under a false Fragonard, had often camped *à la belle étoile* in the waste places of Central Asia; thrice he had passed through the D.C. as calmly as he would swim the Hellespont or toss off a beaker of rosy Comet-Wine; with his girlish hands that Duchesses envied he had grappled lions in the jungle, and would think nothing of waiting for hours, heedless of frost and rain, to bring down some rocketer he had marked in a warm corner at Crichel or Longleat. Familiar with Cairene Bazaars as with the matchless deer-forests of Dunrobin, with the brown fens round Melton Mowbray as with the incomparable grace and brilliance of the Court of Hapsburg; *bienvenu* in the Vatican as in the Quirinal; deferred to by Dips and Décorés in all the salons of Europe, and before whom even Queens turned to coquettes and Kings to comrades; careless, caressed, *insouciant*; of all men the beloved or envied; inimitable alike in his grace of person and in the perfection of his taste; passing from the bow-windows of St. James's to the faded and fetid alleys of Stamboul, from the Quartier Bréda to the Newski Prospect, from the citron-groves of Cashmere, the gay fuchsia-gardens of Simla, to the hideous chaos of Illinois, a region scorched by the sirocco, swept by inextinguishable prairie-fires, sepultured in the white shrouds of remorseless blizzards, and—as though that were not enough—befouled with the fumes and crushed with the weight of a thousand loathsome cities, which are swift as the mushroom in their growth, far more deadly than the *fungus fatalis* of the Midi—it was here, passing from easy nonchalance as the foal passes from one pasture to another, with a flight swifter than the falcon's, luxurious in its appurtenance as a Shah's seraglio; it was here, in these whirling circles of intrigue and pleasure and romance, and in this span of an illimitable nomady, that flew the nights and days of Philip, nineteenth Marquis of Vaulerois, as the world knew him—'Fifi' of the First Life.

I am glad that in her later books Ouida has not deserted 'the First Life'. She is still the same Ouida, has lost none of her romance, none of her wit and poetry, her ebullitions of pity and indignation. The old 'naughtiness' and irresponsibility which were so strange a portent in the Medio-Victorian days, and kept her books away from the drawing-room table, seem to have almost disappeared; and, in complement of her love of luxury for its own sake, there is some social philosophy, diatribes against society for its vulgar usage of luxury. But, though she has become a mentor, she is still Ouida, still that unique, flamboyant lady, one of the miracles of modern literature. After all these years, she is still young and swift and strong, towering head and shoulders over all the other women (and all but one or two of the men) who are writing English novels. That the reviewers have tardily trumpeted her is amusing, but no cause for congratulation. I have watched their attitude rather closely. They have the idiot's cunning and seek to explain their behaviour by saying that Ouida has entirely changed. Save in the slight respect I have noted, Ouida has not changed at all. She is still Ouida. That is the high compliment I would pay her.

J. A. CHAPMAN
1875–

Wordsworth and Literary Criticism

The Russell Lecture, 1931

The chief difficulties of an attempt to understand and judge Milton [or any other great poet] are difficulties inherent in the nature, not only of all criticism in the large sense, but also of all reading. In this association with great spirits which we call reading we receive but what we give, and take away only what we are fit to carry.—SIR WALTER RALEIGH in *Milton*.

> Who reads
> Incessantly, and to his reading brings not
> A spirit and judgement equal or superior
> (And what he brings what needs he elsewhere seek?)
> Uncertain and unsettled still remains,
> Deep versed in books and shallow in himself, . . .
> MILTON.

We are all poets when we *read* a poem well.—CARLYLE.

(i) AT the beginning of the critique of *Othello*, in his *Characters of Shakespeare's Plays*, when Hazlitt is considering tragedy in the light of the old saying (Aristotle's) that it 'purifies the affections by terror and pity', he says presently:

> The habitual study of poetry and works of imagination is one chief part of a well-grounded education. A taste for liberal art is necessary to complete the character of a gentleman. Science alone is hard and mechanical. It exercises the understanding upon things out of ourselves, while it leaves the affections unemployed, or engrossed with our own immediate, narrow interests.

To a man sufficiently prepared by his life-experience and his studies, it would be enough just to make such a statement as that. Others, and among them especially those of you who are specializing in scientific studies, might reasonably demand some proof of the rightness and truth of the statement. If it be not the proper conception of this lecture that it should contain matter of proof of any kind, and not rather suggestion and stimulation, a word or two may be said about Hazlitt's statement. As that if, to those who have recognized the overwhelming practical importance to their race and country that scientific study should be pursued in it, it should sound harsh to call science 'hard and mechanical', it is to be understood that it is so only relatively, and in comparison with those studies that interest the affections and the emotional nature rather than the intellectual, or than the applying and inventing faculties, which again are of the intellectual part of a man.

It is further to be noted that Hazlitt says no more than that the study of poetry and works of imagination, which after all is a study, every one will admit, much better as a preparation for the study of religion (the greatest purifier of the affections) than is the study of such as chemistry and physics, is one chief part of a well-grounded education. He does not say that it is the whole, or even *the* chief part, but only *one* chief part. It is of interest, further, to reflect that men and women, fathers now or mothers, and by way of being long ago done with their education, spend as a fact most of the time that they give to study, it being study only 'of a kind', over works of imagination. So do not quarrel with Hazlitt's statement, and let us get on with the lecture.

It might happen that one was born to love reading more than anything else among the occupations that our life offers. There have been many such men. It might be that one of those men should be brought by the accident of his life into close contact with one of the very best readers of his own generation and race, and that out of that contact a long continuing friendship should spring. These two things, he has long felt, happened to the author of this lecture. After being born with what grew into a stronger disposition to read than to follow any other occupation, he was brought, at an age when men are still eager to learn, to a friendship with that Charles Russell, for the perpetuation of whose name and memory your lectureship was founded. It soon became plain to the younger man (that is, to myself) that Russell had the very rarest gifts as a reader. What follows may seem a somewhat strange way of showing how great were Russell's gifts in that respect; but it is only an illustration. Let it be considered then, and not immediately rejected. Hazlitt, when he has to show with what intellectual and other mental power Shakespeare has endowed Iago, as well as speaking of Iago's 'indefatigable industry and inexhaustible resources', of his head as 'acute and active', of his being 'an extreme instance of intellectual activity', albeit, every one knows, of the kind that applies itself to mischief, will say that Shakespeare

... knew that the love of power, which is another name for the love of mischief, is natural to man. He would know this as well or better than if it had been demonstrated to him by a logical diagram, merely from seeing children paddle in the dirt or kill flies for sport.

That at first takes one's breath away. What, the common mind will think, is the connexion between the love of power in certain men and the instinct that drives children to paddle in the dirt? Then the connexion is seen. After that you remark two things—that amazing intellectual power and intellectual resource *are* characteristic of Iago; secondly, that Hazlitt, to have seen into Shakespeare so clearly (witness the so much else that is proof of that, as the analysis of Shakespeare's delineation of a romantic heroine that comes at the very beginning of *Characters*), must have had a mind to read with almost as powerful as Iago's mind was for the purposes in which he employed it. Russell as a reader had a mind of the same great power. Except perhaps in one direction, he always knew the whole ambit and content of any piece of writing. It was not merely that hard meanings, as when a Hegel or another is dealing with recondite and really difficult thought, were no hindrances to Russell. They certainly were none: he read difficult writings with ease. Much better than that though—he felt the writer wonderfully behind the words, his character, the feeling in him, his passion, which is far the most important thing in reading of certain kinds; when the text is a work of literature or the imagination. He showed all this plainly, being a man who lived with openness. He was not only fond of reading a book by himself: he as much enjoyed reading a book aloud to a friend. He was equally fond of talking about books, whether the book he had read aloud to you, or some other that he had read by himself. He talked all round the subject, talking easily, being so interested. He was as ready to tell you what there is in Hazlitt's writing about a famous rackets player (what the point of it all is), or to show, piece by piece, the humour of Wordsworth's describing himself as running to chapel, ostrich-like, not to be late the morning after too many libations in Milton's old rooms, as to tell you what are all the points of (the lines are Donne's):

.... as the Heathen made them severall gods,
Of all God's Benefits, and all his Rods,
(For as the Wine, and Corne, and Onions are
Gods unto them, so Agues bee, and Warre)
And as by changing that whole precious Gold
To such small Copper coynes, they lost the old,
And lost their only God, who ever must
Be sought alone, and not in such a thrust: ...

or to discourse to you runningly on *Hamlet*, *Othello*, or *King Lear*. He would speak of many small things as well as the great. He would dwell, for instance, on the satisfaction, for the present-day mind, of Donne's use of 'thrust' there. Always he showed (this seems the point best worth making) that he was seeing the writer through the words, until one felt that that must have been the way of every good reader. He was even more concerned with the writers (but not in little-worth, gossiping books about them) than with their texts; always more concerned, too, with the nobility of writers than with their weakness. All that, of course, except when the book was such as Bagehot's *Lombard Street*, a book he would read for the information in it bearing on a matter that he was studying, and wished to understand deeply.

Russell was a hard student, and one all his life; but that in which he most excelled was the same that Hazlitt had excelled in—'the ability to enter into the spirit of works in literature', an ability of which Wordsworth (those are his words that I have just spoken) has said:

... it must depend upon a man's feelings, his imagination and his understanding, that is upon his recipient, upon his creative or active and upon his judging powers, and upon the accuracy and compass of his knowledge, in fine upon all that makes up the moral and intellectual man.

No more appropriate subject, then, could be chosen for a lecture in memory of Charles Russell, especially by one in all whose way of reading and in all whose discourse on books there is a great deal of repetition of what Russell taught him, than the ability to enter into the spirit of works in literature. What is the value of that ability, to say more than Hazlitt said in those words quoted at the beginning—that it belongs to a chief part of a man's education? The answer can well be given again in words of Wordsworth:

It is an awful truth, that there neither is, nor can be, any genuine enjoyment of poetry among nineteen out of twenty of those persons who live, or wish to live, in the broad light of the world—among those who either are, or are striving to make themselves, people of consideration in society. This is a truth, and an awful one, because to be incapable of a feeling of poetry, in my sense of the word, is to be without love of human nature and reverence for God.

That is an emphatic answer.

The subject of that ability, then, is of the very greatest and highest; for the cultivation and use of the ability lead to the greatest measure of the love of human nature and reverence for God that it is possible for a man to reach; except, of course, by the continued contemplation of the Divine and Infinite Mind itself.

(ii) One should not overlook the fact that when Wordsworth speaks of one's being incapable of a feeling of poetry, it is in *his* sense of the word poetry. A great deal might be said, and in a way ought to be said, about his sense of what poetry is, but there is not time. It must be enough to say, that to Wordsworth poetry is always less what the words mean than the 'certain colouring of imagination' (the words are his own) thrown over the things that the words speak of, it being to that colouring that the affections respond. So a living critic will speak of 'the misted opulence, the unsmutched bloom of ripeness', that lies on all the work of Keats that was done, when his genius was at its supreme. He will speak of the thought also, the 'unhesitating thought, rich, flexible, swift, and unerring', but what he feels most is something added to the thought; a ripeness, something to make men think of the mist of loveliness that Nature will spread over river and forest and mountain. Hazlitt, thinking of the same aspect of Shakespeare's poetry, uses the phrases 'a lustre', a 'romantic grace', 'radiant light'.

To read the poetry that only such men can write; that is, to be stirred in one's emotional nature, as a Shakespeare, a Wordsworth, or a Keats in his, by that 'colouring of imagination' or that 'misted opulence', is not easy. That is the point—that it is not easy. How little easy it is, how greatly difficult it is in fact, may be judged by this—that Wordsworth will speak of whole classes of men as unable to read his poetry, their imagination having slept, while, he goes on, 'the voice which is the voice of my poetry, without imagination, cannot be heard'.

It is probable that, for any effective use of it in a man's life, as also if the power is to be cultivable, some portion of the ability must have been born in the man. To cultivate it, even when some measure of it has been born in him, may be difficult; but no one need despair. So at least Wordsworth thought. He will quote Sir Joshua Reynolds as having declared that an accurate taste in poetry, and in all the other arts, is an *acquired* talent, which can only be produced by thought and a long continued intercourse with the best models of composition. The talent, Wordsworth thought himself, *can* be produced, or he would not be found quoting one who had said that it could be produced only by certain means. So no one need despair.

There is another saying of Wordsworth, this one a famous one, and there is a certain encouragement to be drawn from it. 'Never forget', he says in his letter to Lady Beaumont,

what, I believe, was observed to you by Coleridge, that every great and original writer, in proportion as he is great and original, must himself create the taste by which he is to be relished; he must teach the art by which he is to be seen; this, in a certain degree, even to all persons, however wise and pure may be their lives, and however unvitiated their taste.

The writers themselves create the taste for their poetry. They do this by operating on the men who read their poetry, those men, or some of them, operating on others in their turn. Any great poet will create a taste for his poetry in any one of you, if you will spend time enough in reading him. So there is the encouragement of knowing that; but let it not be overlooked that Wordsworth clearly thought that one's being wise and pure in one's life would aid the poet in teaching one the art by which he is to be seen.

The ability to read poetry finely has been chosen as the subject of this lecture, if, as you will know must be the case, only a small part of the topic can be covered in it. The object of anything said is to help you to read more as those fine readers have read, men like Hazlitt, or that Charles Russell who was once your Principal; of whom let it be said here, as a last word about him, that his ability to read finely came partly of that wisdom and purity in a life of which we were thinking but a moment ago.

The subject is the ability to read finely, but I have chosen to point rather to instances of indifferent or bad reading than to examples of fine and good, thinking that that would mean an argument less difficult for you to follow. Even so, it will not be an argument easy to follow. You must none of you be disappointed, if you leave this hall with a good deal of uncertainty as to what I have been trying to insist upon. The lecture will be printed: you will therefore have an opportunity, those who should think it worth while, to study the matter more at leisure. If Wordsworth, to say a word in conclusion of this part, is to be believed and trusted, no man's effort to learn to read poetry finely can be too great, or would or could be such as he would feel afterwards had been a waste of time. In ways that you none of you can be expected now to understand, because you are still too young, such even as the political future of your country is bound up with India's power to read poetry finely, and each of you has an opportunity to add to that power, to increase it. Therefore listen to me patiently.

(iii) This is the argument. Let men think of the poetic criticism of the past, other than the criticism of the poets themselves, or of the best of it, for much even of it is poor enough. Let them think of that professional criticism, as it may be called, in the light of the saying of Wordsworth that

if my conclusions are admitted, and carried as far as they must be carried if admitted at all, our judgements concerning the works of the greatest Poets both ancient and modern will be far different from what they are at present, both when we praise, and when we censure: and our moral feelings influencing and influenced by these judgements will, I believe, be corrected and purified.

Or let men think of the professional criticism of the past in the light of this other saying of Wordsworth, when he is addressing Christopher North:

You have given me praise for having reflected faithfully in my Poems the feelings of human nature. I would fain hope that I have done so. But a great Poet ought to do more than this; he ought, to a certain degree, to rectify men's feelings, to give them new compositions of feeling, to render their feelings more sane, pure, and permanent, in short, more consonant to nature, that is, to eternal nature, and the great moving spirit of things.

Let men begin with such thoughts as those, especially with the thought of what Wordsworth so returns to—his conviction that the moral feelings influence and are influenced by men's judgements of poetry; of poetry as rendering men's feelings more sane, pure, permanent, and consonant to eternal nature. Beginning with such thoughts, let men follow all the indications there are in Shakespeare's plays, Milton's,

Wordsworth's, Keats's, and Shelley's poems, in all their critical writings, in their Letters (they will follow instead the indications in the great writings of their own literature, if they are not Englishmen), of what the great poets have thought of us and our reading and our judgements. Let men then think of the main positions of Criticism at this day (to personify criticism), and of the practice of the leading contemporary critics, those excepted who should be excepted. They will then surely be left saying that most non-poet criticism, to use a phrase of Shakespeare, is 'choughs' language, gabble enough, and good enough', or, with Parolles:

that the muster-file, rotten and sound, amounts not to fifteen thousand poll; half of which dare not shake the snow from off their cassocks, lest they shake themselves to pieces.

Very little English poetic criticism, unless it has come from a Dryden, Wordsworth, Coleridge, Keats, Shelley, Arnold, or another poet, will bear handling; for, if it is touched, it falls to pieces like the paper of those books that have been too long in the libraries in India, and have become as brittle or more brittle than glass.

While that is the fact about most non-poets' criticism—that, if handled, it falls to pieces—the more one examines the criticism of, say, Wordsworth, the clearer it grows on one that he has not really said one single word that is not worth thinking over, and valuable. He *knew* about poetry. If he had not Coleridge's readiness of mind, and power of intellectual display, he knew much more about poetry in the deepest way of knowing. It may take him five or six different trials, in as many separate pieces of writing, to get out all his say about poetic diction, and poetry generally; but the essential points are all made, or at least shadowed forth; those that are not made. The core of his criticism is as inspired as his greatest poetry. It is, in the main, to the same subconscious mind that the world owes both. There is the same utter sincerity, earnestness, passion, and truth in both. There is, for example, no sincerer or truer word in any poem of his than the word, in the second of the three articles on epitaphs, with which Wordsworth sums up what he saw as proper to be said about the epitaph that Lord Lyttleton wrote for his wife, and what is said there has a bearing on all poetry, and so admits of quotation here:

So that a great portion of original genius was necessary to embolden a man to write faithfully to Nature upon any affecting subject, if it belonged to a class of composition in which Pope had furnished examples—

the man had to have, to add a word of one's own, as great a portion of original genius as was found in, say, Blake.

No man has ever written in English anything excelling the courage about, and the clearness of insight into, the corruption of poetry—those two combined—shown in another passage that you must let me quote from Wordsworth. It occurs in the same essay on epitaphs, and soon follows those words that I have just quoted:

... to an unpractised Reader the productions of every age will present obstacles in various degrees hard to surmount—

I may break off to point out that Wordsworth is there thinking of poor or even bad reading; that he set the example. He continues:

a deformity of style not the worst in itself but of that kind with which he is at least familiar will on the one hand be most likely to render him insensible to a pith and power which may be within, and on the other hand he will be the least able to see through that sort of falsehood which is most prevalent in the works of his own time.

'To see through that sort of falsehood', let it here be said, is the last and most difficult of the tasks, not only of the unpractised reader, but of the professional critic also. Wordsworth speaks there of the unpractised reader. It is not only he, ever. Throughout his critical writings Wordsworth is most tender of the feelings of the critics of his day—not Hazlitt, Coleridge, Lamb, be it understood—but those whom his arguments were likely to offend. It leaves his readers with a word to add at times to what he has said.

Wordsworth is one for all to learn from, the professional critic, indeed, more than one just a reader. He will show remarkable differences in his practice from that of the professional or journeyman critic. Thus when stating, in the *Preface to Poems* of 1815, what powers are 'requisite for the production of poetry', he will declare them to be (1) Observation and Description, (2) Sensibility, (3) Reflection, (4) Imagination and Fancy, (5) Invention, (6) Judgement. That is a pretty comprehensive catalogue, which makes it all the more to be admired that he should have kept it for a mere footnote in which to say:

> As sensibility to harmony of numbers, and the power of producing it, are invariably attendants upon the faculties above specified, nothing has been said upon these requisites.

The 'faculties above specified' are, of course, Observation and Description, Sensibility, &c.

A professional or journeyman critic might claim to have been of the same opinion as long as Wordsworth in 1815—the opinion, that is, that what need not be dwelt on is the requisite in a poet of the power of producing harmony of numbers, that power that is invariably attendant upon true poetic powers. If you should inquire into his practice at all closely, however, you will almost certainly find that he has no 'practical faith' (an expression of Wordsworth's) in his opinion. He cannot speak long upon any poet's work without speaking of his power of producing harmony of numbers, and other kindred matter; poetry's bones; poetic form. One comes upon so much like this, and the practical following up of the opinion expressed:

> The discussion of poetic form is apt to be tedious, but that cannot be helped. If poetry be a fit subject for Academic lectures, surely form must always be the main part of the business. There is nothing more important for the understanding of poetry than a study of form, . . .

where the last words show that the lecturer did not wish to draw any distinction (if he had, would it anyway have made much difference to his sense?) between academic lectures on poetry and those of other kinds. This might be thought much truer to say than what that lecturer did say—that while there can be nothing more important for the understanding of poetic form than the study of that form, in the deepest sense there is nothing to be learnt of poetry itself from that study.

To continue this part—what do the poets do? They say themselves that they *teach* us; but not of form, but of wisdom, and they do that by appealing to men's affections. When Keats thinks of the Bards of Passion and of Mirth who have gone before, he says:

> . . . then
> On the earth ye live again;
> And the souls ye left behind you
> Teach us, here, the way to find you—

in heaven, that is, where men do not think of poetic form but of wisdom. He goes on:

> Here, your earth-born souls still speak
> To mortals, of their little week;
> Of their sorrows and delights;
> Of their passions and their spites;
> Of their glory and their shame;
> What doth strengthen and what maim:—
> Thus ye teach us, every day,
> Wisdom, . . .

The true business of the lecturer on poetry, be his lectures academic or not, is with the wisdom of poetry.

If Keats *should* touch on form, it will be incidentally; when he is thinking of the thought and imagination of poetry. Thus, when he has copied *Bards of Passion and of Mirth* and *Ever let the Fancy roam* in a letter, he may go on with:

> These are specimens of a sort of rondeau which I think I shall become partial to—because you have one idea amplified with greater ease and more delight and freedom than in the sonnet,

where his main thought is of the ease, delight, and freedom of the amplifying of ideas. In another part you will have him thinking of poetry as 'a Spear bright enough to throw a light to posterity', which may fitly be compared with the main ideas of *Bards of Passion and of Mirth*.

The fact would appear to be that, unless the critic is also himself a poet, and has learnt in writing his own poetry what, one may venture to say, only the writing of poetry can reveal to a man, he never knows about it deeply. He may have the most enthusiastic love of poetry, and be constrained to be speaking about it. He may very well be able 'to study poems, and prove that he has entered into the spirit of them' (another of Wordsworth's phrases) by declaring his passionate love of them; but he cannot, if he knew it, go beyond that any more than men generally; and, except in a world of easy toleration, which ours is, he would seldom be allowed even to try.

In a passage that there will be a further use for Hazlitt says: 'We do not say that a man to be a critic must necessarily be a poet.' Some men's poetry, to put it so, comes as prose; the poetry of even poets sometimes comes so; so that you may have a man saying such a thing as this of Keats: 'The Poetry which came . . . on this memorable morning was Prose.' It seems often hard to believe, in face of the evidence, that a man can be a critic of any importance unless at times there can come from him at least the poetry that comes as prose. There must be that, it seems, for any depth of knowledge.

Let this be an illustration, where illustrating is not easy. Many a man has loved the sight of those delicate, dark-green reeds that grow by the edges of stretches of shallow water. A man might be haunted all his life long by a sense of the unexpressed poetry in reeds, especially as seen in the lights of evening. Keats apparently was. All the love in the world, however, nor it trebled or made a hundredfold, would not enable him to deliver lectures on the poetry of reeds. For him to be able to do that, he would have to be changed into a reed, as in some Greek fable, and live out the life of a reed, if not even that of a reed-poet, and then be changed back into a human poet.

It would be no lecture on the poetry of reeds, if the man filled out his blank spaces with the botany of reeds, for that is science and not poetry. That is surely, however, what professional critics do—they fill out the blank spaces of their lectures on poetry with the science of it It was their love of poetry made them critics, but not being poets themselves, of any sufficient kind, they do not see deeply enough into poetry. When they speak, they must fill out their spaces with the technique of poetry, or some other part of its science.

Let there be this other illustration. A man might say with truth that he has always loved music fully as much as any professional critic has ever loved poetry; but that, beyond the limits of parlour conversation, he cannot talk of the greatness of Mozart, Bach, or Beethoven, because he does not know well enough in what it consists, or on what it rests. A man is kept from speaking of music—one who has really nothing valuable to say about it—by the obvious difficulty of thinking of a word to say. Poetry looks easy to talk about: that is what misleads folk. It is really almost as difficult to talk about —beyond the limits of conversation—as ever music is; but it looks easy to talk about, or parts do. The critics talk of those parts; but, if I may now repeat a little what has already been said, without its perhaps making a very strong impression on any of you, one notices that, unless it is a Dryden speaking out of his own mind about Shakespeare or Chaucer, not this time merely translating or paraphrasing a foreign author, or Milton speaking, or Wordsworth, or another inspired man, the critic's book is all about those parts of poetry, as the versification, that harmony of numbers, the structure of a poem or a play in verse, about which the Drydens, &c., are either altogether silent, or speak only in footnotes.

Thence it follows (because of the impression made by all these critics' speaking) that poetry, in the general opinion and estimation of men, is not infinite, as Shelley has declared it to be. Listen for a few moments to him: in the beginning of the words I am to quote he is speaking of Dante:

His very words are instinct with spirit; each is as a spark, a burning atom of inextinguishable thought; and many yet lie covered in the ashes of their birth, and pregnant with a lightning which has yet found no conductor.

I would break off in the middle of the quotation to say that there is a good example of poetry that came to a man as prose; to say also that Shelley has all that written over again as verse (even as more poetic poetry, but that was no matter of course, but only as it happened) in the last stanza of the *Ode to the West Wind*. Shelley goes on, speaking of poetry as being infinite, with:

All high poetry is infinite; it is as the first acorn, which contained all oaks potentially. Veil after veil may be withdrawn, and the inmost naked beauty of the meaning never exposed. A great poem is a fountain for ever overflowing with the waters of wisdom and delight; and after one person and one age has exhausted its divine effluence which their peculiar relations enable them to share, another and yet another succeeds, and new relations are ever developed, the source of an unforeseen and an unconceived delight.

If I go on to say what I do, and if there appear to be a kind of licence in it, it is that you may be encouraged not to be overawed, as the young are only too likely to be, by the long roll of names of professional critics. You are all the more likely to be overawed by the names, in that the authorities of your university, following the example of many other universities—so at least

I understand—prescribe the critics' books for the study of some of you.

This is what I was intending to say. There is this part of a scene in *Romeo and Juliet*, where Peter, after punning on 're' and 'fa', and 'Do you note me?' when he is answered in kind, presently says:

> Answer me like men:
> 'When griping grief the heart doth wound,
>   And doleful dumps the mind oppress,
>   Then music with her silver sound'—
> why 'silver sound'? why 'music with her silver sound'?
> —What say you, Simon Catling?

That is 'choughs' language, gabble enough'; but does not professional criticism go about saying of poetry, 'Why "silver sound"?' 'Why "music with her silver sound"?' then answering to the best of its ability, when there really is no answer? There are things that a man can know *enough*, and those are what a Wordsworth will write of. There are others, as poetic form, with the discoursing about which I have already dealt. There are still other possible matters of discourse, as 'Why "silver sound"?' but such are questions that no one really can find answers to, and so no Wordsworth will speak of them. They are just, however, what professional or academic criticism will also be talking of. Then its results or half-discoveries are fanciful, fantastical, or flimsy.

(iv) The more one reads professional criticism, the farther one is apt to be led from any thought of that 'ability to enter into the spirit of works in literature', on which Wordsworth has dwelt.

I shall have led you away from that thought myself. Let me lead you back to it. What Wordsworth thought the power to enter into the spirit of poetry depended on is shown in a passage that, though I have already quoted it once, I wish to bring in here; and let it this time be this longer passage:

If a man attaches much interest to the faculty of taste as it exists in himself, and employs much time in those studies of which this faculty ... is reckoned the arbiter, certain it is his moral notions and dispositions must either be purified and strengthened or corrupted and impaired. How can it be otherwise, when his ability to enter into the spirit of works in literature must depend upon his feelings, his imagination and his understanding, that is upon his recipient, upon his creative or active and upon his judging powers, and upon the accuracy and compass of his knowledge, in fine upon all that makes up the moral and intellectual man.

The trouble is that a man's feelings, imagination, and understanding; his recipient, creative, active, and judging powers, may all have had imposed upon them such a limiting fetter as the prepossession that the favourite style of his age is the very best one. As for the favourite style of his or any day, Wordsworth will say:

... the favourite style of different ages is so different and wanders so far from propriety, that if it were not that first-rate writers in all nations and tongues are governed by common principles, we might suppose that truth and nature were things not to be looked for in books.

Man, then, Wordsworth thought, is little

better than a slave—from being as easily played on as a child, a child being one easily played on and deceived from having had no experience outside its own little world, and therefore knowing nothing. Do men differ from children so much? What do we know of the unrealized world of great literature until the poets themselves, in that operation on our minds that is completed only after long reading, or is not even then completed (more would be done, if we did not too soon give the reading up), have opened that world to us? We know little more, in what was plainly Wordsworth's view, than any body of self-deceivers and deceived are likely to know. Wordsworth did not express the matter with the convincingness that is only now beginning to be possible; that is beginning now to be possible from the greater stir and activity of present days in psychological studies.

To go back for a moment before going on, and to let the testimony of Keats be added to that word of the poets opening their world to us. He will say, speaking of Wordsworth:

In regard to his genius alone—we find what he says true as far as we have experienced, and we can judge no further but by larger experience—for axioms in philosophy are not axioms until they are proved upon our pulses. We read fine things, but never feel them to the full until we have gone the same steps as the Author.

Wordsworth, as a critic relying on his intuition and understanding; that is to say, what men call his inspiration, when they are talking of his finest poetry, had arrived at the clear view that, first, the best writers in all tongues are governed by the same principles; secondly, that all the other writers are governed, not at all by principle, but by varying and passing fashions. *Their* works are not merely inferior to the best, but are not of the same kind as the best. All this is accounted for and explained, if it be true that the best writings come from the activity of the subconscious mind, all the others being due to, and springing from, the general imitativeness of man, and so being a birth of the conscious mind, the only mind that ever imitates. Wordsworth's position was one that could only be reached *then* by intuition or inspiration, but that now could perhaps be reached by an experimental psychologist. At least there might now be an appeal to the psychologist. We could summon him to witness whether the intuitions of such as Wordsworth, Shelley, and other acknowledged geniuses, writing about poetry out of their fullest minds, are not borne out in the main by his laboratory studies.

Suppose that those intuitions *are* borne out; that it is seen that there is no rightness in ranking works of literature as first-rate, second-rate, third-rate, &c., the proper division being into inspired and imitated, a mass of confusing weight would be lifted from men's shoulders. What stands out from all Wordsworth's writing, not about poets and their poetry but about men generally as readers of poetry, but his conviction of there being an imperative element in their knowing the best, the only real thing, from all the rest? Except for that conviction, he would never have written a line except about poets, and its being necessary and right that they should write their own poetry, and not be dictated to by a public enslaved by fashions. He would never have written a word about men as readers; he who wrote so many. So many, at least, to come from a man so little disposed to write prose; so little disposed to write anything that could not be written in his head, as he tramped out-of-doors.

If that mass was cleared away, it would be then, to give an illustration, as with one who should have been trying to keep all the flowers in a meadow of June clear and distinct in his visual memory, but who should now be assured that only the blue flowers need be attended to, and remembered. What before was impossible, from the great mass and confusing variety, is now possible. The man can hold the flowers clearly and distinctly in the visual memory. If only, too, he can do that long enough, there is the possibility of his learning. That is only one's illustration: it is not to be looked at too closely for a sense in itself.

(v) Have we not now been led close to the question: How much help is it right to look for from the critics of the past in one's effort to cultivate one's natural ability to enter into the spirit of works in literature, it being agreed that the very best way of all is to read poetry habitually, so letting the poets operate on our minds as teachers? Part of the answer to the question is that no help is really to be looked for from those critics of the past, whether poet-critics or professional, who were poor or bad readers. If, for instance, Hazlitt was right, in a passage, a line of which has already been quoted, in saying that Dr. Johnson—

was neither a poet nor a judge of poetry. He might in one sense be a judge of poetry as it falls within the limits and rules of prose, but not as it is poetry . . . We do not say that a man to be a critic must necessarily be a poet: but to be a good critic he ought not to be a bad poet. Such poetry as a man deliberately writes, such, and such only will he like—

if Hazlitt was right in saying that, then no help is to be looked for from the study of Dr. Johnson's poetic criticism; or to the extent to which what Hazlitt says is true, to that extent Dr. Johnson's criticism is ruled out. It may be read for other interest; but you cannot learn to know better from it what poetry is; neither from it, nor from all the criticism like it.

That is part of the answer. So much of the rest of the answer as it seems necessary to give now, is that the student, not awed by any name, but prepared to find (for that he *will* find it so a man may be absolutely convinced) that the greater mass of criticism of the past is really worthless for men's higher purposes, must feel out for the proofs that the critic whose work he is studying, did or did not use his faculties in the order, to put it so (I can think myself of no better way of putting it), in which Wordsworth places them, and not in the reverse order. He places them in this order—feelings, imagination, understanding—and not in the reverse of that. Again his order is—recipient, creative or active, judging powers—not judging, creative or active, recipient powers.

To use the judging power first, and not first to feel and be stirred in one's imagination, emotional nature, and affections, is in Hazlitt's phrase, to let 'one's general powers of reasoning overlay one's critical susceptibility'. That is fatal. A man who has let that happen to him will see nothing in poetry that really matters. He will merely, to express the matter after Hazlitt, see the prose of it. And there is this too, if it is not better to say, *for* there is this too—that to use the judging power first is almost always to end in using it and no other power, until the other powers die out of a man one by one. Human powers that are not used do die. From first to last what is to be relied on, and if possible increased, is not the judging power (unless, indeed, it is controlled by the supremer powers), but what you will find certain poet-critics of the past thinking of as a man's measure of 'organic sensibility'. If, as men have heard Wordsworth declare, without an unusual measure of organic sensibility true poetry cannot be composed, so without some really active measure of it poetry cannot be read; consequently the greater the measure, or the pulse of its activity, the finer the reading.

A man's organic sensibility, then, is what he must rely on mainly, and what he must rely on is what he should strive in all ways to cultivate. Not until that sensibility has been cultivated to the very utmost possible, is the man as fully equipped as he ever could be for that 'habitual study of poetry and works of imagination' that Hazlitt was quoted at the beginning as declaring 'one chief part of a well-grounded education'.

(vi) To the question—How a fine ability to enter into the spirit of poetry and works of the imagination is to be ranked, when compared with the other abilities that men spend time in acquiring?—if the answer may once more be given in words of Wordsworth, one might choose some words that occur in his 'Letter' to 'The Friend', where he is speaking of THE FRIEND himself. There he says:

> He speaks now of the general superiority of thought to action;—as preceding and governing all action that moves to salutary purposes; and, secondly, as leading to elevation, the absolute possession of the individual mind, and to a consistency or harmony of the being within itself, which no outward agency can reach to disturb or to impair;—and lastly as producing works of pure science; or of the combined faculties of imagination, feeling, and reason;—works which, both from their independence in their origin upon accident, their nature, their duration, and the wide spread of their influence, are entitled rightly to take place of the noblest and most beneficent deeds of heroes, statesmen, legislators, or warriors.

The poets themselves will do more for you than you will ever do for yourselves, if you will submit your minds to them. There is also your own part, and remember that it is not an easy one. The most perfect fruit, in human affairs, comes of the purest discipline. The purest discipline has been described in many words. Many of those words are undoubtedly better than some words that I will immediately quote. Many of those words are better in themselves; but those that I am to quote are more appropriate to end a lecture in English on poetry and literary criticism. It is Mr. Middleton Murry speaking of Keats. He says:

> To yield to Life: this was, for Keats, the secret of Poetry and of the human living. To receive, to lie open, to grow; yet also to strive, to seek, to endure: to strive to the uttermost, and when the organism can no more, to sink back through numbness, and pain, and despair, into the warm darkness of Nature's womb, thence to emerge re-born.

Of poetry itself, to the study of which every word said here is intended as an aid, and in that has all the value that it could have, let this now be said: that Keats, thinking of the England before Chaucer, the England that was without English poetry, and comparing it with the England that he knew himself, addressed the Muse of England in *Endymion* in these words:

> O, thou hast won
> A full accomplishment—the thing is done,
> Which undone, these our latter days had risen
> On barren Souls.

Of all the earthly possessions of any race its poetry is the greatest possession. The poetry of this earth is the best of it.

H. W. GARROD
1878–

The Profession of Poetry[1]

The Profession of Poetry, 1929

And therefore here I stand forth, only to make good the place we have thus taken up, and to defend the sacred monuments erected therein, which contain the honour of the dead, the fame of the living, the glory of peace, and the best power of our speech; and wherein so many honourable spirits have sacrificed to memory their dearest passions, shewing by what divine influence they have been moved, and under what stars they lived.—SAMUEL DANIEL: *A Defence of Rhyme.*

IN a history of more than two hundred years, it has happened, I think, only twice before—and in living memory once only—that the Chair of Poetry should become vacant by death; and accordingly, though there are still living and working among us scholars whose names have added lustre to this Professorship, I feel obliged, breaking, I fancy, with precedent, to say a few words of my immediate predecessor. Few words they shall, and should, be. Ker was himself a man who hated the waste of words, and he would better have liked that we should remember him here with kindness than speak a panegyric upon virtues which his shyness made always some study to conceal. Moreover, to many of those here, he was better known than it was my fortune

[1] An Inaugural Lecture, delivered before the University of Oxford, 13 February 1924.

to know him—it is not for *me* to cry the last hail and farewell. And yet again, and above all, there was that in the manner of his death which would make it poor in us to lament and knock the breast. Let no man deceive us; nor our own hearts. It is a good thing, to die in the profession of poetry. *Felix ille quem in hisce litteris meditantem mors occupat.* It is a good thing, to die amid the great spaces of sky and mountain, the everlasting consolation of poets. And once more, it is a good thing, to die young at seventy. I think, indeed, that in saying *that*, I have said already all of Ker that there needs. He was a man full of poetry; and it is to the poetry in them that men and nations for ever owe the renewal of their youth.

> Trust to good verses, then;
>   They onely will aspire,
> When pyramids, as men,
>   Are lost i' th' funerall fire.
>
> And when all bodies meet
>   In Lethe to be drown'd,
> Then only numbers sweet
>   With endless life are crown'd.

This is a very old nation; and there are many causes which operate at the present time to oppress it with the sense of age. The years just gone have been fraught with loss beyond precedent in history; and the years which wait are shadowed with difficulties to expedite which there will need, not genius only and courage, but, if I may borrow a term from an allied profession, grace. Perhaps to some I shall seem to be speaking academically; and yet I feel myself to be touching deep realities, when I say that I find, in this disquiet of the times, no circumstance of happier augury than the fact that more than at any other season, as I think, in our history, poetry, and the study of poetry engage interest and inform action.[1] The causes of this I will not venture here to explore. Let me only say, in parenthesis, that I am not much inclined to credit the facile generalizations of those who believe that literature is either made, or made better, by the operation of great wars. Indeed, if we were either able to read poetry, or willing to read history, more truthfully than our habit is, we should find some reason, as I fancy, for thinking that the God of Battles is three parts of him a Philistine. For myself, at least, I mistrust in literary history that temper which awaits, from the issues of battle, with equal complacency economic distress and spiritual affluence, worse homes and better poetry. Such conjunctions are, when they occur, at least more mysterious than our easy comment upon them. That there is at the present time more poetry written and read, and more experimentation in poetry, than there has ever been at any other time—that is, I believe, true, and important; but just because it is both, it behoves us to be circumspect in our comment. That all this poetry, or most of it, is good, or this experimentation

[1] In saying that they 'inform action' I am thinking especially of their share in the formulation of the new and large demands for political and moral liberty which, whatever justice they have, are an important activity of the times.

as new as it seems, I should not like to affirm. To one of his friends Lamb ascribed the amiable quality of being unable to believe 'that there could be anything bad in poetry'; his friend, indeed (it was George Dyer), had carried this temper so far as to greet with joy the *Epigoniad* of Wilkie on the ground that 'there must be some good things in a poem of 8,000 lines'. That is not a proper temper, you will, I hope, agree, in a Professor of Poetry; yet it is certainly a better temper than a bad temper— by which I mean a criticism ungenerous and inexpectant. One quality the new poetry has without which great poetry cannot be: it has immense faith in itself; and not to believe that from this high confidence, infused through so wide a range of youth, there must necessarily ensue great consequences for the national life and art is to be either very old or seriously deficient in poetry. The directions taken by a large part of this poetry are interesting in themselves and significant beyond themselves. Of that part of it which is either most interesting, or interesting to the greater number of students of poetry, some of the characters are written plain. It is for the most part lyrical, and its verse vindicates a freedom believed to be new. Its language affects an extreme plainness; and its content is informed by the dogma that whatever is is good enough for poetry. Its purposes are whatever may be its results; or at any rate its final cause does not stand in ethical theory. Its conception of the character of the poet is different, perhaps, from any that has hitherto had wide currency. I know not how better to hit this difference than if I say that the race of long-haired poets is dead. The bardic has gone the way of less noble affectations; and our makers of music and dreamers of dreams seem almost intolerably trim and brisk. That with all these characters of the new poetry I feel equal sympathy, I will not pretend. I have that innocent trust in 'good verses' which makes me like them better when they scan; and I am too scrupulous to call either new or free types of verse which, in truth, repeat some of the oldest metrical pedantries known to me. I confess, again, to a sneaking liking for what great poets, I know, have decried, 'poetic diction'. I am tempted, indeed, to borrow the comment of a poet who, though he employed a diction notably vicious, was an excellent critic of all poetry except his own. 'As to prosaicalness in general,' says Leigh Hunt, 'it is sometimes indulged in by young writers on the plea of its being natural; but this is a mere confusion of triviality with propriety; and is sometimes the result of indolence.' Upon the subject of the purposes of the new poetry I could say much, but nothing in a spirit not diffident and perplexed. You will divine already that I have been bred in a very stick-in-the-mud poetics; and I find myself still stuck in two of its dogmas: the one, that among the purposes of poetry, is pleasure; and the other, that there is very little, in literature or life, that affords permanent pleasure which has not some hold in ethics. The most famous of my predecessors in this Chair was thought in nothing so much to have abused its authority as when he hazarded the dictum that 'poetry is a criticism of life'; nor much to have mended matters when he added that it is a criticism 'mainly upon the side of morality'. I may be forgiven perhaps, if, in this 'home of impossible loyalties', I am so far loyal to a critic who caught my youth, and a poet whose poetry I grow old in admiring, as to pay to this half-forgotten dictum the proper homage of a truism—which is, not to argue it. It was a part of Matthew Arnold's nature that he rather enjoyed being misunderstood. What, indeed, should it profit a man to have founded a society for the promotion of Sweetness and Light—of which he was the only member—if he were readily intelligible to the dark and sour souls who constitute the great body of his countrymen? I will not to that degree vex his ghost as to try here to make him understood; but I will content myself with observing that he was certainly not commending didactic poetry, and that he was careful to lay it down that the term 'morality' was as wide as life. What is the matter with didactic poetry, of course, is not that it is didactic, but that it is not—there is nothing to be learned from it. All other poetry is didactic; just as life and our friends are, though in a fashion nobler, less obtrusive, more ingenious.

I hope that I shall not, to youth aspirant of immortal garlands, seem to hold out injurious deterrents, if I suggest that, of the great mass of students and practitioners of poetry—never before so numerous—not all, or not enough, have figured to themselves how difficult the business of poetry has become. I am not sure, indeed, that the poetry of to-day sufficiently asks itself what it would be at. Mainly lyrical, it is content to depict moods; and that these are important moods, moods that matter, or that they are the moods of men who matter, of this we are given often, I think, only imperfect assurance. Poetry seems ill-paid, indeed, but easy. Yet never, I fancy, was it harder. Easy, no doubt, it was, once upon a time. Once upon a time, the world was fresh, to speak was to be a poet, to name objects an inspiration; and metaphor dropped from the inventive mouths of men like some natural exudation of the vivified senses. Life was a rhythm, a magical flowing, and every motion was untaught metre. Poetry was not a criticism of life, but life itself. That youth of man and nature has gone; and only by some critical labour of poetry can we either recapture it or even believe in it. The world and its life grows every day harder to express: no day but, as our newspapers record it for us, is big with omens of defeat for poetry. So intractable has our material become that already one part of our poetry is dead altogether, and almost without our knowing it; that part, I mean, which consists in the union of speech and music, and which we call song. Once the poet greeted easily with song all seen things. But to-day a song wants two men's work, and one of them does it badly. Where among the songs of the last two centuries, if you except perhaps portions of Burns and Blake, will you find that vital union of music and words which you feel in the songs of Shakespeare? For Shakespeare, his songs still sang themselves as he made them.

> What is love? 'Tis not hereafter;
> Present mirth hath present laughter;
>   What's to come is still unsure:
> In delay there lies no plenty;
> Then, come kiss me, sweet and twenty,
>   Youth's a stuff will not endure.

There are words made, not for, but with, music; and the art is dead, and it is a chance if anything like it will again revisit literature. The body of our joy has sensibly shrunken. From the old Greek, and the old human, unity of words, music, and dance, we have dropped to mere verse; and already we are asking whether it need scan, and yet again, whether poetry need be in verse at all. About the answer, I have no doubts. It need not; perhaps one day it will not. But the soul of man will have lost, in that day, something of its lilt. Of the fortunes of poetic speech, of the actual words which poets employ, the account is more difficult. Words wear out faster than numbers, than tunes; quicker cease to be vital, and pass into convention. Hence periodic revolutions in diction; when some great and original poet takes us back to simpler elements, to a more human speech; and perhaps with the *naïveté* of his class tells us that the speech of poetry and of prose is one and the same thing. Between the language of prose and the language of poetry there is, in fact, no difference at all—save a difference of poetry; and that is why, so long as there is poetry, there will be poetic diction.

None the less poetry works here, still and always, overshadowed by its deadliest peril, the peril of custom. Sick and fevered it respires after freshness, and reaches arms towards eloquence, but

> Custom lies upon it with a weight
> Heavy as frost and deep almost as life.

These pains of poetry which its forms reflect are part of a deeper embarrassment. That poetry is a particular manner of expressing life, or (what is the same) moods of living persons, will probably be conceded by any criticism not entirely captious. The expression which it achieves is more or less adequate according as it can effect adjustments between its means and its material. Its trouble proceeds in part from the mere multiplicity of life, its tangle of connexions. Each day there happen to all of us, and to the world, things that the soul does not need, things that will not fall into their places, that jar a postulated rhythm of the spirit; until first the world refuses to be sung, presently it can be *versed*, if at all, only with difficulty, insensibly driving us down to forms of speech and rhythm not much above prose. 'I look in vain', said Emerson, 'for the poet. . . . We do not with sufficient plainness, or sufficient profundity, address ourselves to life, nor dare chant our own times or social circumstance'; and he goes on to commend, as unexplored themes of poetry, log-rolling, political cabals, negroes, Indians, repudiations, the wrath of rogues, and the pusillanimity of honest men, trading and planting, Texas and Oregon. That poetry should deal with life courageously, God forbid that I should question. But there are many kinds of courage; and these monstrous and bizarre elements of our developing civilization go not out, I fancy—they do not come into poetry—otherwise than by some high courage of prayer and fasting. It is no good being free and easy with them. The glory of poetry is in proportion to the greatness of its strife; and that these elements do not, or may not, multiply themselves, and their combinations, swifter than poetry—which has already abandoned to them song, and some wealth of speech and rhythm—swifter than poetry can adjust itself; that they are not, in fact, gaining on poetry; this is less certain, perhaps, than we suppose. And yet, of poetry, when it endeavours to express life, these are probably not the most formidable trouble. As the world becomes older, and the springs of human consciousness less elastic, the desolating trouble of poetry is, not the things that jar, but the things that do not. Each day, I said, there happen to all of us, and to the world, things that the soul does not need. But equally each day, and in part as a consequence, nothing at all happens; there happens only that cyclic relapse into ordinariness which is so much a part of our lives that, save for the critical admonitions of poetry, we die in living. 'Custom lies upon us with a weight' which only poetry—only that frail efficiency—can lift.

This homily has a purpose humble and practical; which is no more than to suggest that the problem of poetizing the complexity of our material civilization is less easy than a good deal of modern practice might seem to imply. I am even disposed to believe that poetry might be made better by an increased attention to the theory of it. That is only academic innocence; or it may pass as such—I am not sure that, in what follows, I shall not carry my academicism into guilty and sinister connexions. I have spoken of poetry as expressing life, and of some poetry as doing so in a fashion which I think a degree too free and easy; but if you ask me to hint to you a better fashion, I can offer nothing that will not expose the beggarly character of my critical elements. For I own to a long pupilage to that rather crabbed father of all poetical criticism, Aristotle.[1]

Aristotle is credited, as you know, with the dictum that poetry is an imitation of life. All that he wrote upon poetry was, in fact, directed to the refutation of this dictum. Plato had called poetry an imitation, or copy, of life, or things; of sensible things, themselves only copies of meanings; condemning the poet as three times removed from meaning, a creature not only unphilosophic, but anti-philosophic, whom he exiles from his perfect state. Aristotle, more content with a world of imperfect men and half results, brings back the exile, at least partially vindicated. The poet, he says, does not copy life. It is the historian who copies life; the business of the poet is more philosophical, and better worth

[1] I should like the paragraphs that follow to be read in connexion with the lecture *Poets and Philosophers*, where what is here said is amplified, and the emphasis of it qualified.

while. Literature, or at any rate poetry, is not worth while if it merely repeats the fault of a large part of life—if it throws together unrelated happenings. The end of poetry is, truly enough, to present life; but to present it in such a manner as to eliminate what is unessential, unrelated, inorganic; to present it as a whole of which all the parts are seen to be co-operative. It does what life does not—what, because we cannot do it for our lives, makes them so hard: it eliminates the unessential. It hunts the true connexions of things; and in so far as it finds them, its picture of things is a criticism of life.

A great deal of this—which is not difficult—is expressed by Aristotle in language more technical than need be. It was not easy for him to persuade himself that the criticism of art is itself an art; and hunting through art connexions other than those of life, he assumes, more lightly than we feel to be proper, that these connexions are logical. In occasional parentheses of that kind by which nature entraps great minds into more than they mean, he supplies corrections of himself which it is venial in us, I think, to seize over-greedily; as when he puts first among the gifts of the born poet an eye for metaphor; or hazards—rather surprisingly—the doctrine that the poet is a maniacal creature. The gift of metaphor is, as he says, the power to see resemblances which escape the observation of common men, to seize connexions other than, and in some sense truer than, those of life. Let us make the most of these, and other, oracles. Life, for Aristotle, is matter striving after form.

I am tempted to carry that with some recklessness beyond Aristotle, and to say that it is prose struggling into poetry—

> The mortal and the marble still at strife,
> And timidly expanding into life.

This desire of everything that is for self-expression, for meaning, only philosophy, and philosophy only on that unattained eminence from which it beholds all time and all existence, can completely interpret or satisfy. But God did not make man barely philosophical, any more than barely two-legged. He threw in 'mania'; and to a small order of 'maniacal' men, men ecstatic, enthusiastic, possessed, as the Greeks variously called them, he gave eyes divining hidden connexions, the vision of obscured likenesses, the power to recognize things and name them; a faculty of imitative magic, summoning at will, and subduing by spells, the rebellious elements of the world's life.

The poet is, in fact, the prophet of the world's final causes; the interpreter, vexed often and hesitant, but still the only present interpreter, of a creation groaning and travailing after its proper meaning. He, more fully than any other, shares, and is 'possessed' by, the desire of things for good and for intelligibility. It is his art, or talent, or mystery, 'to give' (in Bacon's phrase) 'some shadow of satisfaction to the mind of man in those points wherein the nature of things doth deny it . . . submitting the shews of things to the desire of the mind'.

That not all of this is free from difficulty, I can

hardly be ignorant; perhaps, indeed, I came here to-day to make difficulties; nor do I think that, in the conditions of the time, I can be better employed than in insisting that both poetry and the theory of it *are*, at all points, hard. I do not know that there has, in fact, ever been a theory or a practice of poetry which did not conceive the poet as, in some sense, the master of connexions other than those of common life, connexions, if not more true, at any rate more important. To what, in himself and the world, he owes this mastery, and in what sense the connexions which he seizes, and which he fixes for us, are real—these are questions to which there have been many answers; and that none of them illustrate their subject more than partially—this may at least serve to remind us of what is more important about the poet than anything else: he is a being essentially mysterious. I spoke just now of the new order of trim and brisk and closely cropped poets; and the bardic, I said, had gone from our lives. I am willing to unsay it; for I hope that, in the deeper sense, it is not so. The trustee and repository of the world's hidden connexions is, truly, bardic; and in that spirit, if I may say so, it is his business to regard himself. Upon the veracity of his report of the world, the world, so far as it is beautiful and fit to live in, depends; and the guarantee of his veracity, to him and to us, is himself. It was said of old that poetry is 'the resonance of greatness of soul'; and Milton has told us that 'he who would not be frustrate of his hope to write well hereafter in laudable things ought himselfe to be a true was still under the exclusive domination of the English sensationalists. We too much forget that Shelley and Wordsworth began their philosophy at the same source—Godwin; and from the spells by which that impossible Pretender —the *archimagus* of a metaphysic quackish beyond redemption—bound the most exalted spirits of the time they escaped, by tracks not now clearly discernible, into one resting-place. Both find the ultimate principle of poetic creativeness in what Wordsworth calls 'Spiritual Love', and Shelley, more barely, and more consistently, Love. Thither, for Wordsworth, 'the affections gently lead us on', the every-day affections of common men; thither Shelley is more tumultuously swung or sung, as winds lift the leaf, as light the mists. But examine either for the guarantee of his safety, his ground of assurance; and his only passport is that of the pure senses. All men are naturally free, naturally good, and in them dwells a natural truth. In my reason dwelleth no good thing. But the senses are naturally pure. If the poet differs from other men, it is because, first of all, he has, indeed, 'a more lively sensibility'; and secondly, he has been, from whatever cause, better able than other men to save this sensibility from the contamination of reason, or, what is the same, the infection of custom. Accordingly, he sees things, or feels them—and he says them—not indeed as they are, but as they matter. Poetry describes things, Wordsworth says plainly, not as they are, but 'as they appear to the senses'. Its descriptions are at once less real, and more true; its effects supernatural, because natural. The purposes of Wordsworth's poetry are excellently defined by Coleridge in the fourteenth chapter of the *Biographia Literaria*. They are to 'give the charm of novelty to things of every day, and to excite a feeling analogous to the supernatural, by awakening the mind's attention from the lethargy of custom, and directing it to the wonders of the world before us; an inexhaustible treasure, but for which, in consequence of the film of familiarity and selfish solicitude, we have eyes yet see not, ears that hear not, and hearts that neither feel nor understand'. To Coleridge goes back, you will notice, Shelley's famous phrase, by which he selects as the peculiar function of poetry that it 'makes familiar objects to be as though they were not familiar'.[1] And that is, indeed, its peculiar function, its redeeming office. It redeems us out of life into ourselves; out of all that seems not to matter into a world vital, organic, pulsating.

That is why, in the phrase of a great writer whom I have already quoted, 'the world is always waiting for its poet'. But not for any poet, but for one bardic, daemonic, possessed: possessed, in the purity of his senses, by that colour and rhythm of life, which our mean vision misses, which escapes common hearing, which, only through him, our dull hearts catch at all. No wonder, when so high the office, so fine the

[1] Elsewhere, in the same context, Shelley borrows Coleridge's actual words 'the film of familiarity'; and the *Defence of Poetry* was clearly written when the influence of the *Biographia Literaria* was fresh upon him.

endowment of character, and requiring so long and so subtle a discipline of heart—no wonder if 'the world is always waiting for its poet'. But always the vigil is worth while: for upon the issue of it hangs the world's life.

> Strange vigil of eyelids wan and worn!
>   What thing is this we wait to see?
>   Shall Christ of Cain begotten be,
> Out of our baseness beauty born?
>
> And yet, not idle utterly
>   This watch the anxious ages keep.
>   If ever once we close in sleep
> Our waiting eyelids, lo! we die!

DESMOND MacCARTHY
1877–1952

Robert Burton

Portraits, I, 1931

ROBERT BURTON was the son of Ralph Burton, of an ancient and genteel Leicestershire family; he was born on 8th February 1576. At the age of seventeen he was sent to Brasenose College, and six years later he was elected a student of Christ Church. Henceforth he lived, he tells us, 'a silent, sedentary, solitary, private life . . . saving that sometimes, as Diogenes went into the city, and Democritus into the haven, to see fashions, I did for my recreation now and then walk abroad, looking into the world.' Having little, wanting nothing, all his treasure was, he declared, in Minerva's tower. But sometimes when in low spirits (for he was subject to scholar's melancholy) he used to go down to the Thames to listen to the bad language and back-chat of the bargemen, 'at which he would set his hands to his sides', so Bishop Kennett tells us, 'and laugh most profusely'.

The story reminds us of the qualities which have made his mighty folio fine reading to this day: a humanity which pedantry cannot smother and a great gusto for words. Later Burton was given the living of St. Thomas, in a suburb of Oxford, and of Seagrave in Leicestershire by his patron, George, Lord Berkeley, to whom he dedicated his famous book. He died in 1640, so close to the date foretold in his own horoscope that foolish rumour asserted that he had taken his own life.

During a half-century after its publication (1621) *The Anatomy of Melancholy* continued to be the admiration of the learned, the delight of the idle, and the resource of the curious. It passed through at least eight editions. But with Time's changes it came to be neglected, and remained so for nearly a hundred years, when plagiarists discovered it as a rich forgotten mine. Sterne stole from it freely. Its reputation was revived more directly by praise from Dr. Johnson. 'There is', he said, 'great spirit and great power in what Burton says when he writes from his own mind': he added that *The Anatomy* was the only book that ever took him out of bed two hours sooner than he wished to rise.

The form of commendation is unexpected, for *The Anatomy of Melancholy* is just the book to read *in* bed; almost every page contains something curious and entertaining, yet it is so much of a scrap-book that it can be put down and begun anywhere without loss. It is a book for dippers. Full of fantastic digressions, fantastic stories, vigorous images, racy, quaint and grand in style, it is the richest curiosity shop in English literature. Though I have read in it many times, I cannot have read more than a quarter of it: I shall never finish it or be finished with it.

One of Burton's recent editors speaks of *The Anatomy* as a seventeenth-century equivalent of a modern work on psycho-analysis. It is a comparison at once misleading and true. The intention of the book was similar—to illustrate and explore the causes of extravagant mental distress and irrational behaviour, and to suggest remedies for them. But though it is possible that the case-stories and the analyses of twentieth-century psychologists may seem as fantastic to posterity as Burton's instances and discourses often appear to us, it is incredible that their books should remain like his, interesting and readable, when their theories have been abandoned. Burton's fortunate ignorance of what constitutes evidence, and the irresistible irrelevance of his interest in human nature preserve his book from ever being out of date. He is the Prince of all scribaceous authors, men who read and read and read till learning must find vent, and they have to scribble, scribble, scribble. He lived 'a mere spectator of other men's fortunes and adventures, and how they act their parts, which methinks are diversely presented unto me as from a common theatre scene ... Amidst the gallantry and misery of the world; jollity, pride, perplexities, and cares, simplicity and villainy, subtlety, knavery, candour, and integrity, mutually mixed and offering themselves, I rub along *privus privatus*.'

There lies the charm of his book! His Minerva's tower is a *camera obscura*, in which, peeping over the shoulder of this 'little wearish old man', we observe the fantastic panorama of mankind in agitation. They are so clear and far away, those little pictures. It is like watching people capering and posturing violently to unheard music, a spectacle incomprehensible and comic. And the master of the tower is able to enchant us so completely, just because he has read all about the passions while knowing so very little about them from within. We consequently enjoy with him the kind of detachment which is next best to that of the philosopher, and a much cosier, humbler one; a detachment which allows us the pleasure of an ignorant and secure amazement at the grotesque and extravagant restlessness of life. It is hard sometimes to believe, though Burton tells us this was so, that he himself could have been subject to melancholy, his relish for that spectacle is so constant and so great.

He was at any rate born with the most reliable prophylactic against tedium—consuming curiosity. This is the passion after all that the Universe is most obviously fitted to satisfy. His curiosity was not scientific in method; but one trait he had in common with men of science, he could be happy correlating phenomena. He remarks that 'the Tower of Babel never yielded such confusion of tongues as this Chaos of Melancholy doth symptoms'. But confusion and babel were his joy. The order to which he attempted to reduce them was entirely formal. He divided *The Anatomy* into three main partitions, with a synopsis introducing each with sections and sub-sections and sub-sub-sections, after the manner of learned seventeenth-century writers. The first portion deals with the causes and symptoms of melancholy; the second with its cure, and the third with love-melancholy and religious melancholy. There are digressions, and of these the most important are upon Anatomy, Spirits, the Rectification of Air, and the Misery of Scholars.

The section on love-melancholy is the one to which most readers turn. It contains many extraordinary stories and exhilarating torrents of words. Burton presumes that there will be some 'cavillers and counterfeit Catos' who will take exception to this portion of his work; but he sticks to his course. It is an essential part of his subject. Besides, it is time 'to refresh his weary readers, to expatiate in this delightsome field', and after all 'an old, grave, discrete man is fittest to discourse of love matters'. If objection is taken to some of his stories and quotations, what do objectors think about the stories in the Bible? (This has always been an awkward question for censors.) He will therefore continue his subject unembarrassed, 'call a spade a spade, and sound all the depths of this inordinate love of ours, which nothing can withstand or stave off.'

It is difficult for the reader to collect any general impression from this famous section, for he is apt to be beguiled into delighted impercipience by the extravagance of its detail, and by an eloquence at once comic and grave. But this comment upon it I think holds good: it is clearly a solitary celibate's discourse upon love; that of a born bachelor, who, part terrified, part condemnatory, and part envious—though he thanks Heaven for his own immunity!—stares with fascinated amazement at the disastrous risks which lovers run, and at the wildness of the things they do and think. The dangers of matrimony, though it is the best cure of love-melancholy, are so many and various that it is better, he concludes, to reply with the philosopher, '*adhuc intempestivum*, 'tis yet unseasonable and ever will be'. In fact, he is so sure that bachelors have much the best of life that they ought in gratitude to build and endow colleges for 'old, decayed, deformed, and discontented maids to live together in'.

Admirable, too, is the chapter on Jealousy, that nigh incurable evil. He has not much faith in remedies for this miserable vexation, 'if the nails of it be not pared before they grow long'. We detect a certain scepticism in his reference to the virtues of the Diamond and the Beryll in reconciling men and wives and maintaining unity and love; 'you may try this when you will and as you see cause,' he says. Men still continue to try this, but without giving exclusive preference to those particular precious stones. He ends this chapter with unwonted reticence. 'One other sovereign remedy I could repeat, an especial Antidote against Jealousy, an excellent cure; but I am not now disposed to tell it, not that, like a covetous Empirick, I conceal it for any gain, but for some other reasons, I am not willing to publish it; if you be very desirous to know it, when I meet you next, I will peradventure tell you what it is in your ear.'

His discourse upon the blindness of lovers inclines one to think that his greatest talent lay after all in vituperation. Listen to the passage which follows, and wonder for a moment with me why such loathing should merely awake in us exhilaration and laughter:

Every lover admires his Mistress, though she be very deformed of her self, ill-favoured, wrinkled, pimpled, pale, red, yellow, tanned, tallow-faced, have a swollen Juggler's platter-face, or a thin, lean, chitty-face, have clouds in her face, be crooked, dry, bald, goggle-ey'd, blear-ey'd, or with staring eyes, she looks like a squis'd cat, hold her head still awry, heavy, dull, hollow-eyed, black or yellow about the eyes, or squint-eyed sparrow-mouthed, *Persean* hook-nosed, have a sharp Fox nose, a red nose, *China* flat great nose, *nare simo patuloque*, a nose like a promontory, gubber-tushed, rotten teeth, black, uneven, brown teeth, beetle-browed, a Witch's beard, her breath stink all over the room, her nose drop winter and summer, with a *Bavarian* poke under her chin, ... *Irus'* daughter, *Thersites'* sister, *Grobian's* scholar, if he love her once, he admires her for all this, he takes no notice of any such errors, or imperfections of body or mind. He had rather have her than any woman in the world. If he were a King, she alone should be his Queen, his Empress.

There was really no hatred at all in Burton, so that even when he almost bursts himself in Herculean effort to express his abhorrence, he merely sends our spirits up. I believe that is the explanation. If there was any hatred in him, it hardly amounted to more than an endearing cantankerousness which was swamped in a love, not of men, but of words. Words. He lived like a king, a despot in the realm of words. Outside it he was a bewildered, innocent-eyed, single-hearted old scholar understanding little of the world, next to nothing of its wickedness, and only something of its miseries. Thus it comes about that his book, though it is an exposure of men's crimes, delusions, and follies, is a sweet-natured book; grand, absurd, profuse, and sweet.

E. M. FORSTER
1879–

William Cowper, an Englishman
The Spectator, 16 Jan. 1932

THE bicentenary of Cowper's birth was celebrated last November with befitting mildness. Perhaps there have been too many anniversaries lately, perhaps the autumn of 1931 was an unfortunate period. At any rate, Cowper attracted little attention, as he himself would have expected. The professional men of letters made no noise, for the reason that their paeans had been anticipated by a perfect biography, Lord

David Cecil's *The Stricken Deer*. And even if the men of letters had piped up, the public at large would have declined to listen. For who reads Cowper to-day? This is surely his last appearance upon the general stage. Wordsworth (to mention a spiritual kinsman) still keeps his place; in the great holocaust of literature that is approaching he will survive for a little. Cowper perishes. His magic is too flimsy to preserve him, and his knowledge of human nature is too much overshadowed by fears of personal damnation to radiate far down the centuries:

> Those twinkling tiny lustres of the land
> Drop one by one from Fame's neglecting hand,

he wrote, 'on observing some names of little note recorded in the *Biographia Britannica*', and the epitaph might be his own. The London booksellers, who should know, say that the demand for his poems has not been stimulated by the recent modest ceremonies. There has been a slight increase of sales for his *Letters*. That is all.

It is not an unsuitable moment for him to perish, for England is perishing, and he was English. He was not British or enlightened or far-sighted or adaptable. He was English, and most so when he forgot his nationality and took a country walk. He had his conscious patriotic gestures, and some of them were effective; but there is a stay-at-home air about them which makes them rather ludicrous in our eyes: the poet defies or depreciates the foreigner from his study-chair, as did most patriotic poets before

Rupert Brooke. It is only when he forgets his high mission that he touches our blood and speaks for our land. Out he steps—not forgetting an umbrella, for he understands the climate. Out he steps, accompanied by a lady when the clay is not too tenacious, and he walks over the weeds and under the elms, or across the empty hayfields, or, puffing healthily, he climbs a gentle ascent, from the top of which he can look back upon the River Ouse. None of the walks are very long; the scenery is neither flat nor hilly, the river is always the Ouse. Had it been the Severn or Thames the view would have been grander but less typical. The Ouse is the water of England. It belongs to our soil. We can scarcely imagine it ever leaving us to enter the sea. It is as near as could be a horizontal stream. And Cowper—who found in the placid trinity of Bucks., Beds., and Hunts., such respite as the Furies allowed—is linked with their unostentatious river and with the fields that edge it. He saw the Ouse first at Huntingdon, when the clouds of his preliminary illness were lifting, and the Unwins received him into their affection. He dwelt by it at Olney and Weston Underwood, scenes of his happiness, tragedies, and triumphs. And he bade farewell to it at St. Neots, when all was lost, and he and Mrs. Unwin, both of them insane, were carried away to end their days by the sea. How he mistrusted the sea! He could note its beauties, but it was too restless for him, and too large. And he was equally suspicious of mountains: 'I was a little daunted by the tremendous height of the Sussex hills', and he compares himself to the athlete who could 'leap nowhere well except at Rhodes', since he cannot write well, or even write at all, unless he is at Weston Underwood. As illness increases, the terror of exile from the Ouse grows more acute, and we find him crying from Norfolk as if it was Siberia: 'I shall never see Weston again. I have been tossed like a ball into a far country from which there is no rebound for me.'

Of course he was an invalid, and his attachment to local scenes can be discounted on that account. He had not enough vitality to seek new experiences, and never felt safe until habits had formed their cocoon round his sensitive mind. But inside the cocoon his life is genuine. He might dread the unknown, but he also loved what he knew; he felt steadily about familiar objects, and they have in his work something of the permanence they get in a sitting-room or in the kitchen garden. He does not greet them with surprise nor with any felicitous phrase. It is rather the instinctive acceptance which is part of rural life. Consequently, to read him is really to be in England, and the very triteness of his moralizing keeps us planted there. Brilliant descriptions and profound thoughts entail disadvantages when they are applied to scenery; they act too much as spot lights; they break the landscape up; they drill through it and come out at the antipodes; they focus too much upon what lies exactly in front. Cowper never does this. He knows that the country doesn't lie in front of us but all around. In front is an elm tree, but behind our backs there is probably another elm tree, and out of the corner of each eye we can see blurs that may represent a third elm and a fourth. And so with the country people, the ploughman or the postman, we may not meet them on our walk, but in either case they were somewhere. All this comes out in his work, and we get from it the conviction that we have a humble and inalienable heritage, country England, which no one covets, and which nothing can take away.

Alas, it is a conviction which finds no support whatever in facts. The country Cowper loved is precisely what is going to disappear. The grander scenery of England will probably be saved, owing to its importance in the tourist industry, but it will pay no one to preserve a stray elm, puddles full of ranunculus, or mole hills covered with thyme; and they, not the grandeur, are England. They will be swept aside by pylons and arterial roads, just as Cowper himself is being trodden underfoot by the gangs of modern writers who have been produced by universal education. Excellent writers, many of them. Writers of genius, some of them. But they leave no room for poor Cowper. He has no further part in our destinies. He belongs to the unadvertised, the unorganized, the unscheduled. He has no part in the enormous structure of steel girders and trade upon which Great Britain, like all other Powers, will have to base her culture in the future. That is why his bicentenary fell flat.

LYTTON STRACHEY
1880–1932

Mandell Creighton

Life and Letters, June 1929; Portraits in Miniature, 1931

THE Church of England is one of the most extraordinary of institutions. An incredible concoction of Queen Elizabeth's, it still flourishes, apparently, and for three hundred years has remained true to type. Or perhaps, in reality, Queen Elizabeth had not very much to do with it; perhaps she only gave, with her long, strong fingers, the final twist to a stem that had been growing for ages, deep-rooted in the national life. Certainly our cathedrals—so careful and so unaesthetic, so class-conscious and so competent—suggest that view of the case. English Gothic seems to show that England was Anglican long before the Reformation—as soon as she ceased to be Norman, in fact. Pure piety, it cannot be denied, has never been her Church's strong point. Anglicanism has never produced—never could produce—a St. Teresa. The characteristic great men of the institution—Whitgift, Hooker, Laud, Butler, Jowett—have always been remarkable for virtues of a more secular kind: those of scholarship or of administrative energy. Mandell Creighton was (perhaps) the last of the long line. Perhaps; for who can tell? It is difficult to believe that a man of Creighton's attainments will ever again be Bishop of London. That particular concatenation seems to have required a set of causes to bring it into existence—a state of society, a habit of mind—which have become obsolete. But the whirligigs of time are, indeed, unpredictable; and England, some day or other, may well be blessed with another Victorian Age.

In Creighton *both* the great qualities of Anglican tradition were present to a remarkable degree. It would be hard to say whether he were more distinguished as a scholar or a man of affairs; but—such is the rather unfair persistence of the written word—there can be little doubt that he will be remembered chiefly as the historian of the Papacy. Born when the world was becoming extremely scientific, he belonged to the post-Carlyle-and-Macaulay generation—the school of Oxford and Cambridge inquirers, who sought to reconstruct the past solidly and patiently, with nothing but facts to assist them—pure facts, untwisted by political or metaphysical bias and uncoloured by romance. In this attempt Creighton succeeded admirably. He was industrious, exact, clear-headed, and possessed of a command over words that was quite sufficient for his purposes. He succeeded more completely than Professor Samuel Gardiner, whose history of the Early Stuarts and the Civil Wars was a contemporary work. Gardiner did his best, but he was not an absolute master of the method. Strive as he would, he could not prevent himself, now and then, from being a little sympathetic to one or other of his personages; sometimes he positively alluded to a physical circumstance; in short, humanity would come creeping in. A mistake! For Professor Gardiner's feelings about mankind are not illuminating; and the result is a slight blur. Creighton was made of sterner stuff. In his work a perfectly grey light prevails everywhere; there is not a single lapse into psychological profundity; every trace of local colour, every suggestion of personal passion, has been studiously removed. In many ways all this is a great comfort. One is not worried by moral lectures or purple patches, and the field is kept clear for what Creighton really excelled in—the lucid exposition of complicated political transactions, and the intricate movements of thought with which they were accompanied. The biscuit is certainly exceedingly dry; but at any rate there are no weevils in it. As one reads, one gets to relish, with a sober satisfaction, this plumless fare. It begins to be very nearly a pleasure to follow the intrigues of the great Councils, or to tread the labyrinth of the theological theory of indulgences. It is a curious cross-section of history that Creighton offers to the view. He has cut the great tree so near to the ground that leaf and flower have vanished; but he has worked his saw with such steadiness and precision that every grain in the wood is visible, and one can look *down* at the mighty structure, revealed in all its complex solidity like a map to the mind's eye.

Charming, indeed, are the ironies of history; and not the least charming those that involve the historian. It was very natural that Creighton, a clever and studious clergyman of the Church of England, should choose as the subject of his investigations that group of events which, centring round the Italian popes, produced at last the Reformation. The ironical fact was that those events happened to take place in a world where no clever and studious clergyman of the Church of England had any business to be. 'Sobriety', as he himself said, was his aim; but what could sobriety do when faced with such figures as Savonarola, Caesar Borgia, Julius II, and Luther? It could only look somewhere else. It is pleasant to witness the high-minded husband and father, the clever talker at Cambridge dinner tables, the industrious diocesan administrator, picking his way with an air of calm detachment amid the recklessness, the brutality, the fanaticism, the cynicism, the lasciviousness, of those Renaissance spirits. 'In his private life', Creighton says of Alexander VI, 'it is sufficiently clear that he was at little pains to repress a strongly sensual nature.... We may hesitate to believe the worst charges brought against him; but the evidence is too strong to enable us to admit that even after his accession to the papal office he discontinued the irregularities of his previous life.' There is high comedy in such a tone on such a topic. One can imagine the father of the Borgias, if he could have read that sentence, throwing up his hands in delighted amazement, and roaring out the obscene blasphemy of his favourite oath.

The truth was that, in spite of his wits and his Oxford training, the admirable North-country middle-class stock, from which Creighton came, dominated his nature. His paradoxes might astound academical circles, his free speech might agitate the lesser clergy, but at heart he was absolutely sound. Even a friendship with that daemonic imp, Samuel Butler, left him uncorroded. He believed in the Real Presence. He was opposed to Home Rule. He read with grave attention the novels of Mrs. Humphry Ward. The emancipation of a Victorian bishop could never be as that of other men. The string that tied him to the peg of tradition might be quite a long one; but it was always there. Creighton enjoyed his little runs with the gusto and vitality that were invariably his. The sharp aquiline face, with the grizzled beard, the bald forehead, and the gold spectacles, gleamed and glistened, the long, slim form, so dapper in its episcopal gaiters, preened itself delightedly, as an epigram—a devastating epigram—shot off and exploded, and the Fulham teacups tinkled as they had never tinkled before. Then, a moment later, the guests gone, the firm mouth closed in severe determination; work was resumed. The duties of the day were dispatched swiftly; the vast and stormy diocese of London was controlled with extraordinary efficiency; while a punctual calmness reigned, for, however pressed and pestered, the Bishop was never known to fuss. Only once on a railway journey, when he believed that some valuable papers had gone astray, did his equanimity desert him. 'Where's my black bag?' was his repeated inquiry. His mischievous children treasured up this single lapse; and, ever afterwards, 'Where's my black bag?' was thrown across the table at the good-humoured prelate when his family was in a teasing mood.

When the fourth volume of the *History of the Papacy* appeared there was a curious little controversy, which illustrated Creighton's attitude to history and, indeed, to life. 'It seems to me', he wrote in the preface, 'neither necessary to moralize at every turn in historical writing, nor becoming to adopt an attitude of lofty superiority over any one who ever played a prominent part in European affairs, nor charitable to lavish undiscriminating censure on any man'. The wrath of Lord Acton was roused. He wrote a violent letter of protest. The learning of the eminent Catholic was at least equal to Creighton's, but he made no complaint upon matters of erudition; it was his moral sense that was outraged. Creighton, it seemed to him, had passed over, with inexcusable indifference, the persecution and intolerance of the medieval Church. The popes of the thirteenth and fourteenth centuries, he wrote,

.... instituted a system of persecution.... It is the most conspicuous fact in the history of the mediæval Papacy.... But what amazes and disables me is that you speak of the Papacy not as exercising a just severity, but as not exercising any severity. You ignore, you even deny, at least implicitly, the existence of the torture chamber and the stake.... Now the Liberals think persecution a crime of a worse order than adultery, and the acts done by Ximenes considerably worse than the entertainment of Roman courtezans by Alexander VI. The responsibility exists whether the thing permitted be good or bad. If the thing be criminal, then the authority permitting it bears the guilt.... You say that people in authority are not to be snubbed or sneered at from our pinnacle of conscious rectitude. I really don't know whether you exempt them because of their rank, or of their success and power, or of their date.... Historic responsibility has to make up for the want of legal responsibility. Power tends to corrupt, and absolute power corrupts absolutely. Great men are almost always bad.'

These words, surely, are magnificent. One sees with surprise and exhilaration the roles reversed —the uncompromising fervour of Catholicism calling down fire from Heaven upon its own abominable Popes and the worldly Protestantism that excused them. Creighton's reply was as Anglican as might have been expected. He hedged. One day, he wrote, John Bright had said, 'If the people knew what sort of men statesmen were, they would rise and hang the whole lot of them'. Next day, Gladstone had said 'Statesmanship is the noblest way to serve mankind.'—'I am sufficient of a Hegelian to be able to combine both judgements; but the results of my combination cannot be expressed in the terms of the logic of Aristotle.... Society is an organism', &c. It is clear enough his real difference with Lord Acton was not so much over the place of morals in history as over the nature of the historical acts upon which moral judgements are to be passed. The Bishop's imagination was not deeply stirred by the atrocities of the Inquisition; what interested him, what appealed to him, what he really understood, were the difficulties and the expedients of a man of affairs who found himself at the head of a great administration. He knew too well, with ritualists on one side and Kensitites on the other, the trials and troubles from which a clerical ruler had to extricate himself as best he could, not to sympathize (in his heart of hearts) with the clerical rulers of another age who had been clever enough to devise regulations for the elimination of heresy and schism, and strong enough to put those regulations into force.

He himself, however, was never a persecutor; his great practical intelligence prevented that. Firmly fixed in the English tradition of common sense, compromise, and comprehension, he held on his way amid the shrieking of extremists with imperturbable moderation. One of his very last acts was to refuse to prosecute two recalcitrant clergymen who had persisted in burning incense in a forbidden manner. He knew that, in England at any rate, persecution did not work. Elsewhere, perhaps, it might be different; in Russia, for instance.... There was an exciting moment in Creighton's life when he was sent to Moscow to represent the Church of England at the Coronation of the Emperor Nicholas; and his comments on that occasion were significant. Clad in a gorgeous cope of red and gold, with mitre and crozier, the English prelate attracted every eye. He thoroughly relished the fact; he tasted, too, to the full, the splendour of the great ceremonies and the extraordinary display of autocratic power. That there might have been some degree of spiritual squalor mixed with those magnificent appearances never seemed to occur to him. He was fascinated by the apparatus of a mighty organization, and, with unerring instinct, made straight for the prime mover of it, the Chief Procurator of the Holy Synod, the sinister Pobiedonostzeff, with whom he struck up a warm friendship. He was presented to the Emperor and Empress, and found them charming. 'I was treated with great distinction, as I was called in first. The Empress looked very nice, dressed in white silk.' The aristocratic Acton would, no doubt, have viewed things in a different light. 'Absolute power corrupts absolutely'—so he had said; but Creighton had forgotten the remark. He was no Daniel. He saw no Writing on the Wall.

The Bishop died in his prime, at the height of his success and energy, and was buried in St. Paul's Cathedral. Not far from his tomb, which a Victorian sculptor did his best to beautify, stands the strange effigy of John Donne, preaching, in his shroud, an incredible sermon upon mortality. Lingering in that corner, one's mind flashes oddly to other scenes and other persons. One passes down the mouldering street of Ferrara, and reaches an obscure church. In the half-light, from an inner door, an elderly humble nun approaches, indicating with her patois a marble slab in the pavement—a Latin inscription—the grave of Lucrezia Borgia. Mystery and oblivion were never united more pathetically. But there is another flash, and one is on a railway platform under the grey sky of England. A tall figure hurries by, spectacled and bearded, with swift clerical legs, and a voice—a competent, commanding, yet slightly agitated voice—says sharply: 'Where's my black bag?'

LASCELLES ABERCROMBIE
1881–1938

The Function of Poetry in the Drama
The Poetry Review, March 1912

THE question: What is it that poetry *does* in the drama? is much more than a merely technical question. It is, indeed, a type or particular aspect of a very large question: What is the relation of art to appearance—that is to say, to actual human experience, sensuous, rational, imaginative? But I shall endeavour not to trespass outside the particular problem: that, I daresay, will be sufficient occupation for us—in spite of the fact that nowadays, it seems, the problem is one that is commonly held to have gone beyond the region of profitable discussion. But that is just the reason why I want to discuss it. The prose play is the thing for us to-day, we have often been told; some would say, it is the thing for the future too: to admit a preference for plays composed in verse is to admit oneself hypnotized by an unexamined convention. Well, I propose to examine the convention a little. Just because poetry *is* discredited as a dramatic medium at present, it seems to me that it is specially important so to consider it—so important that the consideration ought to be undertaken (as I shall try to do) in a spirit of the utmost partisanship. Much might be made of the appeal to antiquity, but that is not a very conscionable line of reasoning, and we will stick to theory as long as we can. I shall not endeavour to prove too much. I shall only inquire whether the assumption that prose is the natural and straightforward medium for a play be not profoundly mistaken; whether, on the contrary, it be not poetry that is the natural and straightforward medium. I shall leave it to inference to suggest that a play written in prose is a thing essentially fantastic, unreal, bizarre—in fact, a *tour de force*.

But when we speak of poetry or prose as a *medium* of drama, when we compare plays *written* in prose with those *written* in poetry—we must not let ourselves be imposed on by what is merely a convenience of discussion. The obvious difference between a verse-dramatist and a prose-dramatist is that the one makes his characters talk verse, the other prose; but that is not the only difference we have to consider. That is only the outer sign of a profounder difference, a difference of conception. We must be clear then that a poetic play is not a play that might have been written in prose, but happens to be written in poetry. If we wish to find the excusing virtues of a poetic play, we must assuredly have in our minds something more thorough-going than a play in which the characters are decent, familiar folk who have, for an hour or so, deliberately contracted a habit of urging their mental activity through image, metaphor, and simile, to say nothing of controlling it into metre—a habit which we imagine to be of brief duration, and are quite certain is extremely uncongenial. No: the kind of play I mean is one in which you feel that the characters themselves *are* poetry, and were poetry before they began to speak poetry: it would be a wrench for them not so to utter themselves. They are characters which, compared with ours, have undergone a certain powerful simplification and exaggeration, so that the primary impulses of being are infinitely more evident in what they do and say than in the speech and action of actuality's affairs. This does not prevent them, of course, from being studies of deep and subtle individual psychology (if the poet's preferences in dramatic method lie that way): but as the confusion of forces which make up the impulsion of ordinary life has in these characters been simplified to a firm arrangement of conflict, an orderly disorder, and as every force which moves in them is made thereby to be of intense unobstructed significance—so also the language which is in their mouths has been simplified out of the grey complexity of ordinary speech into an ordered medley of colour, and every word they use is required to have the intense unobstructed significance which words can only have in poetry; the half-felt allusiveness, the dulled metaphor, of common talking, become image, metaphor, and simile unashamed and rejoicing. So, again, with the exaggeration; characters are put before us which are much more vehement and impressive than the persons we know in everyday life, and this is because they have, compared with the blurred outlines known from actual acquaintance, an exaggerated *shapeliness* of personality; their natures have a precision and definiteness of design; and this exaggeration of character-form draws on a corresponding exaggeration in the *shape* of the speech they utter; wherein the shifting rhythms of common talking become formalized into regular metre—fall into metre, in fact, as naturally as blood-flow goes in beats. That, at least, is one reason why metrical speech is seemly in a genuinely poetical play; personalities designed by artistic exaggeration into a shapeliness one does not ordinarily experience, may allow of a metrical kind of speaking which is equally unusual in life, speech designed by art into regular rhythm. But certainly, in addition to all this, metre has another function, on which I shall touch in a minute or two.

I have been trying to suggest the conditions in a play which make poetic speech obviously natural. But whether you agree or not, that it is exaggeration and simplification in character which make dramatically possible that exaggeration and simplification in speech which results in poetry—what is, at any rate, evident, is that in a perfectly successful poetic play the whole of the talking *can* be done naturally in poetry; and we must always feel it to be natural. When, for instance, a man, while proposing marriage to a lady, assures her that he intends providing her with a fashionable equipage, in lines like these:

With milk-white harts upon an ivory sled
Thou shalt be drawn amidst the frozen pools;

we must be able to feel that it is altogether natural to this particular lover to put into such exquisite terms what would in everyday life be a more or less business proposition: he simply could not help visualizing the matter thus deliciously. If you did not feel this, of course it becomes skimble skamble stuff. Or suppose a murderer, after his first venture in the trade, discovered some blood on his hands; actually, his horror would not get into speech beyond some such exclamation as: Good Lord, suppose it won't come off! But in a poetical play we do not allow him to say that this bloody hand would 'the multitudinous seas incarnadine' merely because that is a noble line; it is allowed, it is *demanded*, because only by such verbal means, by such spoken poetry, can the expression of the character be kept in the *scale* of the character himself; in the scale, that is, of what we may call the conceptual poetry. And, of course, the characters must have an appropriate region of events in which to move, answerably imagined, according to the same laws of exaggeration and simplification, into a *design*, therefore into impressiveness and significance. The whole effect obviously is to give an exhibition of life intensified, life supposed at a higher pressure than actuality. There must be grades between character and character corresponding to the grades of actuality; but, in personality, the lowest grade begins where real life leaves off; the whole lot of humanity is lifted up to an intenser pitch of heat: the current of life flows through the characters at a fiercer strength, and so, to use an electrical simile, the *resistance* of the characters to the current, and their consequent incandescence, is also fiercer. Thus we find, for examples, that for sheer impressiveness of personality, Christopher Sly is on a level with—say—our doctors of divinity or university professors; and Lear is on a level with the man Shakespeare when the Shakespeare is most concentrated in him.

That first instance of mine may seem an unfortunate one; for Christopher Sly happens to be a character who speaks prose. But, of course, one must admit that something of the process I have been describing for the conception of a poetic play must also be the process of a prose play's conception—if the play is to run more than a single night. It is when the process is carried out as thoroughly as it possibly can be, that we get what we call a poetic play. But when the process is moderated from the beginning by quite another sort of notion, the notion of imitating life, and strictly controlled so as not to vitiate the imitation, we get the prose play. The questions therefore are, How far can the process be pushed? And why should it be pushed as far as possible—in other words, Why should we have poetical plays at all? Why not be content with plays in which the necessary conceptual process has been so moderated that their characters may talk in decent, comfortable prose, and not go flying off into poetry?

And it would have been just about here, I suppose, that the defender of prose plays would have broken in on the argument. 'All this', he would say, 'is very well. If we are to have poetic plays at all, they must be plays which are altogether poetry, or so conceived that spoken poetry is their inevitable utterance. But by your own admission, so to conceive a play requires a very serious tampering with the material of drama, which is life. The modern soul, however, wants a drama that gets as close to life as possible, reduces it to drama with as little and as scrupulous tampering as may be: it wants the prose play.' Well, it certainly appears that that is what it does want; but into this sociological question I am not now concerned to enter. What I am concerned with is to ask, What, in the name of *aesthetics*, does this desire to get close to life really mean? At bottom, it means, surely, nothing but this: that drama, like all art, *must be credible*: otherwise you might just as well not write it. Furthermore, the stuff of drama must be made out of actual experience, that is to say, of appearances: there is nothing else out of which it can be made. Must it not be, therefore, that in order to be credible, drama must imitate those appearances which we call reality? Plainly, it must do some imitation; and at first it would seem that the difference between poetry plays and prose plays in the matter is something like this: for a poetry play, only so much imitation is employed as to keep the poetizing of experience credible, recognizable as a supposed representation of life. Whereas in a prose play, imitation is the chief of the business, only such formalization being used as will make the imitation bearable. There is truth in this, but not the whole truth. It only applies to direct or external imitation. But more than that is possible, and I think we ought to agree that, if thorough imitation is a crucial point, the poetry play does better than the prose play. I have already assumed the obvious fact, that a prose play cannot absolutely imitate life in its conception, in its plan; because life, the material, must be to a certain extent formalized, if the play is to be tolerable. In the texture, however, in the words used to reveal the conception, perhaps we can get a pretty close imitation of life: but even here it can never be absolute imitation. For every word spoken in a play must do at least two things: characterize and help on the action. But that is not what words do in life. As a rule, there is no action worth mentioning to help on; and as for characterizing, why, in life most people wear such a rough and ready slip-shod conversation, compact of stock phrases, vague allusions, half-bake slang, and half-understood technical terms, that character is to be inferred therefrom only as much as the modelling of a foot may be inferred from the ready-made boot it wears. External imitation in drama is therefore like that mathematical curve which always approaches but never reaches.

But what is it exactly that drama has to imitate? The answer is not simple, because reality is not simple. Those appearances which we call reality are like a set of Chinese boxes, an inner one still fitting inside the last one opened. There is the sensible reality of deeds and words—the outward gestures of character; then there is the reality of reasoned motive and conscience—so to speak, the inward gestures of character; then character itself; then passion, then the social reality: I don't profess to have taken the puzzle to pieces in the right order. Anyhow, the innermost reality, the one with which art is most dearly concerned, is what is commonly called the spiritual reality. For the purpose of this discussion, however, let me use a name which allows it to be more easily handled. Let me call it the emotional reality; by which I do not entirely mean the plane of such named and recognizable emotions as love, anger, hate, but rather the general substratum to all existence, emotion nameless and unappointed. This is the layer of flame which is the closest we can get to the central fire, to the Will to live, or whatever you like to call it. And an impression of this profound emotional reality is what art must convey, together, of course, with its concentric apparatus or expression of all the other realities—the named emotions, reason, the habit of conscience, action, and the rest. Now the great difference between prose drama and poetry drama is that the first concentrates its imitation on the outermost reality, the second on the innermost. Prose drama gives you an imitation of the ready-made boot of existence, gives it you as exactly as it can; and trusts to your familiarity with it, to your knowledge that the boot does contain something, to enable you to *infer* therefrom the inner reality on which it is constructed. And if you cannot perform that inference, the boot, as far as art is concerned, might certainly just as well be thrown at you empty.

Poetry drama, however, except only for preserving the necessary credibility, neglects the outer shells of reality, and directly seeks to imitate the core. Or rather, it seeks to imitate in you the *effect* which would be produced if you perceived with certainty and clarity the grand emotional impulse driving all existence. For this kind of drama uses for its texture a verbal process which, with its numerous provocative and evocative devices, such as imagery, and deliberate metaphor, and consistent metre, is inescapably recognizable as *symbolic* of the emotional reality of life. The primary emotional urge of our being is conveyed directly, immediately into our apprehension; and since we cannot conceive of that impulse without its worldly embodiment in the more familiar, more easily named realities, a strong impression of the original emotion of Being inevitably conveys the impression that the outer shells of actual experience have also been imitated, when in fact they have perhaps been but carelessly indicated. It is here that the wonderfully important function of metre comes in; for metre gives to the poet's words a *form* which is itself a direct expression of the emotion which the words enclose. Not only does the underlying consistent beat keep our answering emotions in the necessary state of excitation, but the sudden varieties and modulations of metre, the momentary deviations from consistency, are most powerful suggesters of shifting changes and unexpected upward rushes of emotion. Plainly, this poetic method of imitation, of going at once to the core of the requirement, is a much more effective and direct method of imitation than the prose method of imitating the sensible and reasonable exterior of life so laboriously and exactly, that the watcher may, with luck, be induced to infer the inner nature of things which art must somehow exhibit, or else fail to be art. The preference for prose plays over poetic plays is therefore a preference for ordinary appearance over spiritual reality: it is, in fact, a form of materialism. The alleged desire to 'get as close to life as possible', the desire which prose plays satisfy, means a desire for that kind of credibility which keeps us familiar with the superficial, and avoids the requirements of familiarity with the inmost formidable energies of existence.

So much for the function of poetry in the drama as far as the imitation of life is concerned. But I suppose no one to-day maintains that imitation is the chief end of drama; though it is going equally wrong to assert that drama need not imitate at all, for only by some kind or other of imitation can credibility be preserved. Nowadays it would very likely be said that the chief end of drama is the *Representation of Life*, which certainly is quite another matter. Indeed, the theory of realism, in so far as it ever had a theory, is probably based on a mistranslation of a famous Greek phrase, 'imitation' being erroneously put for 'representation'. But into that I am not concerned to enter. The drama as representation of life, then, is an attempt to put forth into concrete exterior form our vague feelings and ideas about life: by it we are to comprehend what we can usually only apprehend. And what are the prevalent ideas about life to-day? Well, it appears they come to this: that life is in a bad way, and something must be done about it. Accordingly, it is assumed that drama should diagnose the diseases of life, and suggest cures; at least, it should tend to settle the hesitancy of minds distracted by the problems that beset our actuality, by putting those problems—economic, moral, sociological—into concrete and impressive form. This brings us to the drama as an engine in the criticism of life; and, taking the phrase without too much examination, criticism of life may perhaps, with a stretch, stand for representation of life. But nowadays, in dramatic practice, at any rate, if not in aesthetic theory, criticism of life is taken in hand in a determinedly practical and rationalistic fashion. Well, I am quite willing to leave this region to the exploration of prose drama. I quite freely admit, that to a man hesitating between socialism and anarchy, or between polygamy and eugenics, or between overhead and underground connexions for tramways, *The Tempest* or *Macbeth* would have very little to say of any profit. But I am very far from admitting that we have yet got to the end of what drama can do. We certainly have not got to the end of it with the criticism of life; I have no notion at all of judging a play according to its criticism of life, even at the highest interpretation; you might just as well judge an expedition to the South Pole as a criticism of life. One goes to the play, whatever sort of a play it may be, because one gets there something in the nature of an adventure— adventure for mind or emotion. And the more poetic the play, I might add, the more adventurous it is. Neither can I be content with the more general assumption that drama is merely to *represent life*. I want to know, what do we gain by the representation of life? Every one perceives (or can perceive), and we are told it is a thing universal and inveterate in human psychology, that it is pleasant to see vague subjectivity put forth into clear, impressive objectivity, to see weltering life turned into a harmonious symbol of life. Yes, but why is it so pleasant? Or, rather, since that is probably asking too much, what is the nature of the pleasure? I think the word I have just used—adventure—is some indication of this; but we must try to get closer still. And, as far as I can see, we get as close as possible when we take the ultimate end of drama to be the excitation of self-consciousness, of a state of being in which we find it something of an exultation to know that we are ourselves.

By means of some process which seems too profound to be analysed, drama, like all great art, has a certain evocative power over self-consciousness. It is, perhaps, a kind of exultant sympathy; we sympathize with the dramatist, who has conquered the confused and meaningless actuality of life into ordered significance. Self-consciousness is itself the sign of a certain orderliness, governing the multifarious forces of life in an individual; but the degree of orderliness varies greatly, and consequently the acuteness of self-consciousness: indeed, it might be true to say that we are, in ordinary affairs, more often conscious than self-conscious. Certainly, self-consciousness is not commonly a positive and clearly felt delight in us. But to make it so is the purpose of art. And to witness the triumph of dramatic order over life causes, by a kind of induction, a more prevailing and shapely orderliness in ourselves; and the consequence must be an enhancement of self-consciousness. This, however, is perhaps speculation. But whether this be true or false, what seems to me undeniable is this: that human nature is possessed by a mighty craving to be aware of itself, nay, to be exultingly and delightedly aware of itself. And the paradoxical thing is, that of the actual craving we ourselves are not always perfectly conscious; we only know, when this state of keen and heightened, intensely alert, self-awareness comes upon us, that it is what we profoundly want. So the true explanation of the appeal of drama is, that to witness a spectacle which instinct knows for a genuine symbol of life *does* cause a person to be triumphantly aware of the personality in him. For a genuine symbol of life is, metaphysically, a symbol of our desires for life; it is, therefore, life made orderly and significant; and to see life thus artistically refashioned, makes us keenly aware of our hidden desires by means of this very satisfaction, and so, keenly aware of ourselves. Life cannot satisfy our desires for life; but drama can; and by so doing seems more real than life, and we by witnessing it seem more real ourselves. Hence the fundamental importance of drama is its power of forcing us into a state of astonishment

—astonishment that glows to perceive with unexpected force that terrific splendid fact, the fact *that we do exist*.

Moreover, there is as well a certain sense of mastery. Self-consciousness, that supreme achievement of life, is triumphing in us over the many powers that would obscure it. And with this there naturally goes a sense of pride; we are proud of the life in us. I am not, of course, saying that in the state I mean we are investigating our own psychology and discovering what I have been describing; for the fact is, that a really intense self-consciousness is too much engaged in simply existing for the time being to be investigating itself: self-consciousness at its best is *not* self-analysis: it is a fire that puts out with its brightness the milder flame of analytic reason. It is a state which is on the way to ecstasy: and ecstasy is *not* unconsciousness, but Being supremely and superbly knowing itself for Being.

If, now, I want to find a metaphor that will most clearly suggest this capital function of drama, I find I am compelled to choose—*intoxication*. It is a word, maybe, that has for some of us disturbing connotations; but I cannot help that. Dionysus was more than a wine-drunken god, and Dionysus is the god of drama. And what is the kind of drama that does best as an intoxicant; which is the most efficient cause of that state of consciousness in which life is felt, for all its malices, as an admirable astonishing power, and *we* are made to exult in the part we have in life? It is surely that kind of drama which most daringly handles its materials: drama which is only for exigencies of technique concerned with imitation of life, in which representation of life has become a complete recreating of life's materials into a symbol charged with satisfaction of our profoundest desires—the aesthetic desire for rhythm and order even in the midst of conflict, the moral desire for courage and exultation resisting the irresistible destiny of things: in a word, poetic drama, wherein the speech used can be the most uncompromising kind of poetry. Dramatic poetry is to experience as wine is to the grape: this is true both of the conception and of the speech which is the bodily vehicle of the conception. Prose is the unintoxicating utterance of common experience; in poetry, the utterance has been fermented into metre and heady imagery. To use spoken poetry for the medium of drama is, therefore, to obey, simply and without violence, the fundamental nature of drama right through, from first conception to ultimate expression. Prose drama is an adulteration. But, of course, even adulterated wine can intoxicate, though not so handsomely as the pure vintage; and I would not be understood to imply that avowedly poetic drama is the only one which can appeal to the patronage of Dionysus. But I certainly do mean to imply that the fundamentally enjoyable qualities in prose drama, yes, even in drama dealing with the politics and economics of everyday affairs, are those qualities which have their freest and fullest exercise in poetic drama; and I say that these qualities are diluted in prose drama because the stuff of prose drama—external imitation—is less disturbing, therefore a weaker solvent of our ordinary states of mind, than the stuff of poetic drama, emotional imitation. Ibsen's plays are a good example: for all their criticism of life, they owe their supremacy and their ultimate appeal to the poetry concealed in them; and for impressiveness, for awakening an answering pride of life in *us*, the later plays certainly cannot compare with *Brand*, wherein the poetry had no need to hide, but could nobly have its way with the whole business, just because the play is *written* in uncompromising poetry, written before Ibsen had become obsessed by the theory of the prose-imitation of actual speech. For not only does the use of poetic speech allow the poetic conception a perfectly free scope, it also allows the conception to be much profounder than in a prose play, that is to say, less closely attached to the outer appearance of life, more frankly and earnestly symbolic of those spiritual desires in us which actual life can but imperfectly answer. The poet has all the time the support of his direct imitation of *emotional* reality to maintain credibility, and can therefore play all sorts of comic and tragic tricks with his material; but the prose man cannot depart far from his external imitative process without seriously endangering credibility; he has nothing else to fall back on. This explains the partially unsatisfactory nature of several well-known modern plays, such as Wilde's *Salome* or Maeterlinck's earlier work, which are written in prose yet attempt to transcend the laws of ordinary experience. If they had been done in poetry, they would surely have been far more impressive, more *seemingly* actual, instead of being, as they plainly are, just wonderful arabesque work. But, while I am upholding poetry as the most natural and suitable medium for drama, I do not need to be reminded that a very considerable contribution to the world's dramatic literature is composed in a mixture of prose and verse; yet I think one may easily hold the position that, given consummate handling, the sharp contrast of medium has a very extraordinary effect of heightening the sheer poetic qualities of the whole. There are, however, many Elizabethan plays in which the handling is anything but consummate; instead of a heightening contrast they give us confusion, and the device of mingling verse and prose is evidently a dangerous one to copy.

One more thing remains to be briefly considered. Can a play written in poetry deal conveniently with contemporary life? Well, why not? It has been done before, why not again? I know no comedy which gives me a more tremendous impression of reality than *The Alchemist*—a play transmuting some of the everyday affairs of Johnson's own contemporary surroundings into poetry, poetizing the affairs of cheats, conjurers, panders, knaves, and gulls, and boldly written in verse from end to end. Then there are what historians call the Elizabethan domestic dramas, for instances on the tragic side. I have already admitted that the practical criticism of modern life is no work for poetry; but, apart from that, I see no reason whatever why poetry should not be used for contemporary drama—as, once more, it is used in that great play, *Brand*. Yet poetry will certainly not be the rule here, for it is undoubtedly pleasant to see the particularities of our own manners aped on the stage, and to these poetry cannot much attend. It must take as short a cut through them as it does through the particularities of ancient Roman or Danish or any other manners. For these minutiae are so engaging to the wits of the audience that they must inevitably distract them from that which poetry sets out to say. In a word, direct and close external imitation can hardly co-exist in a play quite simultaneously with direct poetic imitation of emotional reality.

What then, in sum, is the chief function poetry has to serve in the drama? This: it is to be the alcohol to which the human organism answers with an intoxication of sense, mind, and emotion, bringing them into a unity of triumphant and delighted self-consciousness, self-consciousness bright enough to turn for awhile this obscure fate of life in which we are immersed into some clear nature lit through and through *with ourselves*, that is to say, with those desires which are most profoundly ourselves. Poetic drama can induce, in the deepest sense, the joy of life: it strongly reminds its witnesses that they have the power of being conscious of their own lives, and it makes the possession of that power an actual and keenly felt exhilaration. Characters in a play who can speak poetry naturally and inevitably are characters who have in them all the splendour and vigour of life we can imagine; no wonder they face their destiny so greatly; and as we watch them, they infect us with something of their nature; in us, too, the fate of life becomes for a moment a thing on which we can ride not without mastery. A lie, all this, perhaps; but is not life itself a lie?—as far as our poor wits know it, at any rate. The realist is for repeating all the old lies that life itself has been telling over and over again. 'What a lie life is,' says a famous realist, 'what a beastly lie!'—and that is exactly what his plays are. But the poet dramatist, finding he must lie somehow, is determined to tell as fine and as noble a lie as he can, a lie so splendid that it must be believed in—an intoxicating lie. I must not inquire why the diluted liquor of prose plays is the popular one nowadays. Perhaps our heads are getting weak. The fact seems part of a general process which is narrowing down man's methods of intoxication. Already we are practically limited to two forms, in which the intoxicant is still served without being timidly diluted—music and alcohol itself; and it is doubtful whether we shall have both of these for long. I have nothing against them, yet the noblest form of intoxication is, I believe, neither of these, but a species of drama, the species to which *Agamemnon, Œdipus, The Trojan Women, Tamburlain, Lear, The Tempest*, and *Brand* belong. I am at least certain that there is no greater danger for man than to be limited to a very few forms of intoxication. Broaden the basis of intoxication!—that would be my cry if I were a politician. And, first, I would work to bring it back again in undiluted form into the theatre; I would labour for a movement to set going once more the drama which can most mightily intoxicate men to be consciously and delightedly in love with life itself, yes, even with the tragedy of life.

R. W. CHAPMAN
1881–

The Textual Criticism of English Classics

The Portrait of a Scholar, 1922

In the *Proposals for Printing the Dramatick Works of William Shakespeare* Johnson wrote: 'To have a text corrupt in many places, and in many doubtful, is, among the authors that have written since the use of types, almost peculiar to *Shakespeare*. Most writers, by publishing their own works, prevent all various readings, and preclude all conjectural criticism.' Modern research has shown that books published by their authors are yet not immune from corruption; that Johnson himself knew this is shown by his practice. When they were in Skye, Johnson handed Boswell the works of Sir George Mackenzie, and bade him discover an error in the text on the sixty-fifth page of the first volume. 'I was lucky enough to hit it at once. As the passage is printed, it is said that the devil answers *even* in *engines*. I corrected it to *ever* in *aenigmas*. "Sir (said he), you are a good critick. This would have been a great thing to do in the text of an ancient authour."'

The causes to which it is due that the text of Shakespeare is less certain than that of Sophocles are well known. They have, perhaps, never been better stated than by Johnson.

> Of the works of Shakespeare the condition has been far different; he sold them, not to be printed, but to be played. They were immediately copied for the actors, and multiplied by transcript after transcript, vitiated by the blunders of the penman, or changed by the affectation of the player . . .; and printed at last without the concurrence of the author, without the consent of the proprietor, from compilations made by chance or by stealth out of the separate parts written for the theatre; and thus thrust into the world surreptitiously and hastily, they suffered another depravation from the ignorance and negligence of the printers, as every man who knows the state of the press in that age will readily conceive.

Shakespeare's text seemed to the critics of the eighteenth century to be peculiar only from their neglect of his contemporaries. Most of his fellow-dramatists were in a similar plight. Ben Jonson indeed saved his text from mutilation by himself preparing it for the press and by superintending the printing with laborious diligence; but his was a quite exceptional carefulness. Even writers who, unlike the dramatists, were at liberty to publish their works as soon as they were written, often preferred to circulate them in manuscript. Sidney had nothing to do with the printing of *Arcadia*; the publication of *The Passionate Pilgrim* was piratical; very few of Donne's poems were printed in his lifetime. Even those authors who deliberately published their works were at the mercy of printers to whom the method and regularity of the modern press were unknown. No proof was sent to the author. Mistakes were corrected, and fresh mistakes made, while the sheets were at the press. It is doubtful if any two copies of the First Folio are identical.

Conjectural emendation is not the first, but the last, duty of an editor; the first is to assemble and weigh the evidence. What Pope called 'the dull duty of an editor' has been greatly extended by modern diligence, which has found that copies of the same edition do not agree, and that varying texts abound in contemporary manuscript-books. As the accuracy of printing increased, and authors discovered a conscience, texts became less uncertain and an editor's path less perplexed; but variation and error persist. Editors of Gray and Keats must consult the manuscripts; editors of Wordsworth and Shelley must compare numerous editions.

It is generally accepted that the most authoritative edition is the last published in the author's lifetime. This is roughly true of books published in the last two centuries; but what if the author revised only the first edition, or revised no edition? Of the five editions of *The Shepheard's Calender*, each repeats the errors of its predecessors, and adds new errors of its own. Of the Shakespeare Folios, Johnson says, 'whoever has any ... has all, excepting those diversities which mere reiteration of editions will produce'. The second edition of *The Faery Queene* contains changes which were certainly made by Spenser; but the 'faults escaped in the printing', of which a list was printed in 1590, were repeated in 1596.

Even the careful Boswell, with Malone to help him, allowed errors to appear in the third edition 'revised and corrected' of his *Tour to the Hebrides* from which the first is free. It is therefore never admissible to select one edition and neglect the rest, unless the edition judged to be authoritative is the first.

Sometimes editions differ so widely that the constitution of an eclectic text becomes difficult, if not impossible. The Vulgate Shakespeare has been compiled from Quartos and Folio partly by selection, partly by conflation; and combines versions of the same scene, both of which may be Shakespearian, but which Shakespeare could never have intended to stand together. From such a problem some critics seek refuge by selecting one original and editing it as if it were unique. This is legitimate, but does not exhaust the duties of criticism. A Quarto and the Folio may give versions which, as a whole, it is impossible to reconcile or combine; yet if they contain passages substantially the same, the variations must be weighed. There is in Shakespeare a long sentence, which in the Folio is concluded by the words 'and in one purpose'. The text is defensible, though the sentence lacks a verb. The Quarto has 'end in one purpose'. It is now an editor's business to decide, not whether the Folio text is possible, but whether 'and' or 'end' is the more likely to be right. That Shakespeare wrote both at different times is possible—all things are possible—but is not probable; that a printer should confuse 'and' and 'end' is what happens on every page.

Donne is another author whose editors may be tempted to fly to this unitarian heresy. Most of his poems depend mainly upon the posthumous edition of 1633; but there are also many earlier manuscripts, of inferior authority as a whole (they are not the poet's autograph); and the later editions, which, as they include new poems, are not mere reprints, present variants which do not always seem due either to negligence or to conjecture. Such readings must be considered when the edition of 1633 is corrupt or doubtful, as it often is. To take one edition and ignore the rest because that edition is the best is no more defensible than to use one manuscript only of an ancient author because it is in general the most faithful. Yet since Donne is a poet not only obscure but often wantonly perverse, the decision whether specious variations come from a good manuscript source or from the ingenuity or negligence of an editor or printer, will be always doubtful, and sometimes impossible. The text of 1633 we know to have been copied, however ill, from a good manuscript. The tendency to prefer the later and easier reading has given currency to versions which are not Donne, but Donne made smooth.

Boswell's *Journal of a Tour to the Hebrides* was carefully corrected by the author for the second and third editions. The third is the edition which he himself cites in the *Life of Johnson*, and it is obviously authoritative. Dr. Birkbeck Hill accordingly discarded the first and second editions; and in one place corrected a misprint by conjecture which he might have corrected by reference to the first edition. This is a vicious principle. When the variations between the first and third editions are examined in detail, it is found that, though a great majority of the changes are clearly Boswell's, some are certainly the printer's and a few are doubtful. Johnson 'was very severe on a lady, whose name was mentioned. He said he would have her sent to St. Kilda.' (The reference was to another lady who actually had been marooned on St. Kilda, and who had been talked of the day before.) The third edition has 'would have sent her'. This is less probable in itself, and it is most unlikely that Boswell made the change. In another place the first edition has 'will be pleased', the second 'will be please', the third 'will please'. Our unitarians are here committed to the view that it is more probable that Boswell altered 'be pleased' to 'please' than that the printer of the third edition, finding 'be please' in his copy, corrected it by omitting 'be'. 'Of these trifles enough.'

The works of later writers were published under more favourable conditions than were Shakespeare's or Donne's, and leave less room for conjecture; but conjecture is never inadmissible, and emendations may sometimes be probable. Johnson's rule 'always to turn the old text on every side, and try if there be any interstice, through which light can find its way', is sound; and in a writer 'so licentious as Shakespeare' few emendations can ever be considered certain. Less irregular writers, though their text may be less corrupt, may sometimes be corrected with greater confidence. That the text should stand, if it can be made to yield a meaning, is not always true. In Johnson's *Journey to the Western Islands* is this sentence: 'To disarm part of the Highlands, could give no reasonable occasion of complaint. Every Government must be allowed the power of taking away the treason that is lifted against it.' It cannot be said to be impossible that Johnson wrote this; but when it is considered that the expression is awkward, and therefore not Johnsonian; that the book contains some dozen palpable errors, all obviously due to a misreading of the manuscript which the author did not detect; and that 'treaſson' in Johnson's handwriting is very close to 'weapon'—it becomes more probable that the text is wrong than that it is right.[1] In the same book we read: 'Voluntary solitude was the great art of propitiation, by which crimes were effaced and conscience was appeased'. Other writers might call solitude an art, but hardly Johnson; 'act of propitiation' is a known formula, and the confusion of *r* and *c* was exceedingly common.[2] Even in the eighteenth and nineteenth centuries literature has been produced in conditions favourable to corruption. When Johnson wrote his *Rambler* the printer's devil was at the door and took the copy away as it was written. The present writer knows nothing of the text of the *Rambler*, except that in

[1] The writer had before him a copy of the first edition which lacked the *Errata*. This correction is there anticipated.

[2] In Johnson's note on *Henry V*, III. v. 40, it is said that a catalogue of misspelt French names is unaltered 'since the sense of the authour is not aſſerted'. Read 'affected'.

all editions 'temerity' for 'timidity', or 'timidity' for 'temerity' has made nonsense of one of Johnson's periods; but he should expect to find the original issue, at least, not free from error.

The most satisfactory emendation, though not the most gratifying to its author, is that in which not a letter is changed. Such is the ὂν καὶ μὴ ὄν which Bullen disinterred from 'oncaimion' (or some such Roman gibberish) in *Faustus*; the later editions made it 'œconomy'. Such is Macaulay's restoration to grammar of the first page of *Persuasion* by the alteration of a comma.

The present writer claims to have restored dramatic propriety to a place in *Pride and Prejudice*. In the second chapter the words 'When is your next ball to be, Lizzy?' appear at the end of a sentence spoken by Kitty Bennet. It is absurdly improbable that Kitty should be in need of such information. But her father, who had spoken just before, doubtless was ignorant of the date, and he had a reason for wanting to know. The speech can be given to him by a change which is hardly a change; for the word 'when' begins a line, and will begin a new speech if it is shifted to the right by a fraction of an inch.

> Were it not better done, as others use,
> To sport with Amaryllis in the shade
> Or with the tangles of Neaera's hair?

As these lines are commonly read, there is an awkwardness (pedantically called a zeugma) in the collocation of 'sport with Amaryllis' and 'sport with the tangles'; neither 'sport' nor 'with' has quite the same shade of meaning in the two phrases. If 'with' be read to rhyme with 'scythe' (it is not necessary to write it 'withe') both sense and metre are improved.

The writer cannot refrain from quoting an *aperçu* of a learned friend, which is, he believes, still unpublished. There is a line in Marlowe, 'Our Pythagoras' Metempsychosis', which seems unmetrical. By supposing Marlowe to have pronounced Greek as it is pronounced in Greece today, and was often pronounced then, this critic produces a 'mighty line':

Our Pythagóras' Metempsýchosis.

Emendations more temerarious than these will sometimes occur. Sweeping changes are not often worth hazarding, because in books printed when they were first written it is unlikely that the text of the first edition has been corrupted more than once. But in editing Shakespeare and his contemporaries 'conjectural criticism', says Johnson, 'demands more than humanity possesses'. Yet 'the peril must not be avoided, nor the difficulty refused'.

The credibility of an emendation must be judged by estimating the probability of the corruption assumed as well as the propriety of the change proposed. Sir Walter Raleigh somewhere says that the change from 'way of life' to 'may of life' 'makes Shakespeare write like Pope'. But is there anything very unlike Shakespeare in 'my *May* of *life*'? Sir Walter rightly holds that in Shakespeare anything that has a meaning should not be lightly changed. But when it is remembered that an italic *m* inverted is very like a *w*, and that turned letters are very common, the probability of the corruption is so great, and the change so slight, that the emendation deserves consideration. If it is bad in itself, *cadit quaestio*. It is *a priori* probable that corruptions exist in Shakespeare which have never been and will never be suspected, because the lost word has been supplanted by another which makes sense. There is nothing improbable about 'Vaulting ambition which o'erleaps itself'. But when once 'sell' has been suggested, and the probability that 'sell' would be altered to 'self' is considered, it becomes difficult to be sure that 'self' is right. The late Professor Bywater used to say, 'I wish I had made that emendation'.

The practice of conjecture is pleasant, but like other pleasant things is dangerous. A commentator is apt to think that every line needs a note; Johnson said of Warburton that he 'had a rage for saying something when there was nothing to be said'. An emender is apt to acquire a rage for correcting when there is nothing to correct. Yet an editor is bound to satisfy himself that his text makes sense and grammar; and it is remarkable how the eye will mislead, and an inattentive mind acquiesce in imperfect meaning. Printers employ trained readers, because authors do not see small mistakes. They read the right word when the print has the wrong one. In reading Johnson's *Journey* the present aspirant three times missed the word 'reruined', because the catchword on the previous page had told him to expect 'required'. He would perhaps have acquiesced in 'treason' and 'art', if his vigilance had not been excited by 'thirteenth of August' when he knew from Boswell that it must be 'thirtieth'.

A useful and amusing exercise is to correct a reprint of a book, the most careless that can be found, and compare the emendations with a sound text. Vanity will sometimes be hurt; but sagacity will often be rewarded. The writer has seen the late Dr. Verrall's copies of *Jane Austen* (modern reprint) and compared his marginal suggestions with the original editions. Some of them seemed to be unnecessary; of those which seemed probable, almost all were found to be the readings of the first edition.

The privilege of emendation has been too little exercised by modern editors of English classics; but it is true that emendation is only a small part of their duties. The chief is restoration. In this pious work Johnson was a pioneer. 'In this modest industry I have not been unsuccessful. I have rescued many lines from the violations of temerity.' The editors of the later Folios, and such men as Rowe, confounded emendation with what Johnson justly calls adulteration. They 'regulated' the text to suit their own views of propriety and elegance. In lesser matters they made changes as a matter of routine. When they altered 'Enter the two Bishops' to 'Enter the two Archbishops' (because they were Canterbury and York), and 'exit' to 'exeunt', when more than one person left the stage, they did not know they were doing wrong. A witty scholar commenting on this last piece of pedantry remarked, 'We do not say, Smith and Jones made an *affidaverunt*'. We now know the Folio, carelessly printed as it is, to be much better than Johnson supposed: 'I considered the punctuation as wholly in my power'; we now know that it is in the main sound. Johnson thought it permissible to 'smoothe the cadence, or regulate the measure' by transpositions and omissions from which we now shrink. Even the rearrangement of the lines to suit the blank verse has been called in question. There is a place in *Macbeth* where, in the Folio, the lines as printed do not scan; but the famous directions, 'Knock, Knock, Knock' are disposed on the page with such striking dramatic effect that it is hard to believe the arrangement accidental. What if it should follow Shakespeare's autograph?

The petulance and self-conceit of editors have in the past been notorious. The controversies of scholars are still sometimes more acrimonious than the dignity of their subject should warrant. But the editor of to-day is of necessity a humbler person than his predecessors. In the criticism and exegesis of modern, and even of ancient, literature, most of the obscurities that admit of enlightenment, and most of the corruptions that admit of correction, have been explained or mended. There is still room for labour, but not much room for fame. Yet the diligence of editors is still deserving of respect. To restore, and maintain in its integrity, the text of our great writers is a pious duty, and it is a surprisingly difficult task. An editor's business is to arrive at the truth, or as near it as he can; and to do this it is often necessary to spend time and labour on very small matters. 'To an editor', says Johnson, 'nothing is a trifle by which his authour is obscured.' It is often his misfortune that he cannot but seem to come between his author and the reader's enjoyment, by labouring on 'evanescent atoms'. Because he seems to magnify atoms he is not to be supposed unaware of their insignificance. It is true that good judges of literature often make very bad editors; but it is unfair to conclude that an editor who knows his business, and sticks to it, is insensible of higher matters. On this, as on so many topics of criticism, the 'Preface to Shakespeare' has the last word:

> The greater part of readers, instead of blaming us for passing trifles, will wonder that on mere trifles so much labour is expended, with such importance of debate, and such solemnity of diction. To these I answer with confidence, that they are judging of an art which they do not understand; yet cannot much reproach them with their ignorance, nor promise that they would become in general, by learning criticism, more useful, happier, or wiser.

G. M. YOUNG
1882–

A Word for Gabriel Harvey

Life and Letters, June 1930

MYTHS die hard, and a myth which has once formed round a minor figure in history may live for ever, because no one will take the trouble to dissolve it. Gabriel Harvey was a small personage in his life and might very well have been forgotten. But the literary historians will not leave him in oblivion. He has been labelled and laid up for reference. Harvey, G.: pedant: tried to make Spenser write the *Faerie Queene* in hexameters.

Todd started it. Hallam swallowed it. Kingsley gave it currency in a brilliant chapter of *Westward Ho!* It is repeated from one textbook to another.

> Nor can the Muse defend
> Her Son.

The University of Cambridge still believes it. In the Third Series of his *Studies in Literature*—a book full of learned pastime—Sir Arthur Quiller-Couch writes:

'Examine the correspondence between Spenser and Gabriel Harvey and you will see how nearly the *Faerie Queene* came to be attempted in hexameters.'

'I think, Sir, you will find it a good rule always to verify your references.' The correspondence is accessible: it was last reprinted in Professor de Sélincourt's Oxford Spenser, 1912. And any one who refers to it will find to his surprise, first, that there is no evidence that Spenser ever thought of writing the *Faerie Queene* in hexameters, and, second, that if he did, it was Harvey who laughed and bullied him out of his fancy. The proper entry would be: Harvey, G.: acute and independent critic; saved Spenser from wasting his time on classical metres.

The facts are so clear that it is at first sight

difficult to understand how the legend ever grew up. The reproduction of classical metres in English is a quite legitimate pastime. There are Anglo-Saxon hexameters. There were plenty going about Cambridge in the days of Ascham. One pair was handed down for several years as a model.

> All travellérs do gladly report great praise of Ulysses
> For that he knéw mănў mén's mannérs and saw many cities.

Harvey tried his hand, and suggested that Spenser should try his. Spenser, who was occupied with other models, Chaucer and du Bellay, declined. But Harvey discovered that the hexameter in English was not a serious metre: it was good enough for colloquial and satirical poetry, but not for an elevated theme. When he aspired to celebrate the Queen in Royal Cantos he followed Ariosto. When he wanted to satirize the Italianate Englishman—the stock theme of Elizabethan topical verse—he did it in hexameters.

> French Camarick ruffs, deep with a whiteness, starched to the purpose:
> Delicate in speech, quaint in array, conceited in all points:
> In all courtly guiles, a passing singular odd man.

Hexameters which are very much in the manner of Clough at his liveliest:

> Rome disappoints me much: I hardly as yet understand, but
> Rubbishy seems the word that most exactly would suit it.

Meanwhile Spenser had come under a new and more seductive influence. He had entered the Leicester House circle and succumbed to the fascination which Sidney seems to have exercised over every man, except Oxford, who came near him. Sidney was badly infected with the classical mania. He had lived in Paris: he spoke French to perfection: he may have known Baïf: he certainly knew about his experiments. At this time—in 1578 and 1579—while Spenser was working at the *Shepherd's Calendar*, Sidney was turning out hexameters, pentameters, asclepiads and hendecasyllables by the hundred. Spenser was carried away and submitted the results of his new studies with some complacency to Harvey.

Harvey fell on them tooth and nail. He had scholarship to back his blows. He told Spenser that, unless he proposed to pronounce virginals, virjnálls, his iambics

Unhappy verse, the witness of my unhappy state

did not even scan. As for his *Epithalamion Thamesis*, he had tried the experiment and found that, with very little prompting, his young brother John could do that kind of thing just as well.

This is where Todd, a very dull man, went astray, and led a multitude after him. He published part of the correspondence, with his own deductions. Scott complained that he had not given the whole. If he had the myth would never have come into existence. Scott, at any rate, knew a joke when he saw one, and Harvey's jokes were certainly not subtle.

Here are some of the hexameters which John Harvey produced between breakfast and dinner:

> While your barns are fat, while coffers stuffed with abundance,
> Friends will abound: if barn wax bare, then adieu Sir, a God's name.
> See ye the doves? They feed and breed in gorgeous houses.
> Scarce one dove doth love to remain in ruinous houses.

And here is Todd's scholium:

> It is the production, it seems, of his pupil in this art of versifying: which however he transcribes with apparent ecstasy and complacently adds, in respect to the barbarous transformation and to other specimens of his disciple's rapid progress 'not passing a word or two corrected by me'.

Even Professor de Sélincourt, who is fairer to Harvey than most critics, speaks of his 'enthusiastic praise' of Spenser's classical experiments. If this is praise! And this is not all. In another set Spenser is introduced in the Bishop of Rochester's garden addressing a laurel tree:

> What shall I call this tree? A laurel? O bonny laurel!
> Needs to thy leaves must I bow my knees and vail my bonetto.
> Who but thou the renown of prince and princely Poeta?
> T'one for crown, for garland t'other thanketh Apollo.

Fifteen lines of this elicit an answering groan from the victim:

> But what saith Daphne? *Non omnis dormio*, worse luck.

It was rough fooling, but it was effective. Spenser wrote no more hexameters and the *Epithalamion* was recast as the *Marriage of Thames and Medway*.

The oddest thing about the myth is this. Apart from his rather clumsy satire, Harvey stated his objections to classical scansion in English with perfect lucidity and seriousness. In the mass of bewilderment and borrowed erudition which make up the greater part of Mr. Gregory Smith's *Elizabethan Critical Essays*, Harvey's few paragraphs are conspicuous for their good sense. The problem that was exercising Leicester House was the second syllable of *Carpenter*. Dr. Drant's Rules, improved by Sidney, made it long. What was it, Spenser asks, in Harvey's Rules? Harvey's reply was conclusive. A syllable is as long or short as 'God and his English people' have made it. 'It is the vulgar and natural mother prosody that alone worketh the feat, as the only supreme founder and reformer of Position, Diphthong, Orthography or whatsoever else.'

If this is pedantry, a little more of it would be welcome in prosodic discussions. But poor Harvey can do nothing right. 'At Cambridge', Professor de Sélincourt writes, 'Chaucer was widely read, but Harvey at least would not have regarded him as a fit poetic model.' Harvey adored Chaucer, and his 'brave fine sweet poetry'. And it ought always to be remembered that Harvey came safely through the hardest test that can be put to a critic who is also an unsuccessful author: he could appreciate his contemporaries. He was the first critic to notice that the peculiar grace of the Spenserian stanza lay in the final Alexandrine, and who else was prepared to see, in 1600, that Shakespeare was not only a best-seller but a poet to be taken seriously?

===

CHARLES WILLIAMS
1886–1945

Robert Bridges

Poetry at Present, 1930

Of the fourteen laureates from—and including —Dryden, if we take him as the first, some five (if we include Southey) have been notable poets. With the exception of Dryden himself and of Wordsworth none of them has been a greater than Mr. Robert Bridges. Tennyson is not to be considered a greater, for his verbal achievement is no finer, and his philosophic (if the two can be divided) is very definitely less. None of them has contributed a greater mass of lyric beauty to our literature.

It may very well be held that Mr. Bridges is not only a lyric poet; he has written dramas, a sonnet-sequence, a long narrative poem, and of the volume *New Poems* at least four are more in the nature of philosophic poems than of lyric. But as his lyric verse is more popular, so also it contains so much of intellect that attention may, in such a short tribute as this, be very well concentrated upon it.

Mr. Bridges has been said, by various good judges, to be our greatest lyric poet since Shelley. He was born twenty-two years after Shelley died. But the poetic difference between him and Shelley is immense. There remains something not quite unfair in Matthew Arnold's famous description—'an ineffectual angel beating in the void his luminous wings in vain'. The angel may, merely by virtue of his being an angel, be not entirely ineffectual; the void may be rather an abyss of poetical ether. But Shelley, of all our poets, seems peculiarly unattached to the earth— except in *Œdipus in Thebes* and a few fragments— and peculiarly impatient of intellectual study. A philosophy is to be found in him, but it is not convincing in its poetic intensity. Reason interprets that inspiration too feebly; abstractions become more abstract and aerial and walk less certainly upon our earth.

Mr. Bridges's poetry produces exactly the opposite effect. It is perhaps not without significance that he abandoned a medical career for poetry. For the Laureate is one of the very few living poets who when they speak of abstractions seem to speak of living and significant things. To speak of Beauty, with that capital B, has become almost the defining habit of the minor poet. Mr. de la Mare has dreamed of her, Mr. Abercrombie has cried to her, each convincingly. But neither of these poets has spoken with more assured quietness or with more certain knowledge than Mr. Bridges; neither of them more persuades the reader of the real existence of that Beauty.

And what is true of Beauty is true also of those other abstractions—Virtue, Honour, Truth. What has given to Mr. Bridges's verse this singular prerogative?

Two things—which are indeed one: the concrete instances of these abstractions which he has given us in so many places, and the general quality of his verse.

To give examples of the first would necessitate continued and lengthy quotation. They are to be found in every anthology; they include the famous *London Snow*, *Asian Birds*, and such poems.

But it is not beauty—of landscape or human figure or great poetry or other art, 'the Virgilian muse' or 'the gaiety of Mozart'—that furnishes the chief hidden theme of this verse, nor is it beauty (merely so undefined) that is its peculiar quality. It is rather beauty in restraint; still more it is the strength of beauty in restraint; or, to press it one farther step, it is the consciousness of the strength of beauty in restraint. Dull as the phrase is, and unworthy to approach the high loveliness of this Muse, all four terms could be justified.

The deliberate act by which Mr. Bridges laid aside the profession of medicine for (what to him must have seemed) the equally arduous profession of poetry was a symbol of his general approach to poetry in all its ways. The deliberate and learned interest which he has taken in the manners and habits of prosody, in the Society for Pure English, in handwriting and phonetics, continue to express that approach. His mind seems to know all the time what it is doing; it judges seriously, if lightly; it is aware of its rejections as well as of its acceptances, even when those rejections appear so natural that almost any other poet would have forgotten them altogether, or perhaps been hardly aware that they existed. Joy, for example, which, in so many poets, seems but an accident of their mood, is here a conscious choice, almost a duty, and even, sometimes, an effort. That some of the finest of his lyrics rise into an attitude of pure delight is no contradiction of this; rather, it is its reward. 'Man's duty is to be happy,' said Dr. Johnson; Mr. Bridges's verse might almost be said to have fulfilled that duty after many a conflict and in spite of many an adversary. That it had an original leaning that way is to say no more than that Mr. Hardy's has had a leaning towards a thwarted happiness or Mr. Kipling's towards a fatalistic morality. But Mr. Bridges omits the consideration of evil fortune less than Hardy omits the consideration of good fortune. 'The master Reason' rides always on the right hand of his Muse when she goes through the cruel habitations of the earth, and directs her attentive glance not only to them but also to the satisfying stars. That the stars have been by now a little touched by the literary taint makes the metaphor only the more just. For a great deal of the happiness in this poetry arises from the recollection of great art.

> Days that the thought of grief refuse,
> Days that are one with human art,
> Worthy of the Virgilian muse,
> Fit for the gaiety of Mozart—

these are the terms in which he praises the 'brighter days' of the sea in one poem; and in another (*Dejection*) he warns his soul, 'revolving hopeless strife,

> Pointing at hindrance, and the bare
> Painful escapes of fitful life . . .

> 'O soul, be patient: thou shalt find
> A little matter mend all this;
> Some strain of music to thy mind,
> Some praise for skill not spent amiss.'

But this too, since literature nowadays is never unselfconscious, accentuates the inward and retired deliberation of this admirable verse. However frequent, however exact, the delight in external things may be, it is within that such delight justifies itself by reason and virtue.

This deliberation accentuates the momentary nature of Joy which is in certain of the lyrics so intensely expressed.

> Haste on, my joys! your treasure lies
>   In swift, unceasing flight.
> O haste, for while your beauty flies
>   I seize your full delight.

Poets enough have lamented a fugitive joy; not many have realized, as Mr. Bridges has done, that such a flight is indeed (in our present mode of being) of its very nature—that, without it, Joy apparently could not be at all. To such a dogma speculation can offer objections enough; it is, beyond all speculation, confirmed by experience. And it is from profound experience that this verse arises. In a great poem (No. 13

of the *Shorter Poems,* Book III) the gospel, and almost the mysticism, of Joy is expressed.

> Joy, sweetest lifeborn joy, where dost thou dwell?
> Upon the formless moments of our being
> Flitting, to mock the ear that heareth well,
> To escape the trainèd eye that strains in seeing,
> Or home in our creations, to withstand
> Black-wingèd death, that slays the making hand?
>
> The making mind, that must untimely perish
> Amidst its work which time may not destroy,
> The beauteous forms which man shall love to cherish,
> The glorious songs that combat earth's annoy?
> Thou dost dwell here, I know, divinest Joy:
> But they who built thy towers fair and strong,
> Of all that toil, feel most of care and wrong.
>
> Sense is so tender, O and hope so high,
> That common pleasures mock their hope and sense;
> And swifter than doth lightning from the sky
> The ecstasy they pine for flashes hence,
> Leaving the darkness and the woe immense,
> Wherewith it seems no thread of life was woven,
> Nor doth the track remain where once 'twas cloven.
>
> And heaven and all the stable elements
> That guard God's purpose mock us, though the mind
> Be spent in searching: for his old intents
> We see were never for our joy designed:
> They shine as doth the bright sun on the blind,
> Or like his pensioned stars, that hymn above
> His praise, but not toward us, that God is Love.
>
> For who so well hath wooed the maiden hours
> As quite to have won the worth of their rich show,
> To rob the night of mystery, or the flowers
> Of their sweet delicacy ere they go?

Nay, even the dear occasion when we know,
We miss the joy, and on the gliding day
The special glories float and pass away.

Only life's common plod: still to repair
The body and the thing which perisheth:
The soil, the smutch, the toil and ache and wear,
The grinding enginry of blood and breath,
Pain's random darts, the heartless spade of death;
All is but grief, and heavily we call
On the last terror for the end of all.

Then comes the happy moment: not a stir
In any tree, no portent in the sky:
The morn doth neither hasten nor defer,
The morrow hath no name to call it by,
But life and joy are one,—we know not why,—
As though our very blood long breathless lain
Had tasted of the breath of God again.

And having tasted it I speak of it,
And praise him thinking how I trembled then
When his touch strengthened me, as now I sit
In wonder, reaching out beyond my ken,
Reaching to turn the day back, and my pen
Urging to tell a tale which told would seem
The witless phantasy of them that dream.

But O most blessèd truth, for truth thou art,
Abide thou with me till my life shall end.
Divinity hath surely touched my heart;
I have possessed more joy than earth can lend:
I may attain what time shall never spend.
Only let not my duller days destroy
The memory of thy witness and my joy.

But Joy, so desired, so experienced, so hoped, is not his only subject, or rather it has another name, and that name was given it in the title of his early sonnet-sequence, *The Growth of Love*.

Within that sequence are contained many implicit or explicit declarations of his temperament, his will, and his aim: for example, the lines—

> Nor surer am I water hath the skill
> To quench my thirst

is almost a definition, by its sound and simile, of his own verse—so cool, so simple, is it. So also the fifteenth sonnet may be quoted here because it seems to describe so well the sort of mind which the reader may conjecture lies behind that verse.

Who builds a ship must first lay down the keel
Of health, whereto the ribs of mirth are wed:
And knit, with beams and knees of strength, a bed
For decks of purity, her floor and ceil.
Upon her masts, Adventure, Pride, and Zeal,
To fortune's wind the sails of purpose spread:
And at the prow make figured maidenhead
O'erride the seas and answer to the wheel.

And let him deep in memory's hold have stor'd
Water of Helicon: and let him fit
The needle that doth true with heaven accord:
Then bid her crew, love, diligence and wit,
With justice, courage, temperance come aboard,
And at her helm the master reason sit.

Love, diligence, wit, justice, courage, temperance, reason—these are the qualities Mr. Bridges praises and recommends to the young adventurer. They are, transmuted into poetry, the qualities of his verse; they are the analysed elements of its beauty as it praises Beauty. They are the method of his experience, and the things his genius chooses to experience are selected by them. Besides great art, a few things are pre-eminent in his poetic knowledge—the English landscape, man in society, Hellenism, solitude, piety. These things, communicated by those virtuous Pleiades named above, cause a profound and still delight. But it is a delight which may require a certain similarity of temperament or a certain prolonged discipline before it can be accepted, especially from a reader used to more violent effects. Violence attends on the steps of a number of our poets, and, so long as it is only allowed to act at its master's bidding, even violence may have its work to do. But it is an uncertain slave, and one whom Mr. Bridges would never spend a farthing to buy or shelter.

One of the best examples of his peculiar strength is one of the finest love-poems of the last century. *Awake, my heart, to be loved: awake, awake—*

> Awake, the land is scattered with light, and see,
> Uncanopied sleep is flying from field and tree:
> And blossoming boughs of April in laughter shake;
> Awake, O heart, to be loved, awake, awake!

The stanza is carried on its wide and awakening vowels. How many poets have welcomed morning in their love-songs, but never before had we seen how, in that world which is neither wholly mental nor wholly actual, being poetry's, never before had we known that sleep fled being uncanopied, nor how, among the new shadows, light is flung over the land, nor felt all this as a simile of awakening and hastening love. 'Uncanopied' is one of the most unusual epithets Mr. Bridges's temperance allows him; as a general rule his adjectives are as near the expected as a poet's could be. But they are always there to do their business, never from mere idleness or the needs of the line. 'Sunny hair', 'stout roots', 'branchèd trees', 'red roofs', 'whirling snow', 'delicious notes', these descriptions are there precisely because it is those separate facts which make beautiful whatever it is we see.

His diction, his feeling for words, is a part of his whole 'duteous chastity'; their potentiality in his verse is that rather of putting off their secular inheritance than expressing it. They mean what they say; that they mean no more than they say is a part of their exquisite simplicity. They are therefore peculiarly fit to convey those landscapes which are so distinct a part of this verse, the visions of 'England in the peace and delight of her glory'. No month of all the year is alien, nor is it easy to say that any month is a more welcome guest to this full-hearted host than any other.

But 'uncanopied sleep' has to fly from our minds yet more completely than in a recognition of the just diction of passionate love or sensitive country-side if we are to appreciate Mr. Bridges's verse properly. It is a marvellous training for the ear. This is no place to discuss his classical prosody, his book on Milton's prosody, or his scazons; they would form a too specialist dispute. But poem after poem in the *Shorter Poems* contains the most delicate rhythms, the most exquisite play of pauses, stresses, and variations. His sonnets, for a gross example, are not poems more or less accommodated to fourteen lines; they are sonnets. In them, perhaps more evidently than in the lyrics, the various long traditions of English verse are to be recognized. It is an additional pleasure to discern, for example, how the metaphysical note sounds in Mr. Bridges's own peculiar harmony; how, instead of that manner issuing in a complex and heightened darkness, it becomes a quiet and heightened lucidity. It is a quiet which is almost too profound for most of us to reach or trust. One sonnet begins

> For beauty being the best of all we know,

and it is the implicit challenge offered by such a line to all the easy talk and cheap professions of beauty which go so much abroad in the world that Mr. Bridges's admirers find their own admiration challenged. It will not do, for all its quietness, to take this verse too lightly. It satisfies but it also inquires; its repose is as militant as (it is known) Mr. Bridges can, on occasion, be. No poetry of our day is less pretentious in its doctrine; none is more profoundly doctrinal in its very being. Beauty and love and joy and the rest are here certainly states of existence, but they are also virtues. If the poetry goes often in silver, it is the silver of a natural sanctity, the reward of a persevering and industrious faith. It is as if the genius of Mr. Bridges had determined to know all things in beauty, and as if beauty, here discovered and there imposed, had at last reconciled him to all things.

> Ah heavenly joy! But who hath ever heard,
> Who hath seen joy, or who shall ever find
> Joy's language? There is neither speech nor word
> Nought but itself to teach it to mankind.

Well, perhaps not. But this voice at least might persuade many minds to be still and wait for the full revelation.

End Piece

Sunlight and clear air; the clear air of night—
  is this then the air of earth or heaven, this joy,
    strength with no vehemence, sweetness with no cloy,
but the very sweetness climbing an airy height,
taking again therefrom its heartening flight
  to us whom, hearing that strain, the world's annoy
    may vex with invasion but never so destroy
as that such gay everlasting new delight
dwells not within our minds, 'mid the sanctities
  which Imagination hath for the outer form
    of wisdom made; there paces a courteous Muse,
  her mouth discreet, her brow smooth with the news
of earth's storm subdued and heaven without a storm,
strong-minded, strong-hearted, healthfully so at ease.

T. S. ELIOT
1888–

Johnson's 'London' and 'The Vanity of Human Wishes'

Introduction to the Haslewood Books Edition, 1930

THERE is an essay to be written on the quotations which Sir Walter Scott used for the chapter headings of his novels, to illustrate the wide reading and critical good taste of that novelist. It is a great many years ago—about thirty years ago—that I was struck by a quotation of four lines; I cannot now remember at what chapter of which of Scott's novels it is placed:

> His fall was destin'd to a barren strand,
> A petty fortress, and a dubious hand;
> He left the name, at which the world grew pale,
> To point a moral, or adorn a tale.

It was not for a good many years after, that I read *The Vanity of Human Wishes*, but the impression which the whole poem made upon me was only a confirmation of the impression which the four lines had made upon me long before. These lines, especially the first two, with their just inevitable sequence of *barren, petty*, and *dubious*, still seem to me among the finest that have ever been written in that particular idiom.

It is as dangerous to generalize about the poetry of the eighteenth century as about that of any other age; for it was, like any other age, an age of transition. We are accustomed to make a rough tripartite division between the poetry of the age of Pope, the poetry of sentimental philosophizing—Thomson, Young, Cowper—and the early Romantic movement. What really happened is that after Pope there was no one who thought and felt nearly enough like Pope to be able to use his language quite successfully; but a good many second-rate writers tried to write something like it, unaware of the fact that the change of sensibility demanded a change of idiom. Sensibility alters from generation to generation in everybody, whether we will or no; but expression is only altered by a man of genius. A great many second-rate poets, in fact, are second rate just for this reason, that they have not the sensitiveness and consciousness to perceive that they feel differently from the preceding generation, and therefore must use words differently. In the eighteenth century there are a good many second-rate poets: and mostly they are second rate because they were incompetent to find a style of writing for themselves, suited to the matter they wanted to talk about and the way in which they apprehended this matter.

In such a period the poets who are still worth reading may be of two kinds: those who, however imperfectly, attempted innovations in idiom, and those who were just conservative enough in sensibility to be able to devise an interesting variation on the old idiom. The originality of Gray and Collins consists in their adaptation of an Augustan style to an eighteenth-century sensibility. The originality of Goldsmith consists in his having the old and the new in such just proportion that there is no conflict; he is Augustan and also sentimental and rural without discordance. Of all the eighteenth-century poets, Johnson is the nearest to a die-hard. And of all the eighteenth-century poets, Goldsmith and Johnson deserve fame because they used the form of Pope beautifully, without ever being mere imitators. And from the point of view of the artisan of verse, their kind of originality is as remarkable as any other: indeed, to be original with the *minimum* of alteration, is sometimes more distinguished than to be original with the *maximum* of alteration.

Certain qualities are to be expected of any type of good verse at any time; we may say the qualities which good verse shares with good prose. Hardly any good poet in English has written *bad* prose; and some English poets have been among the greatest of English prose writers. The finest prose writer of Shakespeare's time was, I think, Shakespeare himself; Milton and Dryden were among the greatest prose writers of their times. Wordsworth and Coleridge may be cited, and Keats; and Shelley—not I think in his correspondence, but certainly in his *Defence of Poetry*. This is not a sign of versatility but of unity. For there are qualities essential to good prose which are essential to good verse as well; and we may say positively with Mr. Ezra Pound, that verse must be at least as well written as prose. We may even say that the originality of some poets has consisted in their finding a way of saying in verse what no one else had been able to say except in prose written or spoken. Such is the originality of Donne, who, though employing an elaborate metric and an uncommon vocabulary, yet manages to maintain a tone of direct informal address. The talent of Dryden is exactly the same: the difference is only that the speech which he uses is that of a more formal age. Donne makes poetry out of a learned but colloquial dialogue speech, Dryden out of the prose of political oratory; and Pope out of the most polished drawing-room manner. And of Goldsmith and Johnson we can say the same; their verse is poetry partly because it has the virtues of good prose.

Those who condemn or ignore *en bloc* the poetry of the eighteenth century on the ground that it is 'prosaic' are stumbling over an uncertainty of meaning of the word 'prosaic' to arrive at exactly the wrong conclusion. One does not need to examine a great deal of the inferior verse of the eighteenth century to realize that the trouble with it is that it is not prosaic enough. We are inclined to use 'prosaic' as meaning not only 'like prose', but as 'lacking poetic beauty'—and the Oxford and every other dictionary give us warrant for such use. Only, we ought to distinguish between poetry which is like *good* prose, and poetry which is like *bad* prose. And even so, I believe more prose is bad because it is like bad poetry, than poetry is bad because it is like bad prose. And to have the virtues of good prose is the first and minimum requirement of good poetry.

If you look at the bad verse of any age, you will find most of it lacking in the virtues of prose. When there is a period of good verse, it has often been preceded by a period in which verse was bad because it was too poetic, too artificial; and it is very commonly followed by such another period. The development of blank verse in the hands of Shakespeare and some of his contemporaries was the work of adapting a medium which to begin with was almost intractably poetic, so that it could carry the burdens and exhibit the subtleties of prose; and they accomplished this before prose was highly developed. The work of Donne, in a lesser form, was the same. It has prose virtues, and the heavy toil of his minor imitators was wholly to degrade the idiom of Donne into a lifeless verse convention. Speech meanwhile was changing, and Dryden appeared to cleanse the language of verse and once more bring it back to the prose order. For this reason he is a great poet.

The idiom of the Augustan age could not last, for the age itself could not last. But so positive was the culture of that age, that for many years the ablest writers were still naturally in sympathy with it; and it crushed a number of smaller men who felt differently but did not dare to face the fact, and who poured their new wine—always thin, but sometimes of good flavour—into the old bottles. Yet the influence of Dryden and Pope over the middle of the eighteenth century is by no means so great, or so noxious, as has been supposed. A good part of the dreariest verse of the time is written under the shadow of Milton.

> Far in the watery waste, where his broad wave
> From world to world the vast Atlantic rolls,
> On from the piny shores of Labrador
> To frozen Thule east, her airy height
> Aloft to heaven remotest Kilda lifts.
>
> MALLET: *Amyntor and Theodora.*

> Thus far of beauty and the pleasing forms
> Which man's untutored fancy, from the scenes
> Imperfect of this ever changing world
> Creates; and views, enamoured.
>
> AKENSIDE: *Pleasures of the Imagination.*

But besides this Miltonic stuff, which is respectable only because Cowper, Thomson, and Young made this line the vehicle for reflection and for observation of nature which prepared the way for Wordsworth; and besides the innumerable Odes, of which none but Gray's and Collins's are remembered, there was a considerable output of five-foot couplets of which one can only say that this form of verse is hardly more unsuitable for what the man had to say than any other would have been. Of such is the *Botanic Garden* and its competitors.

> Who that beholds the summer's glistening swarms,
> Ten thousand thousand gaily gilded forms,
> In violet dance of mixed rotation play,
> Bask in the beam, and beautify the day ...
> BROOKE: *Universal Beauty.*

This is decadence. The eighteenth century in English verse is not, after Pope, Swift, Prior, and Gay, an age of courtly verse. It seems more like an age of retired country clergymen and schoolmasters. It is cursed with a Pastoral convention —Collins's Eclogues are bad enough, and those of Shenstone consummately dull—and a ruminative mind. And it is intolerably poetic. Instead of working out the proper form for its matter, when it has any, and informing verse with prose virtues, it merely applies the magniloquence of Milton or the neatness of Pope to matter which is wholly unprepared for it; so that what the writers have to say always appears surprised at the way in which they choose to say it.

In this rural, pastoral, meditative age Johnson is the most alien figure. Goldsmith is more a poet of his time, with his melting sentiment just saved by the precision of his language. But Johnson remains a townsman, if certainly not a courtier; a student of mankind not of natural history; a great prose writer; with no tolerance of swains and milkmaids. He has more in common in spirit with Crabbe than with any of his contemporaries; at the same time he is the last Augustan. He is in no way an imitator of Dryden or Pope; very close to them in idiom, he gives his verse a wholly personal stamp.

The two Satires which follow are Johnson's only exercises in this genre. *London* appeared in 1738; *The Vanity of Human Wishes* in 1749. To my mind the latter is the finer poem; but both of them seem to me to be among the greatest verse Satires of the English or any other language; and, so far as comparison is justifiable, I do not think that Juvenal, his model, is any better. They are *purer* satire than anything of Dryden or Pope, nearer in spirit to the Latin. For the satirist is in theory a stern moralist castigating the vices of his time or place; and Johnson has a better claim to this seriousness than either Pope or Dryden. In the hands of Dryden the satire becomes almost the lampoon; and Dryden had a special gift for farce. Pope also is more personal than the true satirist. In one way, Johnson goes back to an earlier tradition; however inferior as satires Marston's or even Hall's may be to Johnson's, they are surely much nearer to the spirit and intention of Juvenal than are those of Dryden or Pope. Dryden is, in the modern sense, humorous and witty; Pope is in the modern sense witty though not humorous; Johnson, neither humorous nor witty in this sense, has yet 'the proper wit of poetry' as the seventeenth century and the Augustan age had it also. I can better expose this by a few quotations than by a definition.

There mark what ills the scholar's life assail,
Toil, envy, want, the patron, and the jail.

Condemned a needy supplicant to wait,
While ladies interpose, and slaves debate.

Fate never wounds more deep the generous heart,
Than when a blockhead's insult points the dart.

Some fiery fop, with new commission vain,
Who sleeps on brambles till he kills his man;
Some frolick drunkard, reeling from a feast,
Provokes a broil, and stabs you for a jest.

The precision of such verse gives, I think, an immense satisfaction to the reader: he has said what he wanted to say, with that urbanity which contemporary verse would do well to study; and the satisfaction I get from such lines is what I call the *minimal* quality of poetry. There is much greater poetry than Johnson's; but after all, how little, how very little, good poetry there is anyway. And the kind of satisfaction these lines give me is something that I must have, at least, from any poetry in order to like it. It is the certainty, the ease with which he hits the bull's-eye every time, that makes Johnson a poet. The blundering assaults of his contemporary Churchill—a man of by no means poor abilities—do not make poetry; Churchill gives us an occasional right line, but never a right poem.

And the verse of Johnson has the good qualities of his own best prose, and of the best prose of his time. Bolingbroke, for instance, at his best, has some of the same merit.

Those who demand of poetry a day dream, or a metamorphosis of their own feeble desires and lusts, or what they believe to be 'intensity' of passion, will not find much in Johnson. He is like Pope and Dryden, Crabbe and Landor, a poet for those who want poetry and not something else, some stay for their own vanity. I sometimes think that our own time, with its elaborate equipment of science and psychological analysis, is even less fitted than the Victorian age to appreciate poetry as poetry. But if lines 189-220 of *The Vanity of Human Wishes* are not poetry, I do not know what is.

J. MIDDLETON MURRY
1889–

Pure Poetry

Countries of the Mind, 2nd Series, 1931

It is unlikely, let us hope because it is unnecessary, that there should ever be in this country the animated and even violent controversy concerning the nature of 'pure poetry' which broke out in France immediately after the Abbé Henri Bremond concluded his brilliant little lecture on that subject before the French Academy.[1] It was indeed provocative of the then latest and not the least distinguished of the 'forty' to utter so many heresies, to have talked, with the familiarity of

---

[1] *La Poésie Pure.* Par Henri Bremond et Robert de Souza; *Prière et Poésie.* Par Henri Bremond. (Paris: Grasset.)
Prayer and Poetry. By Henri Bremond. Translated by Algar Thorold. (Burns, Oates.)

genuine knowledge, of hurry, to have remembered the subtle de[x] poets, to have père Rapin, to have esta[bli]shed an affinity between the poetic and the m[ystic]al experience, and to have concluded with a [re]fashioning of Pater's famous dictum. There wa[s en]ough in the final paragraph to set the bygo[ne] immortals twittering in the shades. The mag[ic] of poetry was, he said:

Magie recueillante, comme parlent les mystiques, et qui nous invite à une quiétude, où nous n'avons plus qu'à nous laisser faire, mais activement, par un plus grand et meilleur que nous. La prose, une phosphorescence vive et voltigeante, qui nous attire loin de nous-mêmes. La poésie, un rappel de l'intérieur, un poids confus, disait Wordsworth, une chaleur sainte, disait Keats, un poids d'immortalité sur le cœur: *an awful warmth about my heart like a load of immortality.—Amor, Pondus.*—Ce poids, où veut-il nous précipiter, sinon vers ces augustes retraites où nous attend, où nous appelle une présence plus qu'humaine? S'il en faut croire Walter Pater, 'tous les arts aspirent à rejoindre la musique'. Non, ils aspirent tous, mais chacun par les magiques intermédiaires qui lui sont propres,—les mots; les notes; les couleurs; les lignes;— ils aspirent tous à rejoindre la prière.

Here, where we have no Academy to shock, no tradition of rationality to be offended, such a statement would pass perhaps without serious notice and certainly without serious hostility: it accords well enough both with our religious and with our poetic tradition. But in France it awakened on the one side anti-clerical fears, and on the other—more reasonably—a good-humoured suspicion: *timeo Danaos et dona ferentes.*

Between the winds of criticism the controversy was fanned into a blaze.

M. Bremond is a subtle writer, and it is not easy to make clear to ourselves precisely what he was saying. For his peroration is not quite free from ambiguity. In it he is plainly speaking of the effect of poetry upon the reader, and he is saying that 'pure poetry' induces in the well-tuned mind a condition akin to that of the silent mystical contemplation which is the supreme form of prayer. That is not equivalent to the statement which he makes elsewhere that the creation of poetry by the poet has its origin in such a state of rapture. But M. Bremond holds both these positions. There is, in the poet, a mystical or semi-mystical condition: this condition, by the magic of the words, is directly communicated to the reader. And 'pure poetry', if we understand M. Bremond correctly, is the words which allow or enforce this communication. Unfortunately, M. Bremond has linked his discussion up with a discussion by his fellow Academician, M. Paul Valéry (whose path to a fauteuil he was eager to smooth), of a very different sort of 'pure poetry' derived from Mallarmé. The work of the pure poet in this sense of 'pure poetry' consists in the conscious and deliberate construction, upon a theme in itself utterly indifferent, of a musical pattern of words which gives delight. In this sense the 'purity' of poetry consists in its absolute independence of subject: 'pure poetry' is simply verbal 'music'. This conception, by which we have not been greatly troubled in England, despite

M. Valéry's authentic ancestor, Edgar Allan Poe, has no necessary connexion with M. Bremond's; and it is a pity that M. Bremond did not more sharply distinguish them.

M. Bremond's position is a little obscured, not only by his references to M. Valéry's very definite and very different theory of 'pure poetry', but by his Catholic orthodoxy. His appreciation of poetry is so intense that he is inevitably tempted to represent the poet as a Christian mystic who has, so to speak, at the crucial moment taken the wrong turning. Instead of surrendering himself to the silent ecstasy of communion with God, the poet is lured by the demon of expression into utterance of the unutterable. One may point out—indeed, M. Bremond himself lightly indicates as much—that most Christian mystics appear to have been troubled by a similar demon, who lured them into utterance that was not always poetry; consequently, if poets are mystics *manqués*, so are most mystics; and finally, whereas mystics sometimes squander their beatitudes in verbiage, poets do at least produce from them the thing of beauty and the joy for ever. In other words, it may be orthodoxy and not the poets to whom the attitude of *timeo Danaos* in face of M. Bremond's theory would be the more appropriate.

But these are consequences only if the theory be accepted. It needs a closer investigation first. The argument upon which M. Bremond mainly depends to establish a relation between the mystical and the poetic experience is the familiar one that the notional or rational content of a line of true poetry is not of prime importance to its poetic quality. M. Bremond goes further and declares that the notional content is absolutely irrelevant to the poetic quality. He gives for an instance the famous (though perhaps legendary) correction by Keats of 'A thing of beauty is a constant joy' into the first line of *Endymion*. The notional content of the two lines is hardly distinguishable: yet one is poetry, and the other not. Through one, to use M. Bremond's homely metaphor, the current passes; through the other there is no transmission. We must conclude therefore two things: first, that poetry is words by which something is communicated from the poet to the reader, and, second, that this something communicated is not a mere notion or an idea. What is it? Tolstoy said 'an emotion'; Signor Croce says, 'an intuition'; M. Bremond says an incomplete mystical experience; Professor Whitehead, if we understand him rightly, a fragment of the concrete real of primary experience. And, of course, there are innumerable other answers, with innumerable nuances of difference.

What seems most important to have clearly in mind is that the problem is not at all peculiar to poetry in the common sense of the word; it is simply the problem of that 'magic of style' which Matthew Arnold declared to be 'creative' of vision and understanding and virtue in the reader. Perhaps, had M. Bremond been less enchanted by the particular vistas which his approach to the problem seemed to open up, and had he faced it in its full universality as the crux of creative style, he could have gone to the prose-writers of his own country for some less fitful, and less startling, illumination. Stendhal's lucid apophthegm might have warned him against too quick, or too Tolstoyan, a denial that the element of thought in poetry is more than an accidental concomitant of the pure poetry. 'Le style', said Stendhal, 'est ceci: ajouter à une pensée donnée toutes les circonstances propres à produire tout l'effet que doit produire cette pensée.' Whatever the limitations of the dictum, it seems to throw more light than a directly mystical theory on the nature of the process by which Keats transformed 'A thing of beauty is a constant joy' into 'A thing of beauty is a joy for ever'. In both lines the thought is the same; but in the second the harmony of words in which it is expressed enables the thought to produce its full and true effect. There are difficulties in Stendhal's explanation which must be faced; but it takes more account of the facts than any theory which tends to regard the element of thought in poetry as completely irrelevant to it.

We must guard ourselves against pressing the explanation too hard, and remember that 'thought' in Stendhal's vocabulary meant very much more than logical notions or distinct concepts; again, we must be prepared to find that the quantity of distinguishable thought in poetry varies infinitely. The line of Keats, being positively gnomic, is not representative; nor is perhaps the line of Shakespeare, with its elusive thought content,

> After life's fitful fever he sleeps well.

But it brings us by a shade nearer to Stendhal's essential meaning. Every 'thought', at least of those thoughts with which poetry is concerned, has its emotional context, or 'field'. The thoughts which have no emotional 'field' are by nature alien to poetry. Thoughts which for one man may appear to be without an emotional 'field' may be greatly charged with it for another, as, for instance, the Epicurean metaphysic for Lucretius, or the Ptolemaic astronomy for Dante. The full effect that the thought *ought* to produce is, therefore, not absolute; it means the effect that the thought does produce upon the poet's mind, and which, from his point of view, it ought to produce upon the mind of his reader. Poetry will, therefore, be words which do communicate a 'thought' and the emotional 'field' which it excites from the mind of the poet to the mind of the reader.

We may advance a little further. It is obvious that the 'thought' and its emotional 'field' are inseparable from one another; for the emotional 'field' is none other than what happens in the thinking of the thought: it is, we might even say, the actual *thinking* of the thought. Assuredly, the thought and the emotional field are not more distinct than faintly discernible aspects of a single and entire mental act. It would be, in fact, extremely hazardous to say even that the thought came before the emotional 'field'; whatever priority it may have is logical and not actual. And, as a matter of fact, there is good reason for believing that in the activity of many great poets the emotional field is actually prior to the thought, which is, as it were, a condensation of an emotional atmosphere. By this line of approach we preserve what truth there is in M. Bremond's metaphor of 'the current that passes', and avoid what seems to us his premature and dangerous separation of thought and the specifically poetic in poetry. We are not under the illusion that we have explained anything; we have simply prevented a false simplification. Against our caution M. Bremond might adduce once more the line dear to Marcel Proust and himself,

La fille de Minos et de Pasiphaë

and once again deny that it contains any thought whatever. To which we must reply that such an absolute negation of thought is untrue to the fact. The line is not mere incantation any more than is

Jousted in Aspramont, or Montalban.

In both there is an evident distinguishment of quality—exotic rich and rare in both: in Racine's line soft and languorous, in Milton's clangorous and martial. To deny to such a discernment of quality the name of thought would be either to degrade nearly the whole of our mental activity to mere sensation, or to exalt it, unnecessarily and quite improbably, to mystic communion with the ineffable. It would be, we think, altogether more becoming and more convincing to admit that the range of mental acts in poetry is unlimited, and that the element of distinguishable thought can vary from a comprehensive proposition—'We are such stuff as dreams are made on'—to the most tenuous apprehension of a quality physical, or spiritual, or both—'the plainsong cuckoo gray'. What is essential is that the 'thought' should be an intrinsic part of an emotional field in the poet's mind, and that a corresponding emotional field should be excited in ourselves.

There is plenty of mystery in poetry without making it mystical. And we may, perhaps, advance a step further and suggest that the poet is he in whom the vast majority of his 'thoughts' —in the large sense invoked above—occur with vivid emotional fields. It is probably true that in the mental activity of even the ordinary run of men thoughts are always accompanied by such emotional fields, but that they ignore them. They have the best reason for ignoring them, because they have no means of distinguishing them from one another. The poet, on the contrary, from the beginning, possesses such a means. He has the Word. The word in the poet's mind partly arises out of the emotional field, partly is deliberately fitted to convey it. This mating of the word to the entire mental experience of thought and emotional field experienced as one is the specific poetic act. If an ordinary man were visited by Prospero's thought, which came, we may remember, to a troubled brain and a beating mind, he would strive to remember it. He would not be able to remember it. He might say: 'An extraordinary thought came to me. We are like dreams.' Then he would hesitate, knowing that he had betrayed his thought, and add wistfully, 'But it was beautiful'. No doubt it was; but the beauty is lost for ever, for the beauty lay not in the thought, but in the